MILITARY EXPANSION
ECONOMIC
DECLINE

EXPANDED EDITION

MILITARY EXPANSION ECONOMIC DECLINE

The Impact of Military Spending on U.S. Economic Performance

By Robert W. DeGrasse Jr.
Council on Economic Priorities
With a foreword by Lester Thurow

M. E. Sharpe, Inc. ARMONK, N.Y.

This is an expanded edition of a study issued by the Council on
Economic Priorities in 1983, written by Robert W. DeGrasse Jr.
with the assistance of Elizabeth McGuinness and William Ragen,
and edited by Alice Tepper Marlin and Robert N. MacVicar with
managing editor Neal Karrer. The Council on Economic Priorities
is a nonprofit research organization.

This edition of *Military Expansion, Economic Decline* includes
additional statistical materials supplied by the author.

This edition published by M. E. Sharpe, Inc. in 1983 by arrangement with the
Council on Economic Priorities.

Library of Congress Cataloging in Publication Data

DeGrasse, Robert W., Jr.
    Military expansion, economic decline.

    1. Disarmament—Economic aspects—United States. 2. United States—
Military policy—Economic aspects. 3. Defense contracts—United States.
4. United States—Economic conditions—1945-   . I. Title.
HC110.D4D43   1983   330.973'092   83-12680
ISBN 0-87332-258-4
ISBN 0-87332-260-6 (pbk.)

Design by Alison Lee, Inc.
Typesetting by Fine Lines Graphic Services, Inc.
Cover illustration by Joe Lertola

Printed in the United States of America

Table of Contents

Acknowledgments

Many people made substantial contributions to this study. David Gold and Gordon Adams helped structure the research and carefully reviewed the results during various stages of the project. Paul Murphy, Sean Doyle and Benjamin Goldman provided significant research assistance. James Storrow skillfully edited the final manuscript.

The following individuals carefully reviewed one or more drafts of the manuscript: Marion Anderson, Robert W. DeGrasse Sr., Margaret Downs, Richard DuBoff, Lloyd J. Dumas, Michael Edelstein, William Hartung, Edward Herman, Robert Heilbroner, Mary Gardiner Jones, Patricia Kolb, Vice Adm. John Marshall Lee (Ret.), Crosby Milne, Leon Reed, Margaret Simms, Lee B. Thomas, Jr. and two anonymous readers.

The authors would also like to thank the following individuals for the advice, information and support they provided: David Blond, John Braund, George Brown, Jr., James Capra, Carol Chapman O'Cleireacain, David Cortright, Stephen Daggett, Beth Cohen DeGrasse, David Doerge, James Fallows, Joe Franklin, Jr., Richard Greenwood, David Henry, Barbara Hollinshead, Franklyn Holzman, Karen Horowitz, Bruce Carver Jackson, David Johnson, Richard Kaufman, Betty Goetz Lall, David McFadden, Milton Margolis, Jacqueline Mazza, Seymour Melman, Bruce Mizrach, Richard Oliver, Lee Price, Marcus Raskin, Robert Reich, Lester Thurow, James Treires, Ezra Vogel and Edie Wilke.

These people are responsible for many of the best features of this study and liable for none of its faults.

Finally, we are deeply indebted to the following foundations, organizations, and individuals for their generous financial assistance: The North Shore Unitarian Universalist Veatch Program, John Harris IV, the Samuel Rubin Foundation, the Ottinger Foundation, the Louise L. Ottinger Charitable Trust, the International Association of Machinists and Aerospace Workers, John and Elizabeth Morse, the Reed Foundation and two special anonymous donors.

Foreword

When it comes to defense spending, economics is clearly not the only issue. America can afford to spend whatever percentage of the GNP that is necessary for its security. In 1944 about 42 percent of GNP went to the military. Equally clearly, however, there are important economic issues to be taken into account when determining defense spending.

From an economist's view, an MX missile is like a toaster. Both are forms of current consumption; that is, neither contributes to our ability to produce more economic goods and services in the future.

All societies must set spending limits on current consumption, defense and non-defense, to provide for the economic future. If defense spending must go up, then private consumption must come down.

If we pay for defense by drawing the funds out of physical investment, civilian research and development, or educating and training our labor force, we then will be undercutting the long-run survivability of the very economy that we need to sustain defense spending.

The economic world is also changing for Americans. While the United States since World War II has carried a larger military burden than its military allies (as measured by the fraction of GNP devoted to defense), what was once fair and easy has become unfair and difficult.

Where we once had a much higher per capita income and, from the point of fairness, should have been carrying a heavier economic burden, we now have allies with approximately the same per capita standard of living. Where we once had a huge technological lead and did not have to worry about being able to compete in world markets, we now have competitors who are our technological equals in civilian products.

As a result, there are now real questions as to whether we can continue to spend more than our military allies but economic competitors.

Traditionally, "spinoffs" have been suggested as compensating benefits to the costs of military expenditures. Indeed, the original civilian jet airliner was a modified military cargo plane.

But there is reason to believe that whatever the degree of "spinoffs" in the past they are fewer now. Military hardware, as it increasingly moves into space, simply has requirements so specialized that there is little commercial applicability. Although enormous resources have been devoted to the space shuttle over many years, for example, as yet no economically productive uses for it have been generated.

For all these reasons few matters are as important to understand as the interrelationship between our military and our lack of economic success. *Military Expansion, Economic Decline* is an effort to begin to increase that understanding.

Lester Thurow
Massachusetts Institute
of Technology

Introduction

...we must remember that at least 350,000 jobs are at stake and will be lost if there are drastic cuts [in military spending].

Secretary of Defense Caspar Weinberger,
before the National Press Club,
March 8, 1982

The economic aspects of arms spending have often dominated questions of national security. Considering the amount of public funds spent on the military, this is hardly surprising. In fiscal year 1983,* the national defense budget will be $214.8 billion, which is 26.7 percent of the total federal budget and 6.7 percent of the expected gross national product (GNP).[1] Expenditures of this magnitude can have substantial impacts. For example, cuts in military procurement as the Vietnam war wound down left many people unemployed in heavily defense-dependent areas such as Seattle, Santa Clara County in California, and the Route 128 area around Boston. Yet during the war, rapidly increasing arms spending produced an inflationary surge that hurt the entire nation.

Decisions regarding which weapon to build or where to locate a military base should be determined by our security needs. Very often, however, these choices are strongly influenced by economics. Four recent occurrences illustrate this point. Item one: During a campaign trip to Columbus, Ohio, last fall, President Reagan warned that support for the nuclear freeze could hurt the local economy because it would mean cancelling the B-1B bomber, which is partly manufactured in that area.[2] Item two: At the same time, highly visible Democratic Congressional candidates were calling for cuts in the military budget because they believed that rapid growth in Pentagon spending hurts the economy. Item three: Not long before the 1982 elections, Congress was the scene of a pitched battle over who should supply the Air Force with new transport planes. Members of Congress from Washington state fought to have Seattle's Boeing Co. awarded the contract, while members from Georgia worked to keep the project in their state at Lockheed.[3] Item four: During the December 1982 Congressional debate over cutting one of the two nuclear aircraft carriers from the Pentagon's budget,

---

* Fiscal year (hereafter abbreviated "FY") refers to the government's budget year. Before 1977, it ran from July to June. Since 1977, it has run from October to September.

1

numerous members defended the program because it would create employment in America's industrial heartland. One member went so far as to call the aircraft carrier program a "jobs bill."[4]

Before World War II, the notion that economic benefits sprang from military spending had little currency. To the contrary, most people saw military spending as an impediment to economic growth, justified only in wartime. Arms production during World War II began to change that perception as it helped propel the United States out of the Great Depression. Military spending, financed by massive federal deficits, solved the double-digit unemployment that plagued the economy throughout the 1930s.

Keynesian economics provided a theoretical basis for claims that military spending can be good for the economy. It explained how the war helped end the depression. Indeed, in frustration over the failure of western nations to spend enough money on civilian programs to test his theory, John Maynard Keynes predicted in 1940 that: "It is, it seems, politically impossible for a capitalist democracy to organize expenditure on such a scale necessary to make the grand experiment which would prove my case — except in war conditions."[5] The success of military spending as an economic tool helped break down the traditional American opposition to high peacetime military budgets. "Keynesian" economic logic was often employed during key debates over military policy in the Cold War, affirming not only its intellectual but also its political power.

In the late 1940s, by which time the United States had significantly demobilized after the Second World War, a major debate occurred over the need for a large military force during peacetime. Calls for an expanded defense establishment initially went unanswered, but eventually the Truman administration began to increase the size of the military in 1950, prior to the Korean War.

An internal administration document, written during 1949, developed the rationale for the initial Cold War buildup. National Security Council Memorandum (NSC) 68, produced by an ad hoc committee of State and Defense Department officials under the leadership of Paul Nitze, called for a massive military buildup to "contain" the Soviet Union. The memorandum also challenged the traditional view that military spending was harmful to the economy:

> From the point of view of the economy as a whole, the [military buildup] might not result in a real decrease in the standard of living, for the economic effects of the program might be to increase the gross national product by more than the amount being absorbed for additional military and foreign assistance purposes.[6]

While the economic benefits were not the central justification for the buildup, Nitze thoroughly discussed the contents with the administration's leading Keynesian economist, Leon Keyserling, who expressed "full agreement" with the economics of NSC 68.[7]

During the post-Sputnik debate over the "missile gap" in the late 1950s, Keynesian economics was again invoked to counter traditional economic logic. On one side, President Eisenhower, whose military credentials were unimpeachable, argued that the Soviet threat did not justify more military spending, particularly if those expenditures created budget deficits. The other side, backed by Keynesians including James Tobin, argued that Eisenhower's fear of deficits was misguided and that increased military expenditures were necessary to counter the Soviet threat. Tobin, who later served on President Kennedy's Council of Economic Advisors, wrote in 1958 that the Eisenhower administration's "orthodox fiscal doctrines... have brought the nation to the brink of catastrophe, a different and infinitely more serious catastrophe than the internal collapse of 1932."[8] During that debate, others went further than Tobin in ascribing economic benefits to military spending. For example, in an address before the American Banker's Association in 1957, a prominent business executive, Frank Pace, Jr. argued that:

> If there is, as I suspect there is, a direct relation between the stimulus of large defense spending and a substantial increased rate of growth of gross national product, it quite simply follows that defense spending per se might be countenanced on economic grounds   alone as a stimulator of the national metabolism.[9]

While the economic problems of the Vietnam war years eroded the public perception that military spending is good for the economy, the World War II experience has still not been forgotten. Nor have most Americans forgotten that the nation prospered throughout much of the Cold War when military budgets were high. Thus, when President Reagan took office in 1981 promising to revitalize the economy and rearm America, many people viewed these two goals as complementary.

Administration officials, most prominently Secretary of Defense Weinberger, have nurtured this notion among numerous audiences.[10] The Reagan administration, which promised to curtail the Keynesian role of government, has drawn heavily from Keynes to help justify their military buildup. Secretary Weinberger has claimed that military spending is a better way to stimulate the economy than transfer payments.* He has also asserted that cutting the military budget during a recession will cost the economy 35,000 jobs per billion dollars of reductions.[11]

In making those claims, however, the Reagan administration has ignored the short- and long-term "opportunity cost" of a massive peacetime military buildup. Will increased arms production create more jobs than other forms of spending? On balance, will it help or hinder ef-

---

* Transfer payments, such as Social Security, are funds collected by the government as taxes and distributed to individuals based on the law as income.

forts to revitalize our lagging economy? With these questions in mind, we examined the net economic impact of military spending.

In the first chapter we assess the economic power of the Pentagon by examining the size of the military budget in comparison to the overall economy and the federal budget, and by reviewing the distribution of Pentagon expenditures by state and industry. Then we compare jobs created by the military with those created by equivalent private and civilian government spending.

The second chapter contains our analysis of the long-term impacts of military spending during the Cold War. We examine the hypothesis that America's industrial strength has been depleted rather than enhanced by heavy military spending. This hypothesis is tested by comparing the economic performance of 17 non-communist, advanced industrial nations over the past two decades. We also tested four other possible explanations for America's poorer economic performance.

In the third chapter, we assess the technological costs and benefits of military spending. On the whole, has arms production and military research moved our civilian technology forward or hindered our progress? In particular, we review the information available on the role that the Pentagon has played in the development of the semiconductor industry.

The final chapter contains our analysis of the assertion that the present buildup will not damage the economy. Our assessment is based upon a comparison of the Reagan administration's proposed peacetime buildup with the increases in military spending during the Vietnam and Korean wars. We ask why the Vietnam buildup created more problems than did the expansion during the Korean war, even though the Vietnam increase was smaller; then we apply the answers to the current situation.

In sum, by assessing the costs and the benefits of military spending, we have endeavored to provide a "second opinion" on the subject of military economics. While advocates of increased military spending often stress the positive effects of the Pentagon on the economy, there has been little systematic study of the "opportunity costs" that society pays for a large military establishment. This study begins to fill that gap.

Notes

1. *Budget of the United States Government, FY 1984* (Washington, DC: U.S. GPO, 1983), pp. 9-4, 9-53.

2. Herbert Denton, "Reagan Coolly Received on Midwest Swing," *Washington Post*, October 5, 1982.

3. Richard Halloran, "Expansion of Military Air Transport Fleet is Stalled by Dispute in Congress," *The New York Times*, June 20, 1982.

4. U.S. Congress, House of Representatives, *Congressional Record*, December 8, 1982, pp. H 9123 - H 9129.

5. *The New Republic*, July 29, 1940, p. 158.

6. Thomas Etzold and John Lewis Gaddis, eds., *Containment: Documents on American Policy and Strategy, 1945-1950* (New York: Columbia University Press, 1978), p. 426.

7. John Lewis Gaddis, *Strategies of Containment* (New York: Oxford University Press, 1982), p. 94.

8. James Tobin, "Defense, Dollars, and Doctrine," *The Yale Review*, March 1958 reprinted in B. H. Wilkins and C. B. Friday, *The Economists of the New Frontier* (New York: Random House, 1963), p. 44.

9. Frank Pace, Jr., Address before the American Bankers' Association, September 1957, quoted in *Report from Iron Mountain* (London: McDonald & Co., 1967), p. 69.

10. "Cutting Defense Won't Solve Job Problem, Weinberger Says" *The Washington Post*, November 9, 1982, p. 16.

    Peter Meredith, "Shipyard Jobs Tied to Defense Votes," *The Baltimore Sun*, March 6, 1982.

11. George Wilson, "Senators Urge Defense Spending Cut," *The Washington Post*, February 2, 1983, pp. A1, A10.

I

The Military Budget, the Economy and Jobs

Some Senators... have asserted that defense spending has an adverse effect on efforts to improve the current unemployment situation in this country. This rationale, if accurate would lead us to believe that defense spending results in little or no economic benefit. I find this to be a most intriguing argument when, in one breath, Senators will argue for reductions in defense, and then, in another breath, will argue just as strongly that such reductions should not be made in programs located in their states.

Senator John Tower,
Chairman of the Armed Services Committee,
in a letter to Senate colleagues
February 1, 1983

The employment created by military spending has a powerful influence on our defense policy. Despite the fact that numerous members of Congress were calling for deep cuts in the administration's military buildup during the fall of 1982, the proposed FY 1983 Department of Defense budget was cut by only a token amount. Analysts for Prudential-Bache Securities suggest that two economic factors prevented deeper cuts. First, they believe that the broad geographic distribution of Pentagon spending gives even the Congressional "doves" good reason for voting for arms increases. Second, they note that pressure to vote for military programs is greater during a period of high unemployment. Therefore, these Wall Street analysts predict that military spending will continue to grow rapidly and recommend that investors purchase defense stocks.[1]

It is hard to argue with their logic. The pervasive influence of military contracting makes it difficult for our elected representatives to vote against major weapons systems, even when the weapons are of questionable military value. During the 1981 debate over the B-1B bomber, for example, the plane's prime contractor, Rockwell International, informed Congress that components for the system would be purchased from companies in 48 of the 50 states.[2] Although the plane probably will be obsolete by the late 1980s,[3] it was approved by Congress with the support of liberals such as Senators Alan Cranston (D-Cal.) and Howard Metzenbaum (D-Ohio), whose states stand to gain thousands of jobs from the program.

In times of recession, military spending has also gained support as a "Keynesian" mechanism for stimulating the economy. During 1974, in the midst of the last prolonged recession, the Ford administration added over $1 billion to the Defense Department's budget at the last minute as a tactic to pump more money into the lagging economy.[4] As early as 1950, an article in *U.S. News and World Report* summed up the benefit of using military spending in this way:

> Government planners figure that they have found the magic formula for almost endless good times. They are now beginning to wonder if there may not be something to perpetual motion after all. Cold War is the catalyst. Cold War is an automatic pump primer. Turn the spigot, and the public clamors for more arms spending. Turn another, the clamor ceases.[5]

Support for this tactic clearly derives from the fact that arms production during World War II helped jolt the nation out of the Great Depression.

This pump priming tactic can become addictive, however. During the early years of the Cold War, some observers worried that large cuts in military spending might allow the economy to lapse back into a depression. In 1953, for example, James Reston went so far as to suggest in a front page story in *The New York Times* that the Soviet Union's friendlier attitude toward the United States was a ploy to bring about a slump in the West:

> So long as the Kremlin was waging war in Asia and crying havoc all over the world, the Western nations were able to achieve full employment... now, as the experts here see it, one of their objectives seems to be to smile us into disarmament, deflation, unemployment and depression.[6]

Throughout the recent recession, Reagan administration officials have reminded the American people of the economic benefits of higher arms spending.[7] Yet thorough examination of its immediate impact shows that the benefits are dwarfed by the opportunity costs. Moreover, as we discuss later, the real question Congress should be asking is whether the military value of a given program is greater than its long-term economic costs.

This chapter examines the direct effects of military spending in two parts. First, we broadly map the Pentagon's influence in the overall economy. How extensive is the military's impact? Where is it concentrated? Second, we compare the employment created by military spending with employment that would be created by other uses of the same funds. Does the military create as many jobs? Does it help those most in need of employment? We conclude by assessing the role of military spending as an economic stabilizer. Is military spending an effective buffer against depression? Or can we influence the course of the economy more effectively by other means?

Measuring the Military's Impact

The Pentagon is the largest single purchaser of goods and services in the economy. During 1981, national defense purchases by the federal government totalled $153.3 billion.[8] In comparison, the business expenses* of Exxon, the largest corporation in America, were 33 percent less during the same year. The cost of operating the nation's second largest corporation, Mobil, was 60 percent less.[9]

The military has been the largest single source of demand in the economy throughout the last three decades. After adjusting for inflation, there has been little variation in the substantial size of the Defense Department's budget since the early 1950s (Chart 1.1). Excluding the dramatic increases during the Korean and Vietnam wars, military spending has remained high at about $170 billion (in 1983 dollars).

Although Pentagon spending has been a major factor in the economy, the military's proportionate share has declined as the overall economy has grown. While the military budget stayed the same, the gross national product (GNP) has almost tripled in real terms during the past three decades. As a result, the military's share of the GNP dropped from an average of 10 percent during the 1950s to an average of six percent during the 1970s (Chart 1.2).

The military's share of government spending has also fallen, but by a smaller amount. Of the goods and services directly purchased by the federal government during the 1970s, the military consumed 70 percent (Chart 1.3). In the 1950s, the Pentagon's share averaged 85 percent. The military's portion stayed so high because much of the growth in civilian government spending has been in transfer payments, which are not direct government purchases.

While transfer payments do affect the economy, their impact is usually more geographically diffuse than direct purchases. For example, unemployment benefits are paid to anyone who qualifies, no matter where they live. On the other hand, contracting for a tank, or building a

---

* Business expenses are roughly equivalent to the purchase of goods and services.

hydroelectric dam, directly affects a specific area. The difference is politically important. Members of Congress can demonstrate their political effectiveness back home by steering federal purchases into their states. The responsibility that any one Senator or Representative can claim for additional transfer payments is usually less clear.

Since military spending is by far the largest category of federal purchases, it is an extremely important source of political power. Two examples illustrate this point. First, as chairman of the Senate Subcommittee on Defense Preparedness during the 1950s, Lyndon Johnson built his political career calling for a larger Air Force and helping direct aircraft contracts into his home state.[10] Second, in 1969, toward the end of Mendel Rivers' (D-SC) long tenure as chairman of the House Armed Services Committee, there were *nine* military installations located in his district. A Lockheed plant was located there because, as Rep. Rivers explained, "I asked them to put a li'l old plant here."[11]

Regional and Industrial Impact

The military spends its money on a variety of different programs. The four most important categories — military personnel, operations and maintenance (O&M), procurement, and research and development (R&D) — make up over 85 percent of the expenditures (Table 1.1). Broadly, the Defense Department keeps track of the regional distributions of these expenditures in two ways. One is the state-by-state listing of prime contract awards made by the Pentagon. The other is the Defense Department's estimate of expenditures by state, excluding prime contracts.

Prime contract awards* cover purchases from the private sector for a wide variety of goods, ranging from missiles and spare parts to fuel and food. In FY 1981, military prime contracts (above $10,000) with private firms in the 50 states and the District of Columbia totaled $87.8 billion. Over 68.0 percent of the total went for weapons and communications equipment. Fuel was the biggest non-hardware category.

In FY 1981, 29 states and the District of Columbia received more than $500 million in prime contract awards. However, almost 65 percent of the prime contracts went to firms in 10 states (Table 1.2). Corporations

* Prime contract awards only represent obligations incurred by the Pentagon. They do not tell us in which year the money is actually spent. However, in any given year, the amount of contract awards a state receives is roughly equal to the level of spending incurred.

in the top five states received 45 percent of all contract awards. From the limited data available on the subcontract awards of prime contractors, it appears that the second tier of military contracting is more geographically concentrated than the first. Almost three-quarters of the subcontracts that the Pentagon could trace were performed in 10 states during FY 1979, the only year in which these data were collected. Another 5.8 percent of the subcontracting went to companies in foreign countries.[12]

Defense Department expenditures, excluding major procurement awards, totalled $74.0 billion in FY 1981. These expenditures covered virtually all payroll expenses for both civilian and military personnel, about 50 percent of the operations and maintenance budget, 55 percent of research and development expenses, and 75 percent of the military construction budget. Non-procurement Pentagon expenditures are similarly concentrated in only a few states. While 31 states and the District of Columbia received more than $500 million in FY 1981, 56 percent of non-procurement spending occurred in just 10 states (Table 1.3). The top five states received 41 percent of the total.

States come in all sizes; however the raw data do not take size into account, preventing us from comparing the relative impact of military spending among the states. They also do not take into account the fact that individuals and corporations pay taxes to the government for military programs. Therefore, we adjusted the total amount of Pentagon spending each state received in FY 1981 for the number of people in the work force and calculated each state's net Pentagon tax (Appendix A).

After these adjustments, we found that 23 states received less money from the Defense Department in FY 1981 than they paid in taxes (Chart 1.4). Another 10 states received less than $500 more per worker than they paid to the Pentagon. Only 17 states and the District of Columbia received a substantial amount of net expenditures per worker from the Defense Department.

The net impact of military spending is also unevenly distributed by region. None of the seven states in the midwest received more money from the Pentagon than they paid in taxes. Five of the 11 states in the northeast also experienced a net loss. On the other hand, seven of the 14 southern states and the District of Columbia received a significant amount of net military expenditures per worker. Eight of the 18 western states also experienced a substantial net gain.

In addition to being distributed unevenly across regions, Pentagon spending is concentrated in a few industries. The distribution of military purchases among industries can be traced using the detailed input-output table of the economy compiled by the Commerce Department. A breakdown of Defense Department purchases for 1979 shows that the bulk of mlitary purchases — 85 percent — was obtained from only twenty industries (Table 1.4). Ten industries accounted for almost 70 percent of the Defense Department's purchases. The top five industries — aircraft, communications equipment, missiles, ordnance, and ships — accounted for 55 percent alone. Military purchases are also concentrated in the manufacturing sector: 74 percent of all military purchases came from manufacturing industries in 1979. The top ten manufacturing industries provided the Pentagon with 65 percent of all military purchases during that year.

Few industries would be hurt significantly by a major decrease in military purchases. Of the top 20 industries selling to the Pentagon in 1979, only eight depended on the Defense Department for more than 10 percent of all final sales. Only a handful of the over 100 other industries in the economy gained more than five percent of final sales from military purchases.[13] However, four of the top five industries selling to the military depended on the Pentagon for over half of their sales in 1979. The fifth, aircraft, relied on the military for almost 40 percent of its final sales. Many of the companies in these top five industries are heavily dependent on the Pentagon.[14] As a result, defense-dependent companies and industries have a significant interest in preventing reductions in the Defense Department budget. They pursue this interest vigorously through special-interest lobbying and large campaign contributions.[15]

In summary, the economic benefits of military spending are strongly felt only in a few regions and a few industries. During the 1970s, the military also became a smaller part of the overall economy, reducing the role of the Pentagon as a source of demand. However, since the military remains the federal government's single most important fiscal mechanism for directly stimulating the economy, the benefits of military spending still remain a significant political factor. Indeed, because the Pentagon's spending pattern is highly concentrated, the constituencies supporting specific Defense Department programs are probably better organized than if the distribution of expenditures were diffuse.

Military Employment Vs. the Alternatives

Just as with any other form of spending, whether it be by an individual, a corporation, or the government, military spending also creates jobs. The Defense Department alone directly employed more than three million people in FY 1981 — over two million on active duty in the armed forces and another million in civil service jobs (Table 1.5). At least two million more people were employed in FY 1981 by private corporations with military contracts and by other institutions, such as universities.[16]

While military spending clearly creates jobs, a meaningful assessment of the Pentagon's employment impact must include an accounting of the jobs forgone by using our resources to produce weapons. Any form of spending creates jobs; the key question is: How does military spending compare with other uses of the same money? Does it create as many jobs per dollar spent as do other options? Does it provide employment in the occupational categories with high unemployment?

We will focus on the jobs created in the private sector by Pentagon purchases because government employment created by military spending is quite similar to other types of federal employment. Money for civil service workers creates approximately the same number of jobs whether it is spent by the Defense Department or the Department of Health and Human Services. Funds covering the personnel costs of soldiers and sailors would create roughly the same number of jobs if they were spent instead on CETA (Comprehensive Employment Training Act) programs. However, if money for the civil service or military personnel were transferred to the private sector, it would probably not create as much employment. Government jobs, like those in many service industries, require little capital equipment and tend to pay lower wages, particularly in the case of soldiers and sailors. As a result, more people can be hired per dollar spent on the armed forces and the civil service than if the money were spent on subway cars.

Fewer Jobs: However, the comparison between the number of jobs created by military purchases from the private sector and the number created by other forms of private spending is quite different. Most industries selling to the Pentagon create fewer jobs per dollar spent than the average industry in the American economy (Table 1.6). Seven of the 11 manufacturing industries selling the greatest volume of goods to the military create fewer jobs per dollar than the median manufacturing industry. Seven of the nine largest military suppliers create fewer jobs per dollar than the median non-manufacturing industry. More importantly, the three largest manufacturing industries — those accounting for over 40 percent of the Pentagon's total purchases from the private sector — create fewer jobs per dollar than the median manufacturing industry.

Those comparisons, based on data from the Labor Department's employment requirements table, include both direct and indirect employment. Direct jobs are those created in the industry that provides the final product to the Defense Department. Indirect jobs are those created by the final producer's requirements for goods and services. For example, the aircraft industry requires structural forgings, communications equipment, titanium and numerous other intermediate goods to produce jet fighters. Aircraft firms also use outside services such as air transportation and accountants. Such purchases indirectly create employment.

One factor that the lower job-creating manufacturing industries which serve the Pentagon share is a high level of technical sophistication. The aircraft, communications equipment, missile and computer industries all produce very specialized, highly complex products. In each case, the production process requires particularly expensive skilled labor, raw materials and intermediate products. The other three manufacturing industries that create fewer jobs than the average — autos, chemicals, and petroleum products — produce more general goods; however, the production process in each of these industries requires a larger amount of sophisticated capital equipment than is used by the average manufacturing firm. In both cases, the technical sophistication of the industries limits the number and types of jobs created.

The concentration of military purchases in a small number of lower job-yielding industries helps explain why various economic analyses have found that transferring military expenditures to other sectors of the economy creates more jobs. Three econometric simulations of a compensated reduction in military spending done during the 1970s all show that the alternatives — whether greater civilian government spending or a tax cut — create higher employment.[17] More recently, the Employment Research Associates used the Labor Department's employment requirements table to test the impact of shifting $62.9 billion in 1981 from military purchases to personal consumption expenditures.[18] This scenario showed a net gain of some 1.5 million jobs after the shift. The funds created a total of 3.3 million jobs if spent on private consumption, but only 1.8 million jobs if spent on military purchases.

The Employment Research Associates' study indicates that military contracting creates roughly 28,000 jobs per billion dollars of spending (in 1981 dollars). This is slightly less than the 30,000 jobs created by the median industry in the Bureau of Labor Statistics' input-output model (Chart 1.5). Military contracting also provides fewer jobs than public works projects such as new transit construction. It creates significantly fewer jobs than personal consumption and educational services. However, military contracting does create more jobs than industries such as oil refining and car manufacturing.

While military purchases create fewer jobs than most alternative expenditures, they still represent a significant source of demand in the economy for goods and services. The importance of providing an alternative source of demand when arms expenditures are reduced is underscored by the results of econometric simulations that do not compensate for lower levels of military spending by either cutting taxes or increasing other types of spending. For example, a recent simulation by Data Resources, Inc., comparing the Reagan administration's arms buildup to a much slower one, found that the smaller buildup resulted in almost one percentage point more unemployment.[19]

Highly Skilled Work Force: Military purchases also create a very different mix of jobs than other expenditures.[20] Military contractors generally employ a larger portion of technically skilled workers than does the average manufacturing firm. In 11 of the top 15 manufacturing industries producing output for the Pentagon,* the percentage of the industry's work force accounted for by production workers is lower than the average for all manufacturing (Table 1.7).

The extent of the reliance on highly skilled employees is illustrated by more detailed data from the Labor Department on the top five military-oriented industries. In four of the five industries producing the most for the Pentagon, the percentage of professional and technical workers is significantly higher than the average in manufacturing (Table 1.8). Engineers make up the bulk of this category in three of the four. The share of managers in military-related industries is also slightly higher than in the average manufacturing firm. Finally, all five of the top military industries require a smaller than average share of semi-skilled machine operators ("operatives" in Labor Department parlance).

According to Labor Department economists, their figures may understate the percentage of technically skilled employees working in military-serving aircraft and communications equipment firms.[21] Much of the military output produced by those two industries is highly specialized and produced in small batches. As a result their development usually requires more engineering than needed for commercial products. For example, in the guided missile industry, which produces mainly for the government, engineers make up 31.1 percent of the work force. Production of military goods also requires a greater number of machinists and technical workers to create and assemble specialized parts. In the civilian sector of the aircraft and communications industries, larger production runs and greater standardization probably reduce the need for specialized labor. Thus, the skill distribution on the military side of these two industries is probably higher, as in the guided missile industry.

The high cost of technically skilled labor is also a major reason why the manufacturing industries receiving most of the Pentagon's contracts create fewer jobs than the median. While some have speculated that military spending creates fewer jobs because the production process is capital-intensive,[22] this speculation is only true for a small number of industries serving the Pentagon, such as oil refining. In the major suppliers, including the aircraft, communications equipment and missile industries, large parts of the assembly process are often performed by skilled technicians and engineers. Moreover, much of the capital equipment used by large defense firms is very old because there is little incen-

---

* Output differs from final demand, by which we ranked military industries in Tables 1.4 and 1.6, in that it includes the output of all industries, both direct and indirect, required to produce a given product. Final demand is simply the cost of the final product.

tive to make new investments.

Normally, a firm invests to increase production efficiency and reduce costs in order to increase sales and profits. In the defense sector, however, lower cost seldom increases the market for a product and cost overruns are regularly reimbursed.[23] Capital purchases by military contractors are not ordinarily subsidized by the Defense Department. Therefore, there is little incentive to invest. Indeed, numerous reports identify lower productivity growth, resulting from less investment, as a major reason for cost overruns in the defense sector.[24]

On the other hand, Pentagon procurement practices encourage greater use of highly skilled workers. Defense Department officials value high performance above cost.[25] Thus, to gain the edge in selling to the Pentagon, military contractors often hire additional engineers. Moreover, the highly demanding specifications of military components often cannot be met by off-the-shelf items. As a result, many parts must be produced in small batches by subcontracting firms like machine shops and specialty semiconductor producers. These firms use much more skilled labor than firms that mass-produce standard components.

The specialized nature of military employment reduces its economic usefulness. Much of the new employment generated by a military buildup goes to people who need it least. Professional and technical workers have the lowest unemployment rate of any occupational category in the economy. Even during December 1982, when overall unemployment was 10.8 percent, unemployment for professional and technical workers was only 3.7 percent (Table 1.9). Demand for engineers was so great during the 1980 recession that salaries continued to rise dramatically. Indeed, during that recession, increased military spending fueled inflationary pressures in the high-technology sector while the rest of the economy faltered.[26]

At the other end of the spectrum, military spending creates very few jobs for those most in need of work. Meanwhile, unemployment among laborers and machine operators was above 20 percent in December 1982. And, although the present buildup will increase the need for skilled workers, programs to help train the groups with the highest unemployment rates — young people and minorities — have been cut severely.

Conclusion

Clearly, military spending is a limited counter-cyclical aid. It creates fewer jobs than most other industries. It employs highly skilled people who would have relatively little trouble finding jobs elsewhere. Military expenditures are highly concentrated in only a few regions and industries. Moreover, even though military spending creates a substantial demand for goods and services, cutting military spending would not make us more prone to depression. Increasing civilian government programs and/or reducing taxes could replace the purchasing power lost by cutting the arms budget. While large reductions in the current level of military spending would create adjustment problems in selected regions and industries,[27] many of these difficulties could be overcome with planning and specific assistance programs.[28]

When the economy requires federal assistance, programs should be developed to fill the nation's greatest needs, not simply the most convenient pork barrel. The construction industry, hard-hit during the recent recession, will receive a shot in the arm from the recently approved government program to rebuild the nation's deteriorating roads and bridges. Yet the sad state of America's infrastructure leaves us with many other public works options.[29] Instead of creating greater competition for skilled labor by increasing military spending, the federal government might also institute training programs to help those currently unemployed to develop technical skills that will be heavily in demand during the 1980s. If the federal government were to develop a comprehensive mass transit program, we could revive an industry that would employ production workers laid off by the auto makers, and create a hedge against future increases in energy prices.[30] These options clearly indicate that we should not spend money on the military just because it creates jobs.

Some might still wonder if it is possible to create enough public support for civilian government programs to replace military spending as a source of demand.[31] However, we would rephrase the question: Can the U.S. government afford to continue relying on the military budget as the largest public mechanism for stimulating the economy? As we discuss in the next chapter, military expenditures draw wealth from the civilian economy. While we might have been able to "afford" a substantial military burden during the 1950s and 1960s, the loss of skilled labor and investment from the private economy during the 1980s could cost us dearly in export potential. Many American industries could continue to lose markets to foreign producers if U.S. firms do not modernize their factories, and America's technological leadership could continue to slip away if we ask too many of our brightest engineers and scientists to solve military-related problems instead of creating better civilian products. These considerations indicate that, instead of relying on military spending as a source of jobs, we should avoid any military expenditure that is not necessary for our security.

Notes

1. Paul H. Nisbet and Richard L. Whittington, "Defense: Increase Spending or Cut Jobs," *Industry Outlook: Aerospace/Defense*, Prudential-Bache Securities, Inc., December 8, 1982.

2. Frank Greve, "Military Cuts Hard to Find in '84 Budget," *Philadelphia Inquirer*, January 10, 1983, p. 5A.

3. Gordon Adams, "The B-1: Bomber for All Seasons?," *Council on Economic Priorities Newsletter*, February 1982.

4. John W. Finney, "Military Budget Spurs Economy," *The New York Times*, February 27, 1974.

5. See Fred J. Cook, *The Warfare State* (New York: Collier Books, 1964), p. 183.

6. James Reston, "Soviet Tactics Give U.S. Problem of Avoiding Slump if Peace Comes," *The New York Times*, April 8, 1953, p. 1.

7. Herbert H. Denton, "Reagan Coolly Received on Midwest Swing," *The Washington Post*, October 5, 1982.
George Wilson, "Senators Urge Defense Spending Cut," *The Washington Post*, February 2, 1983, pp. A1, A10.
"Cutting Defense Won't Solve Job Problem, Weinberger Says" *The Washington Post*, November 9, 1982, p. 16.
Caspar Weinberger, "Address to the National Press Club," *News Release*, Office of the Assistant Secretary of Defense (Public Affairs), March 8, 1982, p. 3.
"Weinberger Says Military Spending Rise Won't Spur Inflation or Disrupt Economy," *Wall Street Journal*, July 29, 1981, p. 12.
Peter Meredith, "Shipyard Jobs Tied to Defense Votes," *The Baltimore Sun*, March 6, 1982.

8. *Economic Report of the President* (Washington, D.C.: U.S. GPO, February 1983), p. 163.

9. "Fortune 500," *Fortune Magazine*, May 3, 1982, p. 260.

10. Richard Kaufman, *War Profiteers* (New York: Doubleday, 1972), pp. 32-36.

11. Peter H. Prugh, "The War Business, Mendel Rivers' Defense of Armed Forces Helps His Hometown Prosper," *Wall Street Journal*, June 17, 1969.

12. U.S. Department of Defense, Washington Headquarters Service, "Geographic Distribution of Subcontract Awards, Fiscal Year 1979," p. 9.

13. U.S. Department of Commerce, Bureau of Industrial Economics, "Sectoral Implications of Defense Expenditures," August 1982.

14. David Gold with David Brooks, Paul Murphy and Mary Shea, "The Defense Department's Top 100," *Council on Economic Priorities Newsletter*, August 1982.

15. Gordon Adams, *The Iron Triangle:* The Politics of Defense Contracting (New York: Council of Economic Priorities, 1981).

16. U.S. Department of Defense, Office of the Assistant Secretary of Defense (Comptroller), "National Defense Estimates, Fiscal Year 1983," p. 82. This publication estimates that Pentagon contracts with private industry employed 2,230,000 people in 1981. This figure is probably overstated, given the results of input-output analysis performed by Marion Anderson, Jeb Brugmann and George Erickcek, "The Price of the Pentagon: The Industrial and Commecial Impact of the 1981 Military Budget" (Lansing, Mich.: Employment Research Associates, 1982).

17. Roger H. Bezdek, "The 1980 Impact — Regional and Occupational — of Compensated Shifts in Defense Spending," *Journal of Regional Science*, February, 1965. Chase Econometrics Associates, *Economic Impact of the B-1 Program on the U.S. Economy and Comparative Case Studies* (Cynwyd, Pennsylvania: Chase Econometric Associates, 1975).

Norman J. Glickman, *Econometric Analysis of Regional Systems* (New York: Academic Press, 1977).

Each of the above is discussed in Michael Edelstein, "The Economic Impact of Military Spending" (New York: Council on Economic Priorities, 1977).

18. Marion Anderson *et. al.*, *op. cit.*

19. Data Resources, Inc., *Defense Economics Research Report*, August 1982, p. 5.

20. Bezdek, *op. cit.*, p. 195.

21. Richard Dempsey and Douglas Schmude, "Occupational Impact of Defense Expenditures," *Monthly Labor Review*, December 1971, p. 12.

22. Marion Anderson, *et. al.*, *op. cit.*, p. 2.

23. Jacques S. Gansler, *The Defense Industry* (Cambridge, Mass.: The MIT Press, 1980), Chapter 3.

24. U.S. General Accounting Office, Comptroller General, "Appendix I — General Accounting Office Draft Report on Defense Industry Profit Study, Dated December 22, 1970" (Washington D.C.: U.S. GAO, January 1971), p. 51.

U.S. General Accounting Office, Comptroller General, "Impediments to Reducing the Costs of Weapons Systems, Report to Congress" (Washington, D.C.: U.S. GAO November 8, 1979), p. 31. (Hereafter, "Impediments....")

U.S. Congress, Senate Committee on Banking, Housing and Urban Affairs, jointly with the Subcommittee on Priorities and Economy in Government of the Joint Economic Committee, "Department of Defense Contract Profit Policy" (Washington, D.C.: U.S. GPO, March 21, 1979), pp. 1-2.

25. Gansler, *op. cit.*, p. 83.

U.S. General Accounting Office, "Impediments ...," *op. cit.*, p. 23.

Morton J. Peck and Frederic M. Scherer, *The Weapons Acquisition Process: An Economic Analysis* (Boston: Harvard Graduate School of Business Administration, 1962), p. 594.

26. U.S. Congress, House Committee on Armed Services, "The Ailing Defense Industrial Base: Unready for Crisis," a report of the Defense Industrial Base Panel (Washington, D.C.: U.S. GPO, December 31, 1980), p. 13.

27. Wassily Leontieff, Alison Morgan, Karen Polenske, David Simpson, Edward Tower, "The Economic Impact — Industrial and Regional — of an Arms Cut," *The Review of Economics and Statistics*, Volume XLVII, Number 3, August 1965.

Bezdek, *op. cit.*, pp. 188-196.

28. Seymour Melman, "Planning for Conversion of Military-Industrial and Military Base Facilities" (Washington, D.C.: U.S. Department of Commerce, August 1972), draft.

Bernard Udis, ed., *The Economic Consequences of Reduced Military Spending* (Lexington, Mass.: Lexington Books, 1973), Chapters 4 through 7.

Charles L. Shultze, statement before the U.S. Congress, Joint Economic Committee, "Economic Effects of Vietnam Spending," hearings, (Washington, D.C.: U.S. GPO, April 24, 1967), pp. 30-67.

U.S. Congress, Senate Committee on Labor and Public Welfare, "Postwar Economic Conversion," hearings, (Washington, D.C.: U.S. GPO, December 1969), Part 1.

29. Pat Choate and Susan Walter, *America in Ruins: Beyond the Public Works Pork Barrel* (Washington, D.C.: The Council of State Planning Agencies, 1981).

30. Philip Webre, *Jobs to People* (Washington, D.C.: Exploratory Project for Economic Alternatives, 1979), unpublished.

31. Richard DuBoff, "Converting Military Spending to Social Welfare: The Real Obstacles," *Quarterly Review of Economics and Business*, Vol. 12, Spring 1972.

Chart 1.1

Department of Defense Outlays
Fiscal Years 1946 – 1982, Projected 1983 – 1988

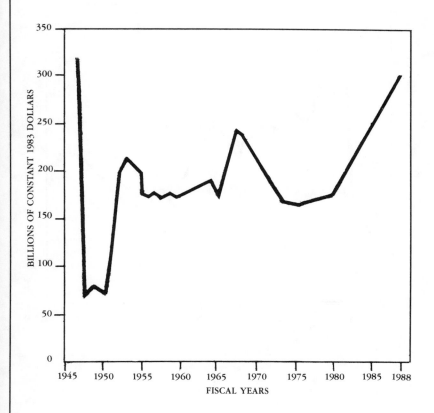

Sources: U.S. Department of Defense, Office of Assistant Secretary of Defense (Comptroller), unpublished data. Estimates for 1983 to 1988 from U.S. Department of Defense, Office of Assistant Secretary of Defense (Public Affairs), "FY 1984 Department of Defense Budget," January 31, 1983, adjusted to 1983 dollars.

Chart 1.2

National Defense Budget As A Share of GNP
Fiscal Years 1947 – 1982, Projected 1983 – 1988

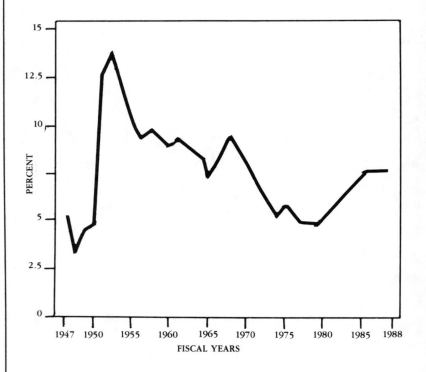

Sources: U.S. Office of Management and Budget, Budget Review Division, "Federal Government Finances," February 1982, Table 12. Estimates for 1983 to 1988 from: *Budget of the U.S. Government, FY 1984* (Washington, D.C.: U.S. GPO, 1983), pp. 9-4, 9-53.

Chart 1.3

National Defense Purchases Of Goods and Services As A Share of Total Federal Purchases
1946 – 1982

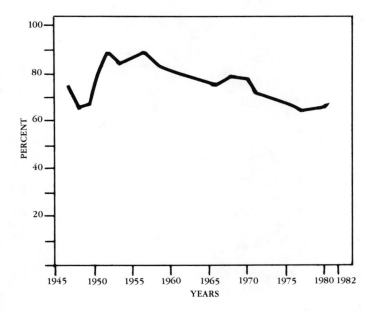

Source: *Economic Report of the President* (Washington, D.C.: U.S. GPO, February 1983), p. 163.

Chart 1.4

Net Pentagon Expenditures Per Worker
Fiscal Year 1981

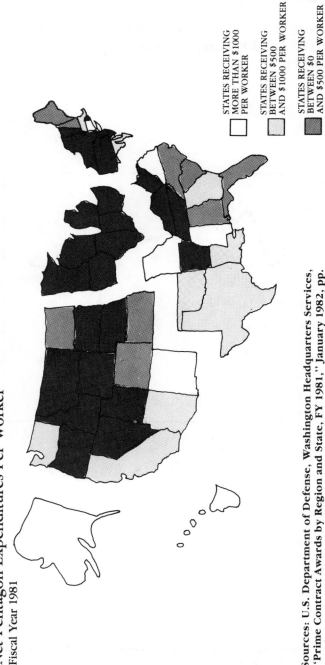

STATES RECEIVING
MORE THAN $1000
PER WORKER

STATES RECEIVING
BETWEEN $500
AND $1000 PER WORKER

STATES RECEIVING
BETWEEN $0
AND $500 PER WORKER

STATES EXPERIENCING
A NET LOSS OF REVENUE
TO THE PENTAGON

Sources: U.S. Department of Defense, Washington Headquarters Services, "Prime Contract Awards by Region and State, FY 1981," January 1982, pp. 13-14. U.S. DoD, WHS, "Estimated Expenditures for States and Selected Areas, FY 1981." Department of Labor, Bureau of Labor Statistics, "Labor Force Status by State," unpublished data.

Chart 1.5

Jobs Created Per Billion Dollars Of Final Demand
Direct & Indirect
(Constant 1981 Dollars)

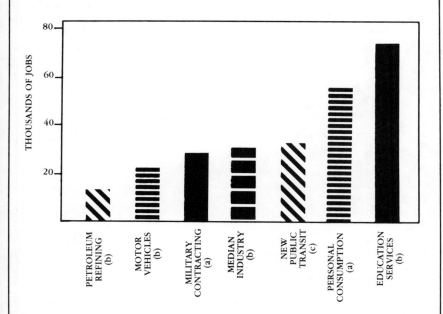

Sources:

(a) Marion Anderson, Jeb Brugmann and George Erickcek, "The Price of the Pentagon: The Industrial and Commercial Impact of the 1981 Military Budget" (Lansing, Mich.: Employment Research Associates, 1982).

(b) U.S. Department of Labor, Bureau of Labor Statistics, "Employment Matrix for 1972 in 1972 dollars," unpublished. Inflated to 1981 dollars using appropriate implicit price deflator from *Economic Report of the President* (Washington, D.C.: U.S. GPO, February 1983), pp. 166-167.

(c) U.S. Department of Labor, Bureau of Labor Statistics, phone conversation with Karen Horowitz.

Table 1.1

National Defense Budget
Fiscal Year 1981

PROGRAM	OUTLAYS (Millions of Dollars)	PERCENT OF N.D. OUTLAYS
Military Personnel	$ 36,409	22.8 %
Retired Military Personnel	13,729	8.6
Operations and Maintenance	51,920	32.5
Procurement	35,191	22.0
Research, Development, Test, and Evaluation	15,278	9.6
Military Construction	2,463	1.5
Family Housing	1,721	1.1
Offsetting Receipts	- 614	- .4
Subtotal (DOD)	156,096	97.7
Atomic Energy	3,398	2.1
Defense Related Activities	276	0.2
Offsetting Receipts	- 4	*
Total	$ 159,765	100.0 %

Totals may not add due to rounding.

* Less than .1 percent.

Source: *Budget of the U.S. Government, FY 1983* (Washington, D.C.: U.S. GPO, 1982), p. 5-10.

Table 1.2

Top Ten States
Receiving Department of Defense
Prime Contract Awards
Fiscal Year 1981

STATE	PRIME CONTRACT AWARDS (Thousands of Dollars)	PERCENT OF TOTAL
California	$ 16,698,825	19.0 %
Texas	7,503,964	8.6
New York	6,520,511	7.4
Massachusetts	4,604,946	5.2
Connecticut	4,494,258	5.1
Missouri	4,411,471	5.0
Virginia	3,611,821	4.1
Florida	3,169,443	3.6
Louisiana	3,045,133	3.5
Washington	2,792,891	3.2
TOTAL	56,853,263	64.7
U.S. TOTAL	$ 87,761,215	100.0 %

Source: U.S. Department of Defense, Washington Headquarters Services, "Prime Contract Awards by Region and State, FY 1981," January 1982, pp. 13-14.

Table 1.3

Top Ten States Estimated to Receive
Department of Defense Expenditures
Excluding Major Procurement
Fiscal Year 1981

STATE	NON-PROCUREMENT EXPENDITURES (Thousands of Dollars)	PERCENT OF TOTAL
California	$ 11,290,539	15.2 %
Virginia	6,709,611	9.1
Texas	6,012,662	8.1
Florida	3,643,437	4.9
Georgia	2,840,364	3.8
Maryland	2,359,111	3.2
North Carolina	2,143,380	2.9
Illinois	2,125,465	2.9
Pennsylvania	2,120,283	2.9
Ohio	2,109,111	2.8
TOTAL	41,353,963	55.8
U.S. TOTAL	$ 74,071,152	100.0 %

Source: U.S. Department of Defense, Washington Headquarters Services, "Estimated Expenditures for States and Selected Areas, FY 1981."

Table 1.4

Top Twenty Industries Serving the Defense Department
1979

INDUSTRY	TYPE	FINAL DEMAND (Millions of Dollars)	PERCENT OF DOD TOTAL	PERCENT OF INDUSTRY TOTAL
Aircraft	MFG	$ 11,754.2	19.0 %	39.6 %
Radio & Communications Equipment	MFG	10,795.9	17.4	51.8
Complete Guided Missiles	MFG	4,277.0	6.9	58.2
Ordnance	MFG	3,747.6	6.0	65.0
Ship Building & Repair	MFG	3,424.5	5.5	50.4
Air Transportation	TRANS	2,045.4	3.3	9.3
Business Services, N.E.C.*	SERV	1,888.7	3.0	10.3
Motor Vehicles	MFG	1,744.5	2.8	1.5
Construction of New Military Facilities	CONST	1,699.7	2.7	100.0
Communications, except Radio and T.V.	COMM	1,474.8	2.4	2.7
Industrial Inorganic & Organic Chemicals	MFG	1,269.5	2.0	16.2
Maintenance & Repair Construction	CONST	1,237.4	2.0	7.0
Wholesale Trade	TRADE	1,207.6	1.9	0.1
Petroleum Refining & Related Products	MFG	1,106.3	1.8	3.4
Computers & Peripheral Equipment	MFG	1,046.7	1.7	4.6
Educational Services	SERV	$ 897.0	1.4 %	3.6 %
Water Transportation	TRANS	808.3	1.3	9.4
Optical & Photographic Equipment	MFG	802.7	1.3	5.0

Cont'd...

TABLE 1.4

Cont'd...

INDUSTRY	TYPE	FINAL DEMAND (Millions of Dollars)	PERCENT OF DOD TOTAL	PERCENT OF INDUSTRY TOTAL
Electric Utilities	UTIL	753.5	1.2	2.2
Scientific & Controlling Instruments	MFG	736.9	1.2	9.8
20 INDUSTRY TOTAL		52,718.0	85.1	NA
DOD TOTAL		$ 61,970.7	100.0 %	NA

Note: Totals may not add due to rounding.

* Not elsewhere classified.

Source: U.S. Department of Commerce, Bureau of Industrial Economics, unpublished data for defense final demand in 1979 in 1972 dollars. Inflated to 1979 prices using the implicit price deflator for defense purchases less compensation from the U.S. Department of Labor, Bureau of Labor Statistics, Government Division, unpublished.

Table 1.5

Defense Department Employment
Fiscal Year 1981
(Thousands of Jobs)

SERVICE OR AGENCY	ACTIVE DUTY MILITARY	CIVIL SERVICE	TOTAL
Army	781	372	1,153
Navy	540		
		321	1,052
Marine Corps	191		
Air Force	570	246	816
Guard & Reserve	19	--	19
Defense Agencies	--	80	80
TOTAL	2,101	1,019	3,120

Source: U.S. Department of Defense, Office of Assistant Secretary of Defense (Comptroller), "National Defense Budget Estimates for FY 1983," March 1982, p. 82.

Table 1.6

Jobs Created Per Billion Dollars of Final Demand
Constant 1981 Dollars

INDUSTRY	DIRECT	INDIRECT	TOTAL
Aircraft	12,318	13,522	25,840
Radio & Communications Equipment	11,556	13,233	24,789
Complete Guided Missiles	7,773	10,481	18,254
Ordnance	12,631	14,722	27,353
Ship Building & Repair	18,051	14,341	32,392
Air Transportation	10,414	11,751	22,165
Business Services, N.E.C.*	24,904	8,006	32,910
Motor Vehicles	6,599	15,587	22,186
Construction of New Military Facilities	NA	NA	NA
Communications, except Radio and T.V.	9,173	4,232	13,405
Industrial Inorganic & Organic Chemicals	6,857	11,819	18,676
Maintenance & Repair Construction	13,175	11,241	24,416
Wholesale Trade	19,769	6,619	26,388
Petroleum Refining & Related Products	2,412	11,024	13,436
Computers & Peripheral Equipment	10,523	14,046	24,569

Source: U.S. Department of Labor, Bureau of Labor Statistics, "Employment Matrix for 1979 in 1972 dollars," unpublished. Inflated to 1981 dollars using the implicit price deflator for defense purchases less compensation from U.S. DOL, BLS, Government Division, unpublished.

INDUSTRY	DIRECT	INDIRECT	TOTAL
Educational Services	53,997	7,202	61,199
Water Transportation	12,617	13,320	25,937
Optical & Photographic	17,231	11,836	29,067
Equipment	7,257	10,061	17,318
Electric Utilities	6,957	8,716	15,672
Scientific & Controlling Instruments	14,452	13,590	28,042
MEDIAN MANUFACTURING INDUSTRY	NA	NA	26,291
MEDIAN NON-MANUFACTURING INDUSTRY	NA	NA	30,030

* Not elsewhere classified.

Table 1.7

Production Workers as a Percentage of the Work Force
In the Top Fifteen Industries Producing
the Most Output for the Department of Defense
1981

INDUSTRY	PRECENTAGE OF PRODUCTION WORKERS
Aircraft	53.1 %
Radio & T.V. Communications Equipment	41.5
Complete Guided Missiles	30.0
Ordnance	64.5
Ship Building & Repairing	76.5
Blast Furnaces & Basic Steel Products	77.4
Industrial Inorganic & Organic Chemicals	54.5 50.4
Motor Vehicles	74.3
Petroleum Refining & Related Products	60.5
Electrical Components	69.9
Semiconductors & Related Devices	41.1
Computers & Peripheral Equipment	38.0
Engineering & Scientific Instruments	48.1
Measuring & Controlling Devices	62.5
Tanks	64.5
ALL MANUFACTURING	69.5 %

Source: U.S. Department of Labor, Bureau of Labor Statistics, "Supplement to Employment and Earnings, Revised Establishment Data," June 1982.

Table 1.8

Percentage of Work Force In Each Occupational
Category
1980

OCCUPATION	AIRCRAFT & PARTS	COMM. EQUIP.	GUIDED MISSILES	ORDNANCE	SHIP BUILD. & REPAIR	ALL MANUFACT.
Professional & Technical	25.4 %	32.3 %	55.7 %	15.2 %	7.0 %	9.1 %
Engineers	11.5	15.0	31.1	5.1	1.8	2.9
Managers	7.4	7.3	7.2	5.3	3.1	5.9
Sales	.8	.7	.2	.4	.4	2.2
Clerical	13.9	15.7	12.3	10.9	7.3	11.3
Craft	21.3	12.4	10.8	22.5	40.9	18.5
Operatives	27.3	27.3	11.2	33.5	31.6	43.4
Service	2.0	1.5	2.1	5.0	1.5	2.0
Laborers	2.0	2.9	.6	7.3	8.3	7.7

Source: U.S. Department of Labor, Bureau of Labor Statistics, "Employment by Industry and Occupation, 1980 and Projected 1990 Alternatives," unpublished data.

Table 1.9

Unemployment Rates
Selected Occupations, Age and Race
(December 1982)

OCCUPATIONS	UNEMPLOYMENT RATE
Overall Rate	10.8
White Collar	5.6
Professional & Technical	3.7
Managers & Administrative (Except Farm)	4.0
Blue Collar	16.3
Craft & Kindred	11.9
Operatives (Except Transportation)	20.5
Laborers (Except Farm)	20.4
Youth (16 to 19 years old)	24.5
Blacks	20.8
Black Youth	49.5

Source: U.S. Department of Labor, Bureau of Labor Statistics, "The Employment Situation: December 1982," January 7, 1983, Tables A-1, A-2 & A-5.

II

Military Spending:
Stimulant or Impediment?

...our research suggests that [military expenditures] are beneficial in the long term to the civilian economy, since much of the additional spending promotes domestic production in our most capital and technology intensive sectors.

Secretary of Defense Harold Brown,
testimony before the U.S. Senate
Budget Committee, February 27, 1980

Since John Maynard Keynes suggested in frustration that a war would be the most politically feasible method for testing his theory, numerous advocates of higher military budgets have asserted that Pentagon spending is a good way to stimulate the economy. As we mentioned above, government officials and industry leaders promoted this theory during key debates over defense policy during the 1950s. More recently, numerous Secretaries of Defense, including James Schlesinger, Harold Brown and Caspar Weinberger, have made similar claims.[1]

This position departs, however, from the historical main stream of economic thought. Military spending has been generally viewed as an impediment to economic progress. Since soldiers and arms producers do not create goods and services that can be consumed by others, many economists see arms spending as subtracting from a nation's total resources. If the "dead weight" of military spending becomes too great, it is assumed that an economy will suffer. The first economist, Adam Smith, presented this position in his famous book, *The Wealth of Nations:*

> [T]he whole army and navy, are unproductive labourers. They are the servants of the public, and are maintained by a part of the annual produce of the industry of other people. Their service, how honorable, how useful, or how necessary soever, produces nothing for which an equal quantity of services can afterwards be procured.[2]

That traditional view was widely held in the United States before World War II. Even after the war, government officials voiced concern about the untoward economic effects of higher military spending. Presidents Truman and Eisenhower, for example, both cited economic dangers as a factor in their decisions to limit arms spending increases.[3] In addition, even among those economists who now support higher arms budgets, a number recognize the costs. Herbert Stein, an advocate of increased military spending and a former Chairman of the Council of Economic Advisors, commented last year, "no one that I know of, except for a few old Marxists, ever thought military spending was good for the American economy."[4]

Even though some highly visible people have warned of the dangers of excessive arms spending, the economic prosperity created by World War II left a deep impression on the American people. Before the war, the United States was mired in the Great Depression. Unemployment, which had been as high as 24.9 percent in 1933, still averaged 14.6 percent in 1940. During the war, unemployment dropped rapidly. In 1942 it averaged 4.7 percent and in 1944 unemployment reached a wartime low of 1.2 percent.[5] As a result, the images of "Rosie the riveter" and America as the "arsenal of democracy" stayed with Americans long after the Second World War was over.

While those memories increased support for heavy military spending, there has been little assessment of the effect that high arms expenditures have had on the U.S. economy during the Cold War. Did high levels of military spending result in better economic performance? Or has military spending contributed to our present economic problems? We assess these questions by examining the evidence regarding the causes of our economic difficulties.

Current Economic Crisis

Since World War II, Americans have come to expect that our standard of living would increase indefinitely. During the 1950s and especially the 1960s, the future promised greater opportunity and prosperity, even though we already enjoyed the world's highest per capita income. In the 1970s, however, the "American dream" began to crumble under the weight of an economy plagued by inflation, unemployment and slow growth.

"Stagflation" during the 1970s eroded the yearly increase in real income that Americans had come to expect. From 1960 to 1973, the yearly increase in per capita disposable personal income averaged 2.8 percent after accounting for inflation. Between 1973 and 1981, however, the average increase was only 1.6 percent. Production and non-supervisory workers fared worse. Instead of increasing, their hourly earnings actually *fell* 1.6 percent a year, between 1973 and 1980, after rising 1.5 percent a year from 1960 to 1973.[6]

During the past decade, unemployment has continued its post-World War II trend — remaining at a higher level after each recession than it was prior to the downturn. In December 1982, unemployment reached a level unmatched since the Great Depression — 10.8 percent.[7] Few economists expect it to fall below 10 percent until late in 1983. Even though unemployment in other industrial nations also rose after the oil crisis, America's unemployment rate remained higher than most (Chart 2.1).

Economic growth in the United States has also been sluggish. America's average inflation-adjusted rate of growth in gross domestic product (GDP)* since 1960 ranks 13 among 17 major non-communist nations (Chart 2.2). As a result of stronger economic growth, eight European nations surpassed America's standard of living by 1980, as measured by the level of GDP per capita.[8] Throughout most of the 1970s, Switzerland, Denmark and Sweden all enjoyed a higher level of GDP per capita. By the end of the decade Germany, Norway, Belgium, the Netherlands and France also passed the United States.

A growing number of economists place a large measure of blame for our economic problems on the declining competitiveness of U.S. manufactured goods in both foreign and domestic markets. "U.S. industry's loss of competitiveness over the past two decades has been nothing short of an economic disaster and goes a long way toward explaining the shrinking standard of living," explained *Business Week* in a special issue entitled the "Reindustrialization of America."[9] During the past decade, American manufacturers have lost almost a quarter of their share of the international market and about three percent of their share of domestic manufacturing sales (Chart 2.3). These declines cost the American economy some *$125 billion* in lost production and at least 2 million industrial jobs. The nation's reduced manufacturing competitiveness occurred even after a 40 percent devaluation of the dollar during the 1970s that made foreign goods more expensive, and American goods cheaper, in the international market.[10]

At the same time American manufacturers were losing ground to foreign competition, the rising cost of imported oil and other raw materials made the expansion of exports an urgent task. Before the mid-1970s, America's positive balance of trade in manufactured goods always exceeded any negative balance in fuels and crude materials. But since the oil crisis began, exports of manufactured goods have offset the

---

* Gross domestic product (GDP) is preferred for international comparisons.

increasingly negative balance in raw materials during only one year, 1975 (Table 2.1). In two of the nine years between 1973 and 1981, the balance of trade in manufactured goods was negative. In the other years, exports of manufactured goods were less than 20 percent greater than imports of such goods (Chart 2.4). By comparison, during the 1960s, such exports were over 30 percent greater than imports in all but the last two years of that decade.

These statistics indicate a serious relative deterioration of U.S. manufacturing competence. As the most advanced industrial nation in the world during most of the last three decades, a wealth of skilled labor, capital and advanced technology should have enabled American firms to produce quality goods at competitive prices. This, however, did not occur. Japanese and European manufacturers are capturing larger and larger shares of U.S. domestic markets, and are displacing American goods in markets abroad. A wide variety of American industries have lost ground to foreign competitors, including: autos, steel, aircraft, industrial chemicals, telecommunications, consumer electronics and machine tools.

The explosion in energy prices significantly contributed to the problems facing U.S. manufacturers by making energy-intensive production techniques more expensive, and thus, less competitive. In addition, manufacturers were forced to use resources, such as engineers and investment capital, to increase energy-efficiency. As a result, product development and improvement suffered. The energy crisis, however, is not the only reason for the lagging fortunes of America's manufacturing industries. A steep decline in the ratio of manufactured exports to imports began in the mid-1960s, years before the dramatic rise in oil prices in 1973 (Chart 2.4). Moreover, other advanced industrial nations were able to offset increased energy prices by expanding the export of manufactured goods.[11]

A variety of other factors has been cited to explain the declining competitiveness of U.S. manufacturers. Some observers believe that increased social spending and expanded government regulations have reduced the amount of new investments made by American firms.[12] Others have argued that lower labor costs have provided our competitors with a key advantage.[13] More recently, some analysts have pointed to shortsighted management techniques employed by major American firms as a reason for our decline.[14] Still others have suggested that industrialization in the United States has proceeded sufficiently to exhaust most of the profitable opportunities in old-line industries, such as autos and steel.[15] Only a few analysts have examined the possibility that military spending has been a major contributor to declining fortunes in the manufacturing sector.[16]

In this study, we concentrate on examining the last thesis. Although not the only reason for our economic woes, arms expenditures robbed the civilian sector of key resources, such as engineers and investment capital, that might have been used to modernize U.S. manufacturing industries. While America's manufacturing firms were becoming less competitive, the United States spent more on arms than all of our NATO (North Atlantic Treaty Organization) allies combined. Even after adjusting for the relative size of each economy, America's military burden was by far the heaviest among major industrialized nations (Chart 2.5). Over the past two decades, America spent 35 percent more of its GDP on the military than did the United Kingdom, which had the second largest military burden. At the other extreme, in relative terms, Japan spent only about one-seventh as much as did the United States.

Statistical Analysis

We explored the assertion that military spending has contributed to America's declining competitiveness by comparing the national economic performance of 17 major non-communist, industrial countries over the past two decades (Appendix B). We thought that patterns in the performance of these industrial nations might help explain why some were more successful than others. We believed that a cross-national comparison would provide the broad illumination needed to assess the main question.

Our analysis was performed in three parts. First, we identified factors that were associated with better economic performance. In particular, we tested the hypothesis that greater investment and faster productivity growth resulted in stronger economic growth and less unemployment and inflation. Second, we examined the hypothesis that among comparable nations, those with heavier military burdens suffered poorer economic performance. We also examined four questions drawn from the current economic literature bearing on our hypothesis:

1. Did greater government spending reduce investment and performance?

2. Did higher labor costs decrease the competitiveness of American manufactured goods?

3. Did the baby boom of the 1950s slow the growth of capital per worker in U.S. manufacturing?

4. Did more heavily industrialized nations tend to grow slower than less industrialized ones?

Finally, we examined the relationships among the various factors that might inhibit performance to see if any of our results could be explained by disguised correlations.

Three factors were considered in choosing countries for our study. Each filtered out differences among nations that could have invalidated our results. First, we excluded those nations in which market mechanisms do not largely determine the distribution of economic resources. Second, we excluded nations that do not have large and diverse industrial capabilities. Third, we excluded nations for which we could not obtain data consistent with the majority of other countries in the study. The nations meeting all three criteria were: Australia, Austria, Belgium, Canada, Denmark,, Finland, France, West Germany, Italy, Japan, the Netherlands, New Zealand, Norway, Sweden, Switzerland, the United Kingdom, and the United States. These countries, located on four continents, produce most of the world's economic output.

From the outset, we recognize that our sample contains nations with significant differences in social customs and economic history. We believe that these differences do not invalidate the study if our findings are interpreted carefully.

We averaged a variety of economic indicators for each of the 17 countries over the period 1960 to 1980. The data were also divided in two sub-periods (1960 to 1973 and 1973 to 1980) to detect any changes likely to be caused by either expanding energy prices or by lower levels of military spending after the Vietnam war.

As discussed in Appendix B, we used three statistical tests to detect associations between variables. First we used simple rank order correlations to catch basic relationships. Then we excluded individual nations, like Japan and the United States, to see whether any one country was primarily responsible for the correlations we found. Finally, we performed multiple regressions on the data to determine which variable, or combination of variables, best explained the trends. The results of those tests suggest that the relationships discussed below do indeed exist. However, it is important to bear in mind that statistical analyses only indicate that relationships exist, they do not explain *why* such relationships occur.

Results of Analysis

I. Reasons for Economic Success

From the outset, we postulated that a large measure of America's decline has resulted from the failure of U.S. manufacturers to keep pace with the rapid growth in productivity maintained by Western European and Japanese firms during the past two decades (Chart 2.6). Between 1960 and the oil price shock in 1973, manufacturing productivity growth in most European nations (except the United Kingdom) averaged twice the U.S. rate. Japan's growth rate was more than three times higher than America's. Even after the oil crunch depressed economic growth in most of the industrialized world, many European countries and Japan still maintained productivity growth rates two to three times higher than the U.S. rate.

Faster growth in output per worker has provided other countries with a significant advantage: They could decrease the price of their goods more quickly than could American firms. Ever since Eli Whitney discovered that interchangable parts made the production and repair of rifles cheaper, the genius of U.S. industry has been its ability to reduce the cost of manufactured goods — making them affordable for most people. Long before the majority of Europeans could buy automobiles, Henry Ford's assembly line produced Model T's affordable to the average American worker. Ford's concept was copied and vastly improved upon by firms in a wide variety of industries throughout the world. Each refinement has been aimed at reducing costs to capture a larger market share. For decades, U.S. firms were unmatched in their manufacturing efficiency. Yet today, many European companies have closed the gap and are now beating us at our own game.

In our analysis, then, we looked to see if nations with faster increases in productivity enjoyed better economic performance during the last two decades. Our statistical tests indicate that productivity growth was closely associated with real economic growth before 1973 (Appendix B), although this relationship deteriorates after the dramatic rise in oil prices. We also found that nations with higher growth in manufacturing productivity tended to have lower unemployment. The probable link here is that increased productivity lowers costs and expands the

41

demand for a product, increasing production and employment. Surprisingly, this relationship is stronger *after* the oil crisis began than it was during the 1960s. Both of tnese findings underline the importance of a strong manufacturing sector to the overall performance of a nation's economy.

Why have other nations been able to sustain higher productivity growth? Increased manufacturing efficiency can be attained by a number of methods, the most important being: 1) replacing older machines with more sophisticated equipment; 2) expanding factory size to take advantage of economies of scale; 3) increasing the skill and competence of the work force; 4) adopting more efficient methods for using people and machines; and 5) replacing expensive materials with cheaper substitutes. Three of these methods — expanding a factory, purchasing new production equipment and substituting materials — require additional investment. In other words, without available investment capital important ways to attain productivity growth are cut off.

Our statistical analysis suggests that investment has been a key factor in productivity growth. Before the oil crisis, productivity growth tended to be faster in nations with higher investment levels. The United States ranked last in productivity growth between 1960 and 1973 and also last in both the share of GDP devoted to new fixed investment and the growth in total manufacturing capital during that period (Charts 2.7A and B). After the onset of the energy crisis, however, our statistical evidence does not indicate that higher investment resulted in faster productivity growth.

New investment also seems to have stimulated economic growth and reduced unemployment. Nations with a larger share of GDP devoted to investment and/or higher growth in total manufacturing capital also tended to have faster real growth in GDP. This relationship remained strong even after the oil crisis began. Furthermore, nations that invested more heavily experienced less unemployment. While this link between investment and lower unemployment is strong prior to the oil crisis, it disappears after 1973.

Initially, we were confused by the differences in our findings for the periods before and after the oil crisis. We were puzzled to find that after 1973, productivity growth did not correlate with investment. Upon reflection, however, these results might be explained by two factors. First, the dramatic boost in oil prices, which made a number of production techniques unprofitable, forced many firms to increase their energy-efficiency. But new investments in energy-efficient plants and equipment did not necessarily increase labor efficiency. Second, firms in nations that had more energy-efficient capital equipment prior to the oil crisis probably did not have to invest as heavily to increase labor productivity as did companies in countries with less energy-efficient equipment. For example, in North America energy prices were controlled during the 1960s, reducing the need for energy-efficient equipment in that period. Thus, even though Canada invested heavily after the oil crisis began, that country experienced the lowest level of productivity growth among the nations we studied. On the other hand, in northern Europe, where energy prices were high during the 1960s, Belgium, Denmark, and the Netherlands all had high productivity after 1973 even though their investments were low.

After energy prices rose dramatically, nations with either higher investment or faster productivity growth generally experienced better economic performance. Countries like Canada, which had higher investment after the energy crisis began, tended to have better economic growth. Nations in northern Europe, which had larger productivity increases usually enjoyed lower unemployment. Moreover, nations such as Japan and France, which had both higher investment and greater productivity increases, also had faster overall growth and lower unemployment. Nations such as the United States and the United Kingdom, which had low investment and low productivity growth, suffered from slow growth and high unemployment.

Inflation was the only performance measure that did not correlate with either investment or productivity growth. While increases in a nation's inflation rate can be particularly detrimental to investment, we found no cross-national association between higher inflation and lower investment. Indeed, while Americans invested less compared with most other industrialized nations, the United States enjoyed one of the lowest inflation rates, even after the energy crisis began (Chart 2.8). Another unexpected finding was that lower unemployment did not correlate with higher economic growth. That overturned our expectation that nations experiencing faster growth would tend to enjoy lower unemployment.

In summary, the measures of investment we used were strongly associated with economic growth in each of the data periods we tested. Investment was also linked to productivity growth and lower unemployment, except after the oil crisis. Ironically, while the association between productivity growth and economic growth disappeared in the post-oil crisis data, the link between higher productivity growth and lower unemployment became stronger in that period. Inflation was not linked with investment or productivity growth, and higher economic growth was not associated with lower unemployment.

While there are limits to cross-national comparisons, our findings offer clues that help explain economic success and failure. Higher investment and productivity growth seem to play a particularly important role in stronger economic performance. However, the difficulties created by rising energy prices have confused these links. Higher investment does not necessarily do as much for one nation as it does for another and faster productivity increases do not automatically mean higher economic growth.

II. Reasons for
Poorer Performance

Having broadly sketched in the hallmarks of economic success, we look in this section for economic pitfalls that may cause poor performance. In particular, why were investment and productivity growth lower in some nations than in others? To help answer this question, we analyze five different factors that might explain poorer economic performance: the civilian government burden; labor costs; growth in the labor force; industrial maturity; and the military burden.

Growth in Civilian Government: Examining cross-national data on government spending, we found virtually no evidence for the often-repeated claim that government social programs, particularly transfer payments, have contributed to America's declining competitiveness (Appendix B). The burdens imposed on most western European nations by non-military government expenditures far exceed the burden they impose on the United States (Chart 2.9). The United States ranked 13 among 17 industrial nations in the share of GDP consumed by civilian government. America also ranked second to last among 14 nations in the share of GDP transferred by the government from one group to another through programs such as social security (Chart 2.10).

Our statistical tests did not uncover any significant evidence that relative levels of civilian government spending or transfer payments had any relationship to economic performance among advanced industrial nations. Of the numerous comparisons between social spending and measures of economic performance over three time periods, *none* showed any strong negative association. On the contrary, some evidence indicates government spending actually improves national economic performance.[17] Government expenditures that improve the economic infrastructure, such as roads, bridges and mass transit, seem to enhance economic growth.

Higher Labor Costs: Although some believe that cheap labor explains the success of our industrial competitors, pay increases abroad have rendered this argument obsolete. Low wages helped some countries during the 1960s; but by the mid-1970s, European manufacturing labor costs had caught up to American costs. By 1975, Belgium, Sweden and the Netherlands surpassed America's absolute level of compensation per hour in manufacturing (Table 2.2). By 1980, compensation to workers in West Germany also exceeded America's. France, Canada and Italy are close behind. Japan, however, continues to have lower labor costs than other industrial nations.

We did find weak evidence, limited to the 1960s, that nations with higher manufacturing labor costs corresponded to those with three areas of lower growth — in productivity, total manufacturing capital and overall GDP. Yet as compensation rates among nations converged during the 1970s, these associations disappeared. More importantly, we found strong evidence that nations with higher labor costs offset this disadvantage by maintaining higher output per employee. This was particularly true for the United States, which had high labor costs and the highest level of output per employed person throughout the entire period (Table 2.3).

Labor costs in other industrial nations have been growing considerably faster than in the United States. Since 1960, the United States has had the lowest growth in hourly compensation in manufacturing among industrial nations (Chart 2.11). Japan's growth in compensation was over twice the U.S. rate between 1960 and 1981. Most European nations averaged growth rates 50 percent higher than ours. Thus, as labor compensation rates become comparable among industrial nations, it became less plausible to blame our present troubles on cheaper labor in other nations.

Higher productivity growth abroad has helped close the wage gap between American workers and their foreign counterparts. Besides allowing firms to expand their markets by decreasing the prices of their products, growth in output per employee also brings worker demands for a share of the rewards. Labor unions throughout the world have often tied wage demands to productivity growth. Thus it comes as no surprise that our statistical analysis uncovered a strong positive relationship between productivity growth and labor cost increases. Compensation increases were also linked to the inflation rate; however, it is still not clear if labor cost increases trigger inflation or if higher inflation encourages higher wage demands.

Booming Labor Force: We do not dispute that the expansion of America's work force during the past few years has combined with sluggish growth of investment to result in slower growth of the overall capital to labor ratio.[18] To use this fact to explain why our manufacturing productivity growth and international competitiveness have declined during the past decade, however, would be erroneous since most of the new jobs created in our economy were in the service sector.[19]

In the manufacturing sector, employment actually grew more slowly during the last few years than it did between 1960 and 1973. At the same time, growth in total manufacturing capital remained relatively stable. Thus, the growth in the ratio of capital to labor was *higher* during the present period than in the earlier period (Table 2.4). While growth in the capital to labor ratio declined in the service sector, this reduction would not explain the problems in the manufacturing sector. Thus, we cannot blame the decline in manufacturing merely on surges in the number of workers — neither that created by the baby boom generation nor by women who have recently entered the workforce in large numbers.

More Industrialized Nations Grow More Slowly: Another factor that might explain the differences in economic performance among the nations we studied is their relative industrial maturity. It seems likely that countries with more developed economies would tend to have fewer opportunities for growth than less industrialized nations. For example, nations that can vastly improve their production technology by borrowing from more developed nations will grow faster. Also, nations that can shift a large number of people from the agricultural sector to the industrial sector will experience a boost in output. While the differences in economic maturity among the industrial nations we studied are narrow, the distinctions are still important.

To determine whether industrial maturity was a key factor in economic performance, we used two measures of industrialization to compare nations: average output per employed person (productivity) and the share of GDP accounted for by agricultural production. We would expect that nations with lower output per employee would grow more quickly by investing in production technology already employed elsewhere. We also assumed that nations with a larger agricultural sector relative to GDP had a greater number of industrial opportunities to develop. By both of these measures, the United States ranks close to the top on the industrial maturity scale. America has had the highest level of output per employee over the last three decades (Table 2.3) and the second lowest share of GDP accounted for by agriculture (Chart 2.12).

While we found no evidence that the relative level of GDP per employee influenced growth and investment, nations with a larger agricultural component of GDP tended to perform better. Prior to the oil crisis, nations with larger agricultural sectors generally had higher investment plus faster economic and productivity growth. After 1973, the relationship between nations with a larger agricultural sector and faster economic and productivity growth disappears; however, the positive association between a large agricultural sector and a higher investment rate remains. We also found weak evidence that nations with lower output per employee had lower unemployment after the oil crisis.

One interesting finding was that the less industrialized nations in our study tended to experience higher inflation. This result was not unexpected because price increases are generally greater during periods of higher growth. However, it does help clarify why a higher inflation rate does not seem to indicate poorer economic performance cross-nationally.

In conclusion, our tests suggest that America's industrial maturity may be a major explanation for our relatively poorer economic performance, particularly prior to the energy crisis.

High Cost of the Military Burden: Our hypothesis is that a nation which spends a larger share of GDP on weapons and soldiers than other nations is likely to experience less investment and poorer productivity growth. As a result, the competitiveness of a nation's manufactured goods may be eroded by a heavy military burden. Arms production diverts engineers and scientists from civilian projects. Some have suggested that building weapons attracts some of the brightest people within those fields because of the challenges and complexity of the work.[20] Even if it only attracts those of average ability, arms production probably reduces the number of highly skilled people working directly to increase the productivity and competitiveness of a nation's manufacturing sector.

A heavy military burden also tends to "crowd out" civilian investment, particularly when the economy is functioning close to peak capacity, as it was during the Vietnam War. When most of an economy's resources are fully employed, higher spending by the government reduces investment, no matter how the spending is paid for. If a government imposes higher taxes, individuals tend to reduce the amount they save and corporations have less revenue to invest. If the government borrows to cover military spending, increased competition for money may also reduce investment. Finally, if the government prints new money to pay for the armed forces, it creates the classic inflationary condition: too many dollars chasing too few goods. Inflation can reduce the incentive to invest.

Our cross-national comparisons generally support our hypothesis. When we compared the share of output devoted to investment with the share spent on the military in 17 industrial nations, we found that those nations with a larger military burden tended to invest less (Chart 2.13). A negative correlation also exists between military expenditures and the growth in total manufacturing capital. Neither of these relationships deteriorated during the energy crisis.

Nations carrying heavier military burdens also tended to have lower productivity growth. While we found strong evidence that military spending reduced productivity growth prior to 1973, our cross-national analysis did not yield similar evidence for the period after the oil crisis began. This finding may be explained by the fact that virtually every nation we studied had a lower military burden after 1973. It might also be the result of the increasingly complex nature of productivity growth after the oil crisis. We cannot be sure.

We also found weak evidence that higher military spending correlates with lower real economic growth. We suspect that the relationship between investment and real economic growth is at work here. For while it is weak, the negative relationship between the military burden and economic growth does not deteriorate during the 1970s.

Two indicators of economic performance, unemployment and inflation, were not associated with military spending. Given the significance of the negative association between military spending and investment, and the tendency of nations with lower investment to have higher unemployment, we expected to find that nations with higher military spending had higher unemployment. However, this relationship did not appear. Since it seems likely that, in the long run, high military spending leads to poorer performance, this link may be disguised by other factors. We also did not find a correlation between inflation and military spending. We were not surprised by this finding, however, given the lack of significant relationships between the inflation rate and other measures of economic performance.

Overall, our evidence suggests that military spending has hurt America's economic performance, particularly in the period prior to 1973.

III. Relationship Among Factors Affecting Peformance

There were three findings in our cross-national analysis that we thought might be influenced by disguised relationships. First, we examined the possibility that the negative relationship between military spending and economic performance might be explained by the fact that more industrialized nations grow more slowly. Second, we analyzed factors that might explain why civilian government spending did not correlate with poorer economic performance, even though military government spending did. Finally, we looked for reasons why military spending did not seem to reduce personal consumption cross-nationally.

The strong correlation between countries with a heavier military burden and a smaller share of GDP accounted for by agriculture raises a critical question: What was the key factor in poorer economic performance, economic maturity or military spending? Some radical economists have suggested that maturity is the basic problem. In their view, military expenditures are greater in mature capitalist economies because arms production creates both investment opportunities and demand for goods and services at a time when the overall economy is stagnating. They argue that military expenditures are more politically acceptable than civilian programs because the Pentagon does not compete with private industries. Moreover, they believe that large military establishments help protect and expand the range of investment opportunities and markets for goods around the globe.[21] This line of reasoning would seem to suggest that military spending indeed bolsters economic performance during a period of stagnation.

While this is an intriguing suggestion, it is just as likely that the negative impacts of military spending and industrial maturity work in concert. Mature nations may find arms expenditures attractive for a variety of reasons; however, as a nation becomes more economically dependent on military spending, efficiency and ingenuity seem to decline. Engineers working on military budgets become accustomed to an environment where cost is not the central concern.[22] Moreover, defense dependency can discourage risk-taking by providing a stable source of revenues.[23] Combined with the diversion of resources entailed by arms spending, these factors probably contribute to economic decline. Our regression tests generally support this second approach: The military burden consistently explained more of the variation in the performance of countries than did the maturity level (Appendix B).

The second issue we explored could be seen as a major contradiction within our findings: Military expenditures correlate with poorer economic performance but civilian government expenditures do not. Two factors could explain this apparent contradiction.

First, civilian government spending may act as an important prerequisite for private investment. A large portion of civilian government funds are used to build and maintain the public infrastructure, including roads, schools and sewers. Far from being a hindrance, expenditures for transportation, education and sanitation lay the groundwork for a successful economy. It is fruitless to start a new business if there are not enough skilled workers; or if the transportation network is inadequate to bring materials and workers to and from the factory on time; or if there are no public utilities to provide electricity, water, and sewage treatment. While our cross-national data did not indicate that civilian government expenditures aid economic performance, this reasoning could explain why, on balance, civilian government expenditures do not hinder progress.

Another reason for the different impacts of civilian and military government spending may lie in the nature of civilian programs. Civilian spending is often a direct substitute for private consumption spending. For example, in countries that decide that the government should pay for health care, personal medical expenditures will probably be lower. The same is true in the case of government-subsidized education, transportation, day care, libraries, and recreation. Moreover, tax systems tend to enforce this "tradeoff." Indeed, among the nations we studied, those that had higher levels of civilian government consumption usually had lower levels of personal consumption. This link was strong, particularly in the post-oil crisis data.

One additional finding that required review was the lack of correlation we found between the share of GDP spent on the military and the share spent on personal consumption. We might expect a negative relationship between these factors for two reasons. First, nations that devote a larger share of GDP to the military by definition spend less on some combination of the other three components of GDP: consumption, investment and civil government. Second, prior research on this subject indicates that *both* investment and consumption would be reduced by military spending.[24] The American experience since 1947 supports this view as well. During times of higher military spending, consumption and investment seem to have suffered proportionately during the Cold War (Chart 2.14). Thus, we were somewhat confused by our finding.

Given the apparent tradeoff between personal consumption and civil government consumption, we tested the possibility that countries carrying heavier military burdens sacrificed some combination of these two forms of consumption. However, we found no evidence for a negative relationship between military spending and "civil consumption." We were left to surmise that, cross-nationally, consumption is not necessarily reduced as much by higher military spending as is investment.

Other Theories

Clearly, our cross-national analysis could not test all theories attempting to explain America's poor economic performance. We have supplemented our statistical work with short discussions of three additional factors that may have exerted significant influence. Below, we examine the effects of regulation, long-term economic trends and management techniques.

Regulation: Over-regulation by the government is often cited as a reason for America's current problems.[25] It is not clear, however, that the regulatory burden has strongly inhibited economic performance[26] or that the impact of regulation on U.S. industry is worse than it is on firms in other advanced industrial nations. Most European and Japanese workers have greater employment security.[27] Relocating industrial facilities is often more difficult abroad. Government bureaucrats in Europe and Japan are much more actively — though not so adversarially — involved in the decision making of private corporations. And environmental legislation is also great.[28] Indeed, estimates by the Organisation for Economic Cooperation and Development indicate that "Japan spent about four times the fraction of GNP on regulatory compliance as the United States; Germany and Sweden spent about the same proportion; and other countries spent somewhat less."[29] Thus to the extent that regulation increases private costs (for the benefit of the whole society), it would be hard to argue that the impact has been greater in America than abroad.

Past the "Crest:" Another interesting theory sees America's present dilemma as a stage in the broad cycle of economic growth and stagnation that is inherent in market economies. Drawing from the work of Nikolai Kondratieff, economists at M.I.T. have developed an economic model that "strongly suggests that the current economic malaise is an expected part of a long wave — that is not unique."[30] So-called "long waves" develop as the production of new technologies stimulate additional growth opportunities. For example, as the automobile became affordable to more people, it helped to create demand for suburban housing, shopping centers and motels. At the mid-point of a wave, Kondratieff's theory suggests that investment opportunities become increasingly scarce, as the central technology and all the peripheral options are fully developed. In the final stage, the lack of investment opportunities leads to widespread stagnation. If the nation is lucky, a new driving force develops during the late stage of the process to form the basis for a new wave. Our earlier discussion of the "maturity" hypothesis may lend some credence to this theory.

Management by the Numbers: Recently, the theory that American business executives have concentrated on short-run returns on investment rather than long-term growth has gained widespread attention. This notion was ably presented by Robert Hayes and William Abernathy in a widely-praised *Harvard Business Review* article in 1980. Hayes and Abernathy see American managers as contributing to our competitive decline:

> By their preference for servicing existing markets rather than creating new ones and by their devotion to short-term returns and "management by the numbers," many of them have objectively forsworn long-term technological superiority as a competitive weapon. In consequence, they have abdicated their strategic responsibilities.[31]

The failures of both the auto and rubber industries fit into their explanation. Car manufacturers failed to develop reliable, fuel-efficient automobiles because larger models had a higher return. As a result, foreign car manufacturers almost doubled their share of the American market during the 1970s, growing to more than $5 billion in sales a year by 1980.[32] The tire industry followed right along behind the automakers, failing to produce radial tires soon enough to compete with imported radials. They continued to produce conventional tires for American cars instead of risking introduction of a new product.

Hayes and Abernathy also believe that American manufacturers have balked at committing funds for researching opportunities to improve the efficiency of production techniques. But "virtually across the board, European managers impressed us with their strong commitment to increasing market share through internal development of advanced process technology."[33]

In a well-documented study of this issue, Ira Magaziner and Robert Reich summarized the shortcomings of American management techniques:

> Once dominant in most of the world's businesses, many U.S. companies have not kept pace in recent years with changes in the international competitive environment. Our systems for evaluating investment decisions have not sufficiently considered the competitive evolution of business. Our accounting systems have given managers incorrect signals about investments. Our systems for measuring total product costs have misallocated manufacturing and distribution overheads and have failed to provide accurate information on the total costs of improvements in process and quality control. Our pricing policies have allowed foreign competitors to gain advantages in other national markets from which they can better penetrate the U.S. market. In managing our international businesses, we have overemphasized the importance of cheap labor in production at the expense of productivity improvements and long-term market penetration. We have failed to give workers a stake in productivity improvements. Finally, we have paid too much attention to rearranging our industrial assets and too little attention to building our industrial base.[34]

Recently, this theory has been criticized for overlooking the substantial growth in manufacturing investment that occurred in the United States after the oil crisis.[35] However, it seems clear that even if investment increased, short-sighted management decisions have badly hurt American companies in autos, steel and consumer electronics.[36]

Conclusion

While numerous factors influence economic performance, America's heavier military burden seems to have stifled investment, and reduced our economic and productivity growth over the last few decades. During the 1950s and 1960s, higher arms expenditures in the United States probably allowed other industrial nations to close the economic gap separating America from the rest of the world more quickly than if we had spent less on the military. While more industrialized nations tend to grow more slowly, our economy probably would have performed significantly better if the United States had reallocated a portion of the resources used by the military. For example, if the government had more heavily subsidized the development and repair of mass-transit systems in major metropolitan areas throughout the United States, we could have sustained and expanded the now-failing American mass-transit vehicle industry, reducing the need to import subway cars from Europe, Canada and Japan to fill the needs of New York, Boston and Philadelphia. If the government had not spent so much on high technology military products, the engineers doing military work might have developed commercial electronics products to compete more effectively with the Japanese. Our highly skilled people might also have worked on developing renewable energy resources. Moreover, we also could have used part of the "peace dividend" to assist sound economic progress in some of the world's poorest nations,[37] thereby helping open up new markets for our goods and services. Surely, given the wide array of possible alternatives, we would have found productive jobs for the thousands of engineers, scientists and skilled workers who were building weapons for the "electronic battlefield."

Military spending also slowed economic performance during the 1970s. While the rising cost of energy clearly damaged performance across the board in the industrial world, military spending continued to draw away resources that could have been used to develop energy self-sufficiency. Moreover, if more engineers and greater investment had been available to the private sector after 1973, American business might have been able to offset part of the higher cost of energy by expanding exports of U.S. manufactured goods.

Increased arms expenditures during the Reagan administration could have the opposite effect on the economy that they had during the Second World War. As the "arsenal of democracy" during that war, America built its industrial base while other nations saw their industrial power consumed by the fires of war. Yet during the next decade, if we increase arms expenditures in the United States while most other advanced nations concentrate on expanding their industrial strength, we could be left watching our economic health continue to slip away.

54

Notes

1. James Schlesinger, quoted in John Finney, "Military Budget Spurs Economy," *The New York Times*, February 27, 1974.

   Harold Brown, "Statement and Annex," before U.S. Congress, Senate Committee on the Budget, February 27, 1980, p. 5.

   Caspar W. Weinberger, "Address to the National Press Club," *News Release*, Office of the Assistant Secretary of Defense (Public Affairs), March 8, 1982, p. 3.

   Weinberger, statement before the U.S. Congress, Committee on Appropriations, Defense Subcommittee, hearings, (Washington, D.C.: U.S. GPO, February 24, 1982), pp. 86-87.

2. Adam Smith, *The Wealth of Nations* (New York: Modern Library, 1937), p. 315.

3. For a discussion of the Truman and Eisenhower administration's views of the economic impact of military spending see: John Lewis Gaddis, *Strategies of Containment: A Critical Appraisal of Postwar American National Security Policy* (New York: Oxford University Press, 1982), pp. 92-95, 132-136.

4. Herbert Stein, "Military Spending's Bottom Line," Letter to the Editor, *The New York Times*, January 8, 1982.

5. U.S. Department of Labor, Bureau of Labor Statistics, *Employment and Earnings*, January 1976, Table 1.

6. *Economic Report of the President*, (Washington, D.C.: U.S. GPO, February 1982), Tables B-24 & 29.

7. U.S. Department of Labor, Bureau of Labor Statistics, "The Unemployment Situation: December 1982," *News*, January 7, 1983, Table C.

8. *National Accounts of Organisation of Economic Cooperation and Development Countries, 1950 - 1980, Volume I* (Paris: O.E.C.D., 1982), p. 88.

9. The Business Week Team, *The Reindustrialization of America*, (New York: McGraw-Hill Book Co., 1982), p. 10.

10. The Business Week Team, *Ibid.*, p. 11.

11. Ira C. Magaziner and Robert Reich, *Minding America's Business: The Decline and Rise of the American Economy* (New York: Harcourt Brace Jovanovich, 1981), pp. 75-77.

12. N.Y. Stock Exchange, Office of Economic Research, "U.S Economic Performance in a Global Perspective," February 1981.

13. Peter Drucker, "The Danger of Excessive Labor Income," *The Wall Street Journal*, January 6, 1981.

14. Robert H. Hayes and William J. Abernathy, "Managing Our Way to Economic Decline," *Harvard Business Review*, July-August 1980.

    Leslie Wayne, "Management Gospel Gone Wrong," *The New York Times*, May 30, 1982.

15. Nathaniel J. Mass and Peter M. Senge, "Reindustrialization: Aiming for the Right Targets," *Technology Review*, Volume 83, Number 8, August/September 1981.

16. Seymour Melman, *The Permanent War Economy: American Capitalism in Decline* (New York: Simon & Schuster, 1974), Chapters 4 and 5.

    Lloyd J. Dumas, ed., *The Political Economy of Arms Reduction* (Boulder, Colo.: 1982), Chapter 1.

    Mary Kaldor, *The Baroque Arsenal* (New York: Hill and Wang, 1981), Chapters 2 and 3.

Ronald P. Smith, "Military Expenditure and Investment in OECD Countries, 1954-1973," *Journal of Comparative Economics*, No. 4, 1980, pp. 19-32.

R.P. Smith, "Military Expenditure and Capitalism," *Cambridge Journal of Economics*, No. 1, 1977, p. 61-76.

17. Alfred S. Eichner, "Consequences of the Budget: Reagan's Doubtful Game Plan," *Challenge: The Magazine of Economic Affairs*, May/June 1981, Volume 24, Number 2, p. 19-27.

Bryan Wilson, "The Effect of Compositional Changes in Government Expenditures on Economic Growth," unpublished paper, Rutgers the State University, December 17, 1980.

18. George Terborgh, "The Productivity Puzzle" (Washington, D.C.: Machinery and Allied Products Institute, December, 1981).

19. Lester Thurow, *The Zero-Sum Society* (New York: Penguin Books, 1981), p. 46-47.

20. Thurow, "How to Wreck the Economy," *The New York Review of Books*, May 14, 1981.

21. Paul Baran and Paul Sweezy, *Monopoly Capital* (New York: Modern Reader, 1968), Chapter 7.

Michael Reich, "Does the U.S. Economy Require Military Spending?" *The American Economic Review*, May 1972, pp. 296-303.

22. Melman, *op. cit.*, Chapters 2 and 4.

23. Kaldor, *op. cit.*, Chapter 2.

24. Bruce Russett, *What Price Vigilance?* (New Haven, Conn.: Yale University Press, 1970), pp. 137-146.

Kenneth Boulding, "The Impact of the Defense Industry on the Structure of the Economy," in Bernard Udis, ed., *The Economic Consequences of Reduced Military Spending* (Lexington, Mass.: Lexington Books, 1973), pp. 225-252.

25. Murray Weidenbaum, statement before the U.S. Congress, Senate Committee on Commerce, Science and Transportation, Subcommittee for Consumers, "Cost of Government Regulations to the Consumer," (Washington, D.C.: U.S. GPO, November 1978), p. 93.

26. Richard Kazis and Richard Grossman, *Fear At Work*, (New York: Pilgrim Press, 1982), Chapter 5.

William K. Tabb, "Government Regulations: Two Sides of the Story," *Challenge* November-December, 1980, pp. 40-48.

27. Magaziner and Reich, *op. cit.*, Chapter 12.

Joint Report of Labor Union Study Tour Participants, *Economic Dislocation: Plant Closings, Plant Relocations and Plant Conversion* (Washington, D.C.: United States Steel Workers, International Association of Machinists, United Auto Workers, May 1979).

Ezra F. Vogel, *Japan as Number 1* (New York: Harper and Row, 1980), Chapter 6.

28. Quoted in John Kendrick, "Sources of Growth in Real Product and Productivity in Eight Countries, 1960 -1978," unpublished paper prepared for the New York Stock Exchange, Office of Economic Research, Table 13, p. 40.

29. *Ibid.*, p. 41.

30. Nathaniel J. Mass and Peter M. Senge, *op. cit.*, p. 59.

31. Hayes and Abernathy, *op. cit.*, p. 70.

32. The Business Week Team, *op. cit.*, p. 70.

33. Hayes and Abernathy, *op. cit.*, p. 78.

34. Magaziner and Reich, *op. cit.*, p. 5.

35. Richard West and Dennis Logue, "The False Doctrines of Productivity," *The New York Times*, January 9, 1983.

36. Magaziner and Reich, *op. cit.*, Chapters 13 and 14.

37. Wassily Leontieff and Faye Duchin, *Military Spending: Facts and Figures, Worldwide Implications, and Future Outlook* (New York: Oxford University Press, 1983), Chapters 6 and 7.

Chart 2.1

Unemployment Rate
Selected Nations
1973 – 1981

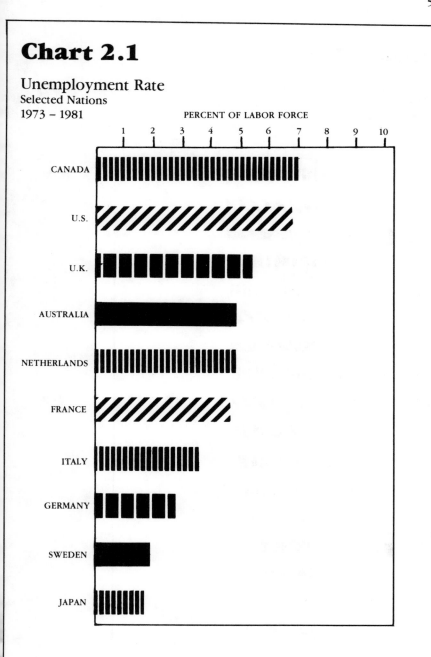

PERCENT OF LABOR FORCE

Source: U.S. Department of Labor, Bureau of Labor Statistics, "Statistical Supplement to International Comparisons of Unemployment, Bulletin 1979," unpublished, June 1982, Supplement to Table 3, p. 10.

58

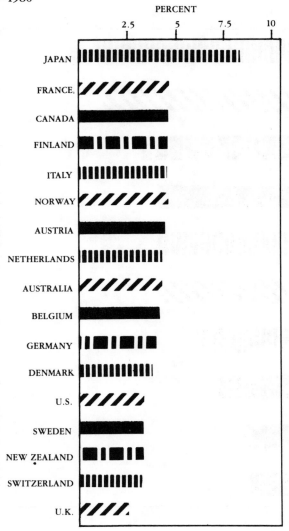

Chart 2.2

Real Growth Of GDP
Selected Nations
1960 – 1980

PERCENT

2.5   5   7.5   10

JAPAN

FRANCE,

CANADA

FINLAND

ITALY

NORWAY

AUSTRIA

NETHERLANDS

AUSTRALIA

BELGIUM

GERMANY

DENMARK

U.S.

SWEDEN

NEW ZEALAND

SWITZERLAND

U.K.

Source: Organisation for Economic Cooperation and Development, *National Accounts of OECD Countries, 1950–1980, Volume I* (Paris: OECD, 1982).

Chart 2.3

How U.S. manufacturing's market
share has been shrinking at home . . .

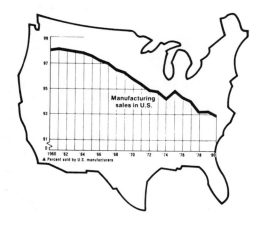

. . . and abroad

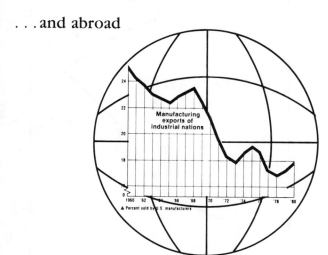

Source: The Business Week Team, *The Reindustrialization of America* (New York: McGraw-Hill Book Co., 1982), pp. 8-9.

Chart 2.4

Ratio Of U.S. Manufactured Exports
To Manufactured Imports
1960 – 1981

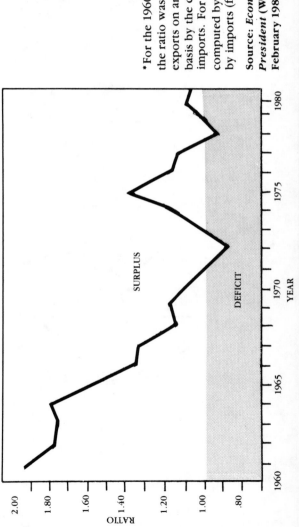

*For the 1960 to 1974 period,
the ratio was computed by dividing
exports on an f.a.s. (fee alongside ship)
basis by the customs value of
imports. For 1974 to 1981, it was
computed by dividing exports (f.a.s.)
by imports (f.a.s.).

Source: *Economic Report of the
President* (Washington, D.C.: U.S. GPO,
February 1982), p. 350.

Chart 2.5

Military Spending As A Share Of GDP
Selected Nations
1960 – 1980

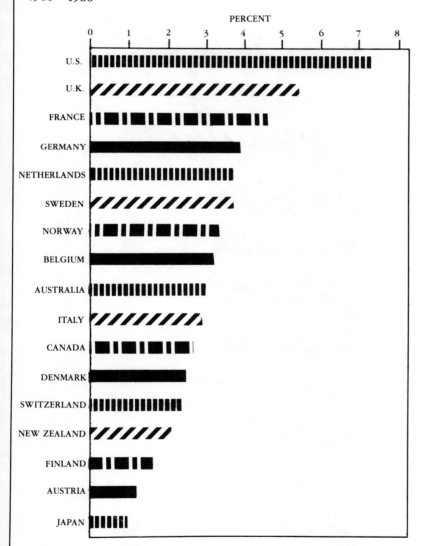

Sources: Stockholm International Peace Research Institute, *World Arma-*
ments and Disarmament, SIPRI Yearbook 1982 (London: Taylor & Francis
Ltd., 1982), pp. 150-151. SIPRI, *Yearbook 1975* (Cambridge, Mass.: MIT
Press, 1975), pp. 122-123, 126-127, 132-133.

Chart 2.6

Productivity Growth In Manufacturing Industries
Selected Nations 1960 – 1973, 1960 – 1981, 1973 – 1981

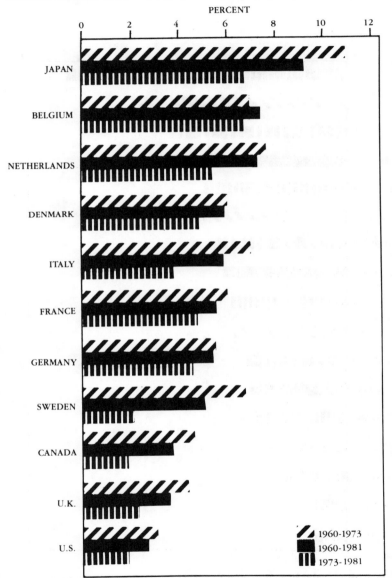

Source: U.S. Department of Labor, Bureau of Labor Statistics, "International Comparisons of Manufacturing Productivity and Labor Cost Trends, Preliminary Measures for 1981," June 2, 1982, Table 1.

Chart 2.7A

Fixed Investment As A Share Of GDP
Selected Nations
1960 – 1980

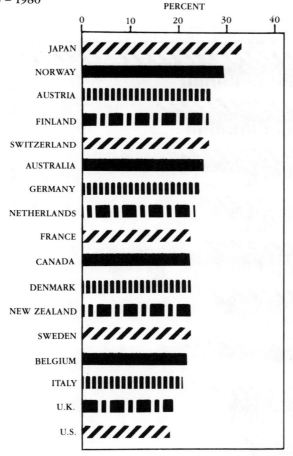

PERCENT

Sources: United Nations, *Yearbook of National Accounts Statistics, 1979*
(New York: U.N., 1980). Organisation for Economic Cooperation and
Development, *National Accounts of OECD Countries, 1950-1980, Volume I*
(Paris: OECD, 1982).

64

Chart 2.7B

Manufacturing Capital Growth
Selected Nations
1960 – 1973, 1960 – 1978, 1973 – 1978

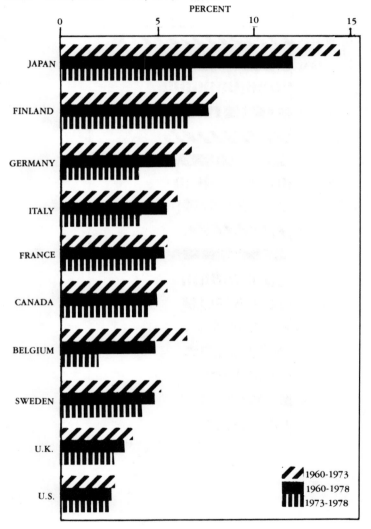

Source: Organisation for Economic Cooperation and Development, unpublished data.

Chart 2.8

The Rate Of Inflation
Selected Nations
1973 – 1981

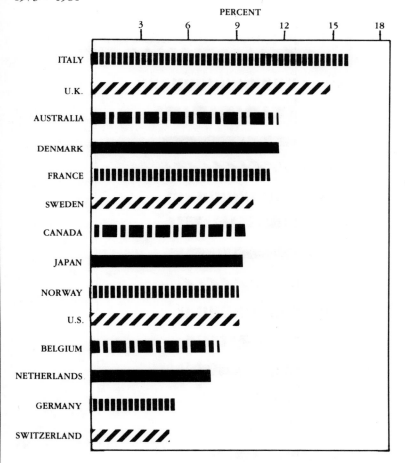

PERCENT

Source: U.S. Department of Labor, Bureau of Labor Statistics, "Consumer Price Indexes, Fifteen Countries, 1950-1981," June 1982.

66

Chart 2.9

Civilian Government Consumption As A Share Of GDP
Selected Nations
1960 – 1980

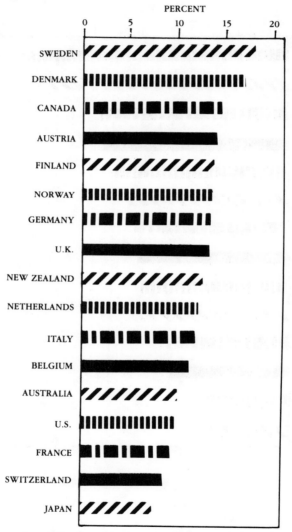

Sources: Organisation for Economic Cooperation and Development, *National Accounts of OECD Countries, 1950-1980, Volume I* (Paris: OECD, 1982). Stockholm International Peace Research Institute, *World Armaments and Disarmament, SIPRI Yearbook 1982* (London: Taylor & Francis Ltd., 1982), pp. 150-151. SIPRI, *Yearbook 1975* (Cambridge, Mass.: MIT Press, 1975), pp. 122-123, 126-127, 132-133.

Chart 2.10

Government Transfers As A Share Of GDP
Selected Nations
1961 – 1978

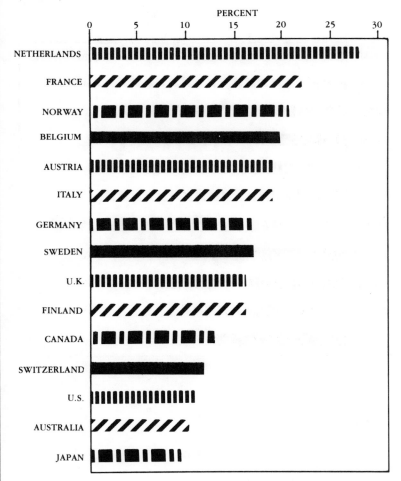

Source: Organisation for Economic Cooperation and Development, *National Accounts of OECD Countries, 1961-1978, Volume II* (Paris: OECD, 1980).

68

Chart 2.11

Growth Of Manufacturing Labor Compensation
Selected Nations
1960 – 1981

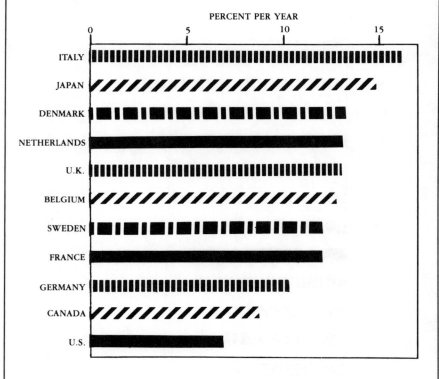

Source: U.S. Department of Labor, Bureau of Labor Statistics, "International Comparisons of Manufacturing Productivity and Labor Cost Trends, Preliminary Measures for 1981," June 2, 1982, Table 1.

Chart 2.12

Agriculture As A Share Of GDP
Selected Nations
1960 – 1979

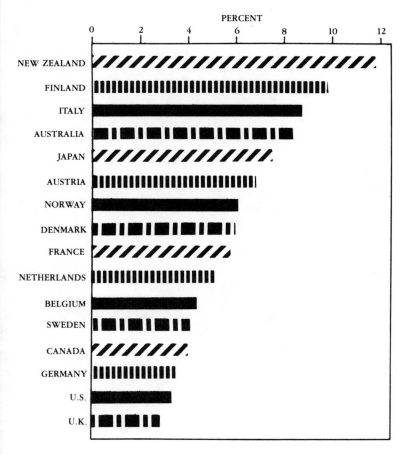

Source: Organisation for Economic Cooperation and Development, *National Accounts of OECD Countries, 1950-1979, Volume I* (Paris: OECD, 1981).

Chart 2.13

Investment Vs. Military Spending
Selected Nations
1960 – 1980

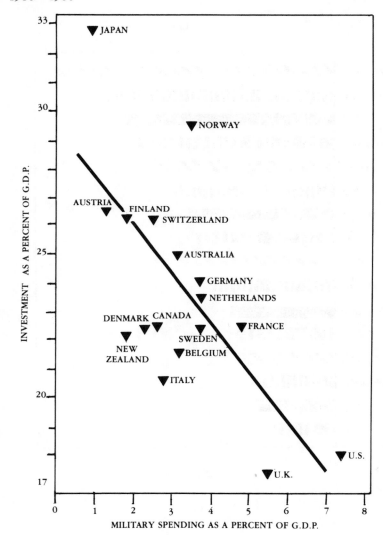

Source: Appendix B.

Chart 2.14

Investment And Consumption In The U.S.
Vs. Military Spending
Selected Years

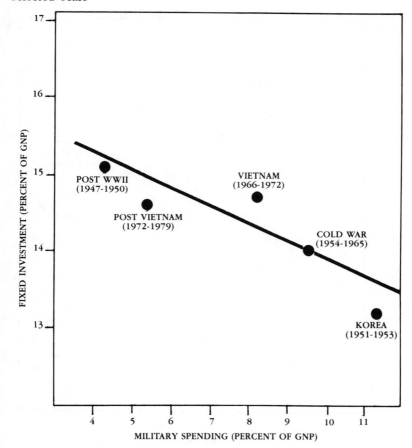

Cont'd...

72

Chart 2.14

Cont'd...

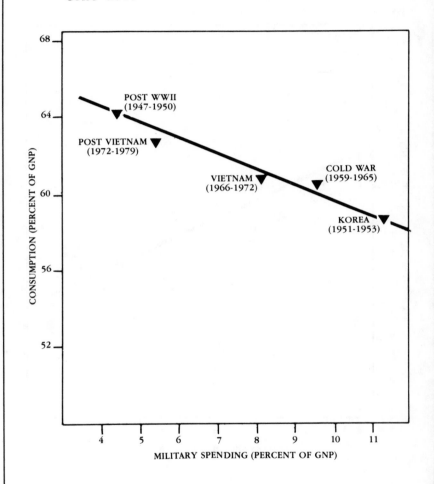

Sources: U.S. Office of Management and Budget, Budget Review Division, "Federal Government Finances," February 1982, pp. 71-74. *Economic Report of the President* (Washington, D.C.: U.S. GPO, February 1982), p. 350.

Table 2.1

U.S. Merchandise Trade Balance By Commodity Group
1960 – 1981
(Millions of Dollars)

	FOOD, BEVERAGES, AND TOBACCO	CRUDE MATERIALS AND FUEL	MANUFACTURED GOODS
1960+	$ -862	$ -476	$ 6,236
1965+	506	-1,167	6,189
1970+	-1,172	150	3,437
1971+	-1.328	827	29
1972+	-810	-1,747	-4,027
1973+	3,703	-2,711	-270
1974+	4,532	-16,040	7,321
1974*	4,524	-16,262	8,300
1975*	6,870	-17,399	19,871
1976*	5,343	-25,379	12,466
1977*	1,736	-34,975	3,597
1978*	4,861	-30,944	-5,844
1979*	6,852	-43,168	4,361
1980*	11,856	-60,254	18,769
1981*	14,830	-60,068	11,739

+ F.a.s. (free alongside ship) value of exports minus customs value of imports.

*F.a.s. value of exports minus f.a.s. value of imports.

Source: *Economic Report of the President* (Washington, D.C.: U.S. GPO, February, 1982), p. 350.

Table 2.2

Hourly Compensation Costs of Production Workers in Manufacturing
Selected Industrial Nations
(U.S. Dollars)

COUNTRY	1960	1965	1970	1975	1980
Belgium	$ .82	$ 1.29	$ 2.06	$ 6.54	$ 13.18
Sweden	1.20	1.87	2.93	7.18	12.51
West Germany	.85	1.40	2.33	6.19	12.26
Netherlands	.67	1.23	2.12	6.53	12.17
United States	2.66	3.14	4.18	6.35	10.00
France	.82	1.23	1.72	4.58	9.23
Canada	2.13	2.28	3.46	6.11	9.04
Italy	.62	1.11	1.74	4.60	8.26
United Kingdom	.84	1.15	1.49	3.27	7.37
Japan	.26	.48	.99	3.05	5.61

Source: U.S. Department of Labor, Bureau of Labor Statistics, "Hourly Compensation Costs and Direct Pay for Production Workers in Manufacturing, Ten Countries, 1960-1981," unpublished data, April 1982.

Table 2.3

Real Gross Domestic Product Per Employed Person
Selected Nations
Based on International Price Weights
(Index: United States = 100)

COUNTRY	1950	1960	1970	1980
Netherlands+	58.3	66.3	79.3	96.5
Canada	84.4	89.7	91.1	93.3
Belgium	55.7	60.0	73.1	91.9
France	42.2	53.5	70.7	91.6
West Germany*	37.2	56.1	70.7	89.4
Italy	27.7	38.0	57.6	68.1
Japan	16.8	25.8	50.0	68.0
United Kingdom	53.5	53.9	56.8	61.3

+ Employment figures for the Netherlands are Dutch estimates of work-years of employed persons.

*Excluding the Saar and West Berlin in 1950.

Source: U.S. Department of Labor, Bureau of Labor Statistics, "Comparative Real Gross Domestic Product, Real GDP Per Capita, and Real GDP Per Employed Person, 1950-1981," unpublished data, April 1982, p. 7.

Table 2.4

Growth in the Capital to Labor Ratio in the U.S.
Manufacturing Sector
Selected Periods
(Annual Rate of Change)

	1960–1973	1973–1981	1960–1981
Total Manufacturing Capital	2.7 %	2.5*	2.6*
Manufacturing Labor	1.6 %	.6	.9
Capital to Labor Ratio	1.1 %	1.9	1.7

*Manufacturing capital data ends in 1978.

Sources: Organisation for Economic Cooperation and Development, unpublished data. U.S. Department of Labor, Bureau of Labor Statistics, "International Comparisons of Manufacturing Productivity and Labor Cost Trends, Preliminary Measures for 1981," June 2, 1982, Table 1.

III

The Technological Impact of Military Spending

...defense spending has been making a substantial contribution to technological developments of great importance to our economy.

Murray L. Weidenbaum,
*The Economics of Peacetime
Defense*, 1974

Government officials, economists and scientists have often claimed that military spending encourages technological progress and results in civilian "spinoffs." Technologies that are cited as having profited from military spending include: aerodynamics, jet engines, computers, electronics, numerically controlled machine tools, lasers and nuclear power. Two broad arguments have been advanced to explain how military efforts enhance technology. In one, military demands are seen as a prod that continually encourages scientists and engineers to expand the frontiers of knowledge. By setting higher performance standards than are typically encountered, military projects are said to increase the "state of the art."[1] As a senior economist in the Pentagon argues:

Defense sets goals that are difficult to meet; and our new programs often tax the limits of technology. Only the Department of Defense's budget is rich enough to experiment with new approaches to complex problems. It is my belief that we cannot foretell exactly the future path that technology must take in the quest for new commercial applications and solutions to nondefense problems. In the same sense that we seed the clouds in the hope for rain, so too we seed our research laboratories in the hope for finding solutions to difficult problems.[2]

A second argument, viewing military spending as a source of demand for new products, typically runs this way: "By providing an initial market and premium prices for major advances, defense purchasers speeded their introduction into use."[3] Transistors and integrated circuits are good examples of innovations that benefited from defense purchases when the

77

price was significantly higher than civilian firms were willing to pay. Purchases of these goods for defense and space applications allowed manufacturers to improve their products and reduce costs by gaining production experience, a phenomenon known in the field as "coming down the learning curve."

The military's substantial funding for advanced weapons systems and research and development has certainly yielded some benefits. To be seen in perspective, however, positive effects must be weighed against any negative influences arms programs may have on technological advancement. At least three broad areas should be considered. First, military-oriented research and production diverts scientists and engineers from civilian pursuits. As a result, we are left with fewer people to develop civilian technologies such as consumer electronics, fuel-efficient cars, alternative energy systems and mass transit. This drawback is particularly worrisome when high technology resources are limited, as they are today. Competition between the Pentagon and private industry for highly skilled labor, key subcomponents and raw materials can drive up the price of American high technology products, making them less competitive in the world market.

Second, military-oriented programs can distort a new technology by encouraging applications that are too sophisticated to be marketed commercially. British and French experience with the Super-Sonic Transport (SST) program is one example of this problem. While the United States wisely chose not to develop a civilian SST, our European allies proved that the military's pioneering research on flying at supersonic speeds did not have widespread commercial application. Nuclear power, with its unsolved safety problems and excessive cost, is another example. As we shall see later, military-sponsored programs designed to spur development of faster integrated circuits and more automated machine tools may also distort their development for commercial markets.

Finally, at the political level, we must assess the implications of according the military significant control over science and technology policy. While many of our politicians, including President Reagan, extoll the virtues of the free market, they still allow the Pentagon to control about a third of all public and private research and development funds and to purchase over 10 percent of the durable manufactured goods produced in our economy. These expenditures influence our technological and economic direction just as Japanese government policies controlling trade, encouraging investment and subsidizing research influence that nation's direction. Japan's goal is economic growth, whereas our government largely aims for technological superiority in armaments.

In this chapter, we first use broad economic data to assess the technological costs and benefits of military expenditures. The key question is: What resources have been devoted to military technology and how has their diversion affected overall technological progress? Next we answer that question in greater depth by examining the role that military programs have played in the development of the electronics industry.

Measuring the Military's Impact on Technology

Between 1960 and 1973, Defense Department contracts for hardware averaged 16.9 percent of the durable manufactured goods sold in the United States (Chart 3.1). Since then, hardware contracts have averaged 10.9 percent of durable manufactured goods production. Of the major hard goods purchased by the Pentagon over the past three decades, at least 70 percent have been components of high technology systems such as aircraft, missiles and space systems, and electronics and communications equipment.[4] As a result, the military's share of industry output in sectors such as aerospace, electronics and communications is considerably higher than for durable manufactured goods as a whole. Although the military's share of industry output was declining during the 1970s, the Defense Department's purchases have significantly influenced the direction of the high technology industries. Moreover, since these statistics exclude production of nuclear weapons and that portion of the space program with direct military applications, these figures could understate the military's claim on total technological resources by as much as a quarter.

The Pentagon further influenced technological development by funding 38.1 percent of all public and private research and development (R&D) between 1960 and 1973 (Chart 3.2). In the post-Vietnam period, this figure fell to 25.6 percent. Space-related R&D, at least 20 percent of which had direct military applications (Appendix C), averaged another 11.8 percent of all R&D between 1960 and 1973. Since then, the space program has accounted for 7.2 percent of all public and private R&D.

Military R&D has been the federal government's largest mechanism for influencing technological growth. Defense Department R&D averaged 61.4 percent of all federal R&D between 1960 and 1973. Since then it has accounted for 52.7 percent. Space research accounted for another 16.7 percent before 1973 and 14.3 percent since then.

Between weapons procurement and R&D, the Pentagon employs a substantial share of our nation's technical personnel. Estimates of the percentage of scientists and engineers engaged in Defense Department-sponsored projects range from 15 to 50 percent.[5] While the higher estimates might have applied to the research and development during the 1950s and 1960s, they could not have covered all production personnel as well.[6]

The most accurate data come from a National Science Foundation (NSF) survey conducted in 1978.[7] NSF's data show that in 1978, 16.2 percent of the nation's engineers and scientists (excluding psychologists and social scientists) worked on national defense as their most important task (Chart 3.3). Another 3.8 percent primarily worked on space research. The percentages are significantly higher for fields directly related to aerospace and electronics. For example, 60.2 percent of the aeronautical engineers and over 35 percent of electronics engineers worked primarily on national defense. Since NSF's data were gathered for 1978, a year in which the share of GNP devoted to the military was at its lowest point since 1950, there is good reason to believe that the average percentage of all scientists and engineers involved in Defense Department programs over the past two decades is significantly higher.

The available data and estimates by other experts lead us to conclude that 25 to 35 percent of America's scientists and engineers worked primarily on Pentagon projects during the 1960s. During the 1970s, this figure probably dropped to between 15 and 25 percent. As a result of the current military buildup, this percentage is likely to rise significantly during the 1980s.

If the economic benefits of devoting these technological resources to the military outweighed the costs, we would expect to find that the technological superiority enjoyed by American industry during the 1960s would have been maintained or expanded. Since the Pentagon has "seeded" our research laboratories and purchased new products when they were too costly for civilian applications, American industry should have been in an excellent position to commercialize high technology goods. We would also expect that technological advancements resulting from our military effort would have enhanced the efficiency of our factories, leading to increases in manufacturing productivity. Indeed, since America's support for military technology was only part of the largest R&D effort undertaken by a major industrial nation (except the Soviet Union) over the past two decades, there is every reason to expect these results. Unfortunately, neither spinoff has occurred. Since 1960, American high technology industries have lost ground to the Japanese and the Western Europeans in the competition for shares of both the U.S. domestic and world-wide markets. Growth in the productivity of American manufacturers has also fallen substantially.

American firms have experienced some of their largest market-share reductions in industries that are heavily engaged in military contracting, including aircraft, electronics and machine tools (Table 3.1). Although these American high technology industries are growing, they are not keeping pace with competition from abroad in civilian markets. For example, Japanese firms have virtually taken over the commercial electronics market, including televisions, stereos, portable radios and cassette players, and newly-introduced video cassette recorders. In

1964, the Japanese did not export color television sets. By 1977, the Japanese captured 42 percent of the world market and 37 percent of the American market for this product.[8] Japanese control over the video cassette recorder (VCR) market is even more one-sided. While the first video tape machines were produced in the United States for the television industry, the Japanese were the first to develop a marketable consumer version. They currently control virtually all sales of VCRs.[9]

More importantly, the Japanese are making a concerted effort to challenge American preeminence in semiconductors. Development and production of these small silicon chips, which represent the "state of the art" in electronics technology, was dominated by American manufacturers as recently as 1974. Yet since that time, Japanese firms have entered the competition to mass-produce an important segment of this market, memory chips. In this quickly-changing field, the Japanese captured 40 percent of the market for the last generation of memory chips — 16K RAMs, random access memories that can store over 16,000 bits of information. In 1978, the Japanese introduced the first reliable 64K RAM, repesenting a four-fold increase in the storage capacity over the 16K RAM. The Japanese currently control about 70 percent of the world and 50 percent of the U.S. market in 64K RAMs and show every sign of becoming the industry leaders in this technology by being the first to introduce the next generation of memory chips: the 256K RAM.[10]

Similar deterioration of America's technological lead has occurred in machine tools and the emerging field of robotics. As recently as 1967, the United States accounted for 34 percent of the world production of machine tools. However, over the past decade, American firms have not kept pace with the growth of machine tool production in Western Europe. By 1981, U.S. manufacturers were responsible for only 19.5 percent of world output. Western European firms, led by the West Germans, now account for 34 percent of the total.[11]

American manufacturers are also failing to keep pace in the development of emerging machine tool technologies. While computer controlled machine tools and robotics were American innovations, helped along by Pentagon-sponsored programs, the Japanese now threaten to dominate the commercial application of these technologies during the next decade. Last year, Japanese machine tool builders accounted for over 50 percent of the sales of numerically-controlled machining centers in the United States.[12] This is a staggering invasion, considering the fact that they accounted for only four percent of the U.S. market in 1974. The situation in robotics is hardly more encouraging. Today, there are 4,500 computer-programmable robots working in the United States, up from 200 in 1970. In Japanese factories, meanwhile, 14,000 robots have already been installed, accounting for 70 percent of the world total.[13]

In the commercial airframe market the European consortium, Airbus Industrie, is challenging Boeing for control of the world market for the new generation of fuel-efficient jumbo-jets. Lockheed has already dropped out of that commercial market and McDonnell Douglas' DC-10 program continues to suffer substantial losses. Potentially more damaging to America's aircraft industry is its failure to develop an entry to compete in the booming commuter airline market. The Congressional Office of Technology Assessment estimates that by the year 2000, commuter airlines will order 6,000 new aircraft. Yet, in a pattern reminiscent of the U.S. auto industry in the 1960s, American manufacturers including Beech, Cessna and Piper have failed to invest in the technology necessary to develop an aircraft that can compete effectively in that market. Consequently, America's commuter airlines are turning to Canadian, French and Brazilian firms to fill their needs.[14]

America's declining productivity growth also suggests that our technological progress has slowed. As discussed in the previous chapter, many factors influence productivity growth. Two of the more important paths to greater manufacturing efficiency are improving production technology and creating more attractive products. Funding for research and development should thus have a positive impact on productivity growth because new tools and new products are nurtured in our research labs. While traditionally the relationship between R&D and productivity growth has been found by economists to be quite significant, recent evidence suggests that the relationship has changed.[15]

Cross-national data comparing R&D expenditures are indicative of this change. While American investment in R&D has been substantial, productivity growth has been weak. The United States has maintained the greatest number of R&D scientists and engineers and the highest proportion of these researchers in the total labor force of any country except the Soviet Union. We spend more on R&D than France, West Germany, and Japan combined.[16] In addition, U.S. expenditures on R&D as a proportion of GNP were higher than four of the five other industrial countries for which data can be obtained — the United Kingdom, France, West Germany and Japan (Chart 3.4). The Soviet Union was again the exception. Yet in spite of this enormous R&D effort, U.S. productivity growth during the 1970s ranked second to last, among those six nations.

If we chart the share of national resources that the six nations devoted to military and space R&D, we find that as that factor increases productivity growth tends to decline (Chart 3.4). The Soviet Union, the United States and the United Kingdom are at the top of the list in military-related R&D expenditures and at the bottom in productivity growth. It seems that while those nations have been locked in a technological arms race, Japan, West Germany and France have been concentrating on developing civilian technology that increases manufacturing efficiency.

One possible reason that military R&D does not seem to stimulate, and may even hinder, productivity growth is that only a small fraction of America's military R&D is spent on basic research. Technological exploration undertaken to expand the frontiers of science is an important source of innovation. The Defense Department, however, has spent only about three percent of its R&D funds for such purposes during the past two decades.[17] While the Pentagon spent almost half of all federal R&D dollars in 1980, three other federal agencies spent more funds on basic research — the Department of Health and Human Services, the National Science Foundation, and the National Aeronautics and Space Administration (Table 3.2).

Although data on the loss of market shares and productivity growth are only suggestive, they cast doubt on the proposition that military spending helps technology more than it hinders it. We recognize that numerous factors influence international competitiveness and production efficiency. Yet the trends of those data support the thesis that the negative effects of military spending on technology outweigh the positive spinoffs. "The decline in productivity and industrial standards in the U.S.," commented one Japanese observer, "is the best argument against the idea that more defence contracts are vital to maintaining 'state of the art' efficiency."[18]

The reason that military spending has probably slowed our technological progress seems clear: Using scientific and engineering talent to solve military problems is an inefficient means of stimulating scientific or commercial advancement. Growth in our base of scientific knowledge comes most readily from basic research without the constraint of specific applications. The development of new products, like fuel-efficient automobiles, alternative energy systems and computer-controlled machine tools, is most quickly accomplished by applying R&D talent directly. While military programs sometimes provide a market for new products and occasionally result in a civilian spinoff, much of the effort expended to develop weapons systems, like laser-guided missiles and electronic jamming devices, does not help the civilian economy. As one of the founders of TRW Corporation, Simon Ramo, puts it:

> [T]he fallout [from military spending] has not been so great as to suggest that for every dollar of military technology expenditure we realize almost as much advance of the non-military fields as if we had spent it directly on civilian technology. Probably our relative productivity increases and our net rating in technology vis-a-vis other nations have on the whole been hurt rather than helped by our heavier involvement in military technology as compared with other nations.[19]

The nature of military spending and the Pentagon's spending patterns heavily contribute to inefficiency. Since the military stresses high performance over cost, technologies developed for the military are often too expensive and complex for widespread civilian use. Many of those that do have civilian application, like radar and nuclear power, had to undergo significant redesign before they were commercially viable. Military contracting also tends to favor larger firms that tend to be less innovative and create fewer new jobs than smaller enterprises.[20] Since the 1950s, about 80 percent of all military contracts (including R&D and procurement) have gone to large firms.[21]

Moreover, military requirements can distort engineering practices by placing greater emphasis on high-performance capabilities than on reducing cost. Evidence of this problem can be found in the difficulties that military contractors have experienced attempting to develop civilian products. For example, attempts to enter the mass transit market by Boeing Vertol (trolley cars), Rohr (subway cars) and Grumman (buses) all failed in part because their products were too complex and unreliable.

We explore the military's impact on technology in greater detail through our examination of the Pentagon's role in the electronics industry.

Case Study: Electronics

The revolutionary advances in electronics over the past few decades have resulted in products that our great-grandparents would never have dreamed of. These new devices, including computers, hand-held calculators, word processors and video cassette recorders, have significantly changed our lives. At work and during our leisure time these innovations have improved our access to information and entertainment; expanded our ability to analyze, process and store data; and increased our capability to control machines and energy use. In connection with new machine tool technologies such as robotics and computer aided design and manufacturing (CAD/CAM), semiconductor-based electronics might very well transform the factory within the next decade as thoroughly as mechanization and transportation changed agriculture during the last hundred years. As one employee of a major semiconductor firm sees it, we have only begun to recognize the possible applications for this new technology: "Any product that uses springs, levers, stepping motors or gears is performing logic and that product should be built of semiconductors."[22]

There is no doubt that the military has helped stimulate the electronics industry's technological growth by acting as a "creative first user" of the industry's products. The Pentagon has purchased innovations before they were commercially marketable and subsidized efforts to improve their quality and reliability. That role is illustrated by the table and chart below. Table 3.3, listing the percentage of integrated circuit sales accounted for by major categories of end-users, shows that government sales were by far the most important market for integrated circuits when they were introduced in the early 1960s. Chart 3.5 displays the percentage of electronic sales in the United States accounted for by the government. These sales, which were overwhelmingly military and space-related, accounted for over *40 percent* of the U.S. total between 1952 and 1969.

In addition to subsidizing high technology products, it has been argued, the development of military hardware has also resulted in concepts, basic knowledge and skills relevant to the civilian arena. As two Massachusetts Institute of Technology scientists explain:

> [M]ilitary requirements initiated other developments. Missile guidance systems were an early source of support for integrated circuit development; requirements for satellite-tracking radars have supported the development of surface acoustic-wave technology and charge-coupled devices, as well as modern signal processing techniques. . . . The need for reliable military communications had led to the... development of satellite communications [and] to small, mobile terminals. On-line computer time-sharing, computer networks, and computer graphics were all initially supported by the military. Finally, we should mention such significant second-order developments as radio and radar astronomy, microwave spectroscopy, and instrumentation for earth-resources satellites and for modern health care, all of which are heavily dependent on concepts and components derived from military electronics.[23]

This broad claim raises serious questions: How should we evaluate the technological impact of military spending? Should we be thankful for *any* civilian advance resulting from military research and production? Or should we weigh the costs against the benefits of these expenditures? However those questions may be answered, we found that unnecessary military expenditures could never be justified on the basis that they will create an indeterminate amount of technical knowledge transferrable to the civilian sector.

While we recognize that miltary programs significantly contributed to the early development of the electronics industry, our assessment indicates that the costs now seem to outweigh the benefits. Four factors are particularly important:

1. The end-products developed for military use, such as missile guidance systems and electronic warfare devices, have few commercial applications.

2. Military research and development has a mixed record in supporting projects that have lead to significant innovations. The difficulty seems to stem from two factors. One, it is hard for

military personnel to judge the most promising projects. Two, the Pentagon tends to support larger, established firms, rather than the younger, smaller firms that have proved more innovative.

3. Military subsidies for new products are increasingly unnecessary. As the cost of electronic circuits has rapidly fallen, massive industrial and commercial markets have overshadowed the military's role as "creative first user."

4. The Pentagon's current attempts to guide the development of semiconductor and machine tool technology raise serious economic and political issues. Military subsidies for new semiconductor technology in the 1980s may hinder development in this field rather than nurture new products. Defense Department programs designed to increase factory automation are financing a narrow approach without input from the workers who will be affected.

Few Transfers: There are only a few examples of electronic devices originally designed for the military that have later found civilian application. Of those transfers, such as navigational radar, substantial redesign was required for the product to meet the far less complex civilian requirements.[24] This barrier arises from the basic differences between the military and commercial environments: There is little sensitivity to price within the military arena, while cost is the central concern of the commercial customer.[25] In addition, the custom-made requirements of the Pentagon conflict with the civilian demand for standardization.[26] Thus, as military technology becomes more costly and complex, fewer civilian applications can be found. As the Wall Street Journal observed about the aerospace industry as early as 1963:

> When the government was creating the old piston-powered warplanes ... this technology could be easily and profitably translated into commercial airliner designs. When the military moved on to jet planes, the translation became far more difficult and costly — as the financial plight of both manufacturers and airlines currently testifies. The supersonic military jet has thus far defied any commercial translation at all, and the government now debates whether it is worth pouring tax money into subsidizing creation of a supersonic airliner. As for commercial transport application of a moon rocket, it defies even day-dreaming.[27]

The trend is similar in the electronics industry. Night vision devices, radar jamming equipment, and missile guidance systems are all examples of technologies that promise only limited civilian applications. While the development of these systems may have yielded some transferable concepts and supported the production of subcomponents with civilian applications, the bulk acted as a drag on the nation's technical resources.

Inefficient R&D: Military research and development in semiconductors has generally not produced basic technological innovations. Although the military dominated R&D spending during the last three decades, numerous studies indicate that far fewer patents resulted from these efforts than from commercially-funded projects. Moreover, of the patents that did result from military R&D, very few found commercial application.[28] In the words of one analyst: "Texas Instruments reported that between 1949 and 1959, only five of 112 patents awarded to the company were developed under government contract, although the government funded two-fifths of R&D spending. Further, only two of the five patents were used commercially."[29]

Counting patents is somewhat misleading because the military usually retains some control over innovations developed with Pentagon support. Thus firms have an incentive to privately finance potentially profitable innovations.[30] Yet it still stands to reason that R&D sponsored by a firm attempting to develop a specific product aimed at the commercial market would be more productive than research designed to solve a military-related problem that may or may not have other applications. As Robert Noyce, a key figure in the development of semiconductor technology observed:

> With very few exceptions, the major motivation behind technology development cannot come from the military...the major motivation, I feel, is the commercial one....I would say that the military created more motivation for doing good research by creating a market for advanced products....[31]

Noyce's observations hold particularly true for the development of semiconductors. None of the major innovations in this field was directly supported by military research; however, many of the new technologies were heavily subsidized by the military through substantial early purchases. For example, the scientists who first discovered the transistor at American Telephone and Telegraph's Bell Labs in December of 1947 were driven, in large measure, by the pure scientific challenge of understanding materials that sometimes did, and sometimes did not, conduct electricity. More pragmatically, John Bardeen, Walter Brattain and William Shockley were searching for a simple electronic switch to replace bulky mechanical devices that limited the size of the telephone network.[32] The inventors were so concerned that the military would classify information about their innovation that they did not reveal the transistor's secret to the military until they were certain that it would become public knowledge, allowing Bell to develop its civilian applications.[33]

Ironically, the military, needing smaller, quicker, and less power-consuming electrical components, soon became the largest purchaser of transistor devices. Another industry that provided a market for the early, very expensive transistor was hearing-aid manufacturers. These firms shared with the military a need for a more compact amplifier than the vacuum tube. The transistor was the perfect answer. Customers for hearing-aids were also generally willing to pay a premium price.[34] Nevertheless, during the early 1950s, when the transistor was unreliable and expensive to manufacture, the military consumed the vast majority of the infant industry's output.

By the late 1950s, when the two innovations occurred that made it possible to place numerous transistors on one silicon chip, the military was heavily engaged in research toward this goal. As it turned out, however, *none* of the three different projects supported by the three military services was instrumental in these discoveries. Neither Texas Instruments' (TI) discovery of the integrated circuit, linking many electrical components on one device, nor Fairchild Semiconductor's development of the planar process for mass-producing silicon chips, was supported by the military.[35] Yet, as in the case of the transistor, the government market for integrated circuits provided the production experience necessary to make these devices commercially attractive. The Minuteman II project subsidized TI's early integrated circuit production and the NASA Apollo program played the same role for Fairchild.[36]

The military's failure to "back the right horse" in the quest to miniaturize electronic components suggests that military-sponsored programs are a less efficient means of stimulating technological innovation than private efforts. Pentagon-sponsored research aimed at miniaturizing electronic components was spurred on by the Soviet Union's successful Sputnik satellite launch.[37] The Army Signal Corps spent $26 million between 1957 and 1963 on the "micromodule" program designed to stack and encapsulate transistors. This program was seen as an attempt to spur the evolution of the transistor. Much of the research was carried out by RCA, a large, old-line electronics firm. The program, which was only marginally successful, ended as the integrated circuit and the planar process became the accepted miniaturization techniques.[38]

The Air Force took another approach. They pursued a revolutionary breakthrough in "molecular electronics." Jack Kilby, inventor of the integrated circuit at TI, described the Air Force's project:

> The Air Force rejected anything that had any connection with existing circuits. . . . They didn't want to get there circuit by circuit. They wanted these new breakthrough devices that would eliminate all that jazz.[39]

Westinghouse, another large electronics firm, received the molecular electronics contract. One industry analyst has suggested that Westinghouse won the contract because "no other company was interested in taking such a leap into the technological dark."[40] While some have argued that the "micromodule" program increased the industry's interest in miniaturization, the research carried out by Westinghouse under this program did not result in any technological breakthroughs.[41]

The Navy backed "thin film" research designed to "print" a circuit and passive components, like resistors, onto a thin ceramic wafer. While this work did not directly contribute to the discovery of integrated circuits, it did advance photoresist techniques. Yet, by and large, military-funded research and development was not particularly helpful in the search for methods to minaturize electronic circuits.[42]

One explanation for this failure, suggested by industry executives, is that the military officers in charge of these programs did not fully understand the technology.[43] This would not be surprising, considering the speed of change in the semiconductor industry. Yet this is probably not the only reason because venture capitalists and industry executives also had difficulty forecasting the direction of semiconductor technology.

Another important factor that may have neutralized the effectiveness of military R&D was the spending pattern: Most of the money went to projects carried out by larger electronics manufacturers. In 1959, for example, 78 percent of government R&D funds went to the eight established vacuum tube producers (by then, also producing transistors) and Western Electric (ATT's manufacturing division). Yet those firms accounted for only about 37 percent of the semiconductor market. New companies entering the field, which by 1959 had captured 63 percent of the market, received only 22 percent of the government's R&D expenditures.[44]

The government's funding pattern ran counter to the trends that made the American semiconductor industry so successful. Most observers agree that the mobility of technical information and personnel, and the ease of starting a new firm were key ingredients in the rapid technological growth of the U.S. semiconductor industry.[45] Established firms were slow to catch on to the potential of the transistor. At the same time, Bell Labs, concerned about anti-trust action, provided relatively easy access to technical information and did not prevent professional staff from leaving to start new commercial ventures. One such person was Gordon Teal, who demonstrated the first silicon transistor after leaving Bell to head the research arm of TI. In describing the failure of European firms to capture a significant share of the semiconductor market, two British observers suggested that "much of the pace of semiconductor development in the United States can be explained in terms of the decline of the old and the rise of the new. . . ."[46]

Indeed, as the technology progressed into the 1970s, this continued. Metal oxide semiconductors (MOS), which made possible low-cost calculators, watches and large-scale semiconductor memories (RAMs), were pioneered by new firms like Mostek (established in 1969) and Intel (1968).[47] Firms such as TI and Fairchild, now part of the establishment, were convinced that the technology would move in another direction. They did not vigorously pursue this technology until after it was demonstrated by the "upstarts."

The more established firms in the industry were convinced that the integrated circuit industry would evolve toward providing "custom" designs for the final product manufacturers, like computer firms.[48] But the development of MOS technology, and Intel's 1972 introduction of the microprocessor, propelled the industry in two separate directions that vastly reduced the importance of the custom market. As mentioned before, MOS made possible numerous highly profitable standard products, such as the calculator chip first developed by Mostek in 1972. The microprocessor, on the other hand, "was a pioneering advance in *flexible* product design which gave the industry a new way out of the custom versus standard battle: By programming the on-chip memory, the microprocessor could be customized for each application."[49]

Neither MOS nor microprocessor research was supported by the Pentagon. A calculator firm supported both Mostek's development of the calculator chip and Intel's microprocessor work. This support foretold a major change in the semiconductor industry: Civilian markets were destined to overshadow the military. Indeed, support from the military, in the form of early purchases of expensive models and assistance aimed at improving the production process, proved significantly less important to this new generation of products than it had been to the integrated circuit and the planar process.[50]

Decreasing Importance of Military as First User: During the late 1970s, numerous analysts concluded that military spending had become much less important to technological progress in electronics than it had been during the 1950s and 1960s.[51] Two observers argued that the Pentagon's role diminished because the increasing emphasis on cost at the Pentagon lessened the support for expensive, emerging innovations.[52] This assertion, however, falls short of explaining the military's changing role. Current cost overruns on major weapons systems are as bad as they have been throughout the Cold War. Moreover, the Pentagon's most profitable support for semiconductor production, the Minuteman II program, was carried out under a Secretary of Defense, Robert MacNamara, who instituted numerous reforms designed to reduce costs.[53]

Other explanations for declining impact of military spending include: 1) increasing reliance on established suppliers, at the cost of ignoring smaller innovative firms; 2) the decreased willingness on the part of all government agencies to consider unsolicited proposals; and 3) the expanding paperwork burden imposed by Pentagon contracting procedures.[54] The first argument clearly does not stand up. Defense Department support for small businesses has remained remarkably stable, and low, at about 20 percent of total contract awards since the 1950s. In fact, the share of contract awards going to small businesses is actually greater today than it was during the late 1950s and early 1960s.[55]

Although the other two factors may have had some impact, each of these explanations overlook the fact that semiconductors have become so cheap and standardized that they can be profitably used in a wide array of civilian products. In the last decade, civilian demand for semiconductors has become large enough that this market, rather than the military, drives technology advancement. Moreover, as the semiconductor industry entered the 1970s, the military's importance as a market declined. The government's share of semiconductor output fell from 36 percent of the total in 1969 to about 10 percent in 1978.[56] This reduction occurred, not so much as a result of falling government demand, but rather because of the explosive growth in the use of semiconductors in industrial and consumer products during that period. As the cost of semiconductor products fell numerous civilian applications were found. Microprocessors were adopted to control a broad variety of machines, from heating and cooling equipment in large office buildings and factories to telecommunications systems and machine tools. Memory chips were quickly adopted for use in word processing machines, home computers and video games.

With the dramatic reduction in the price of semiconductor products and the fast-paced growth of civilian markets, military subsidies for new semiconductor innovations have become much less important. As we mentioned before, the introduction of microprocessors and MOS memories took place without significant government purchases. Microminiaturization, known as very large scale integration (VLSI), has also been pushed along primarily by competition for civilian markets. Indeed, the military is so concerned that they may not be keeping up with the growth of semiconductor technology, that they have initiated a program to encourage producers to develop chips specifically designed for military requirements.[57] As a report to the Joint Economic Committee of the U.S. Congress pointed out, "...the military's needs are not in the mainstream of the industry's evolution."[58]

Japan's recent success in one of the most sophisticated parts of the semiconductor market is clear evidence of this assessment. Until just recently, American semiconductor producers were unchallenged in the world market. Although the Japanese produced transistors and later, semiconductors for export in consumer electronics products, they exported virtually no semiconductors for computers and other industrial purposes until 1974.[59] Yet when they did begin competing for a part of the international market for a sophisticated product — memory chips — the Japanese soon became a dominant force.

In 1978, when the introduction of IBM's series 4300 computer helped create a sudden surge in demand for memory chips that could not be met by American producers, Japanese companies were able quickly to capitalize on the shortfall and capture 40 percent of the market for advanced memories — 16K RAMs.[60] Japanese firms also introduced the first commercially successful 64K RAM device and established an early market lead. Further, they are planning to introduce the next generation of memories — the 256K RAM — within a year. While some observers feel it is too early to tell how large the Japanese share of the U.S. memory market will be, at least one leading semiconductor executive believes that the battle is over and the Japanese have won.[61]

The Japanese have proved that commercial development of an advanced semiconductor product is possible without military subsidies. Still the growth of Japan's semiconductor industry did not occur without government support. Since the 1960s, Japanese government agencies, particularly the Ministry of International Trade and Industry (MITI), have worked cooperatively with Japanese firms to make the development of knowledge-intensive industries a national goal. A recent MITI document is explicit about Japan's aim:

> It is extremely important for Japan to make the most of her brain resources, which may well be called the nation's only resource, and thereby to develop creative technologies of its own. . . . Possession of her own technology will help Japan *to maintain and develop her industries' international superiority* and to form a foundation for the long-term development of the economy and society. . . .[62]

Three elements were particularly important in the Japanese strategy for expanding the semiconductor industry.

1) Protection of the domestic electronics industry from American products until the mid-1970s. In 1968, American firms controlled less than 15 percent of the Japanese semiconductor market.[63] The Japanese also prevented American companies from setting up production facilities in Japan, with the exceptions of TI and IBM (TI's Japanese subsidiary produces semiconductors and IBM's builds computers).[64] Limited access to the Japanese market allowed domestic firms to develop their expertise in the advanced semiconductor industry by providing a built-in market for Japanese products. While consumer product exports subsidized the semiconductor industry's early development, the Japanese needed protected computer and telecommunications markets to move toward the technological frontier.[65]

2) Purchase of U.S. technology and production equipment. To gain experience in this field, Japanese firms purchased American semiconductor technology and production equipment. American firms settled for royalty payments on their patents after realizing that they could not penetrate the Japanese market. By the end of the 1960s, at least 10 percent of the Japanese semiconductor industry's revenues were paid as royalties to U.S. firms.[66]

3) Support for, and coordination of, research and development efforts.
Since 1971, Japan's R&D efforts have been aimed at developing semi-conductors for the computer market. MITI encouraged three paired groups of Japan's six dominant semiconductor firms to pursue different aspects of large-scale integration (LSI) technology in hopes of capturing a share of the international market for the next generation of computers. Each of the three groups received about $200 million in subsidies between 1972 and 1976.[67] Through this program, the Japanese were able to displace American-developed semiconductor products from their domestic market in all but the most advanced applications. They also succeeded in significantly raising the domestic share of installed computers.[68]

In December of 1975, when the Japanese had significantly closed the technology gap, the Japanese government began to liberalize trade policy. While there is skepticism about how far formal liberalization actually opened the Japanese market,[69] it did set the stage for full-scale Japanese participation in the international semiconductor arena. In 1976, the Japanese semiconductor industry and government created the VLSI Technology Research Association to insure that they could successfully compete in that market. This grouping, which included MITI, the Japanese Telephone Company (Nippon Telephone and Telegraph) and five major semiconductor firms, coordinated research on VLSI technology and shared results to prevent duplication. Firms within the group received significant subsidies that, among other benefits, released company funds to invest in production capacity. Through these mechanisms, the Japanese semiconductor industry was quickly able to increase its technological capacity and successfully compete with American firms.

The success of Japan's basic strategy suggests that in the future, military spending will be an ineffective mechanism for competing with Japanese firms in the high-technology arena. While other factors, such as the availability of capital and lower labor costs, have also contributed to Japan's success, the cooperation between industry and government to develop a technology with wide commercial application has proved quite effective. Particularly in semiconductor technology, which has matured sufficiently so that there is widespread recognition of its applications as well as significant production experience and a degree of standardization, there are likely to be few instances where the military's most effective role — creative first user — will be helpful in supporting technological innovation. Indeed, in the semiconductor field the possibility of the military hindering progress, through diverting resources from the civilian realm, is greater than the likelihood of it stimulating growth.

While our anti-trust laws and trade policies prevent many of the techniques used by the Japanese from being copied in the United States, we still should be able to find more effective ways of stimulating technological growth in that field than relying on military R&D. In the United States, it might make sense to expand government support for basic research at universities in fields applicable to semiconductor technology. Loan guarantees for companies developing promising innovations might be another method for achieving this goal. While more specific recommendations, or a more detailed assessment of the reasons for Japan's success, are beyond the scope of this study, our overview indicates that the military is no longer the most effective way for the government to encourage growth in the semiconductor industry.

Distorting Technology: After watching its influence slip away during the 1970s, the military will attempt to expand its involvement in the high technology sector during the next few years. As in the past, the vast majority of the military's programs are oriented toward developing existing technologies rather than adding to basic knowledge. The programs that are scheduled to grow raise far-reaching economic and social questions. Two efforts that deserve close scrutiny aim at: 1) developing quicker integrated circuits for "smart" weapons; and 2) creating increasingly automated production equipment to reduce the cost of weapons systems. Further Defense Department involvement in the semiconductor field could actually hamper attempts to stay even with the Japanese by diverting technically skilled workers from civilian projects. Military programs designed to automate the factory are financing a narrow approach to automation without significant input from those who will be affected.

As the American electronics industry has grown, the military's role as primary customer has declined. So too has its power to direct technological development. To counteract this declining influence, the Defense Department launched the Very High Speed Integrated Circuit (VHSIC) program. The Under Secretary of Defense for Research and Engineering explained the need during budget hearings in 1980:

> Between our funded Science and Technology program and the contractors' independent R&D program, we have an outstanding ability to direct technology resident in the defense industry to high priority defense programs. However, we have little ability to influence those companies whose sales are predominantly commercial. This is a serious limitation in the case of the semiconductor industry, whose products play a crucial role in nearly all of our advanced weapon systems. Therefore, we have initiated a new technology program intended to direct the next generation of large-scale integrated circuits to those characteristics most significant to defense applications.[70]

The VHSIC program is designed to generate interest in the semiconductor industry for the development of chips with ten times the density and 100 times the speed of current chips. The military needs these faster and smaller chips for such sophisticated weapons as precision-guided munitions, air-to-air missiles, cruise missiles, ICBMs, night vision devices and torpedoes. While further research on miniaturization could help the commercial sector, many firms have expressed concern that the VHSIC program will divert resources from civilian efforts and retard technological progress.[71] As one industry executive put it: "Those incredibly complex VHSI circuits the military wants don't seem to have their use elsewhere."[72]

While the military's involvement in the semiconductor field could reduce the competitiveness of American firms, the Pentagon's support for research on factory automation raises a different kind of concern. Is the Defense Department the correct agency to control public funds destined for a program that could have widespread impact on work in America?

In 1973, the Pentagon initiated an effort to develop a fully automated "factory of the future." This program, known as Integrated Computer Aided Manufacturing (ICAM), is exploring ways to coordinate the work of a factory-wide network of machine tools and robots through computers. If successful, ICAM could significantly reduce the number of skilled machinists needed in defense facilities. The jobs that do remain may require far fewer skills. For example, one ICAM prototype facility was able to process 25 percent more material with 44 percent fewer workers.[73]

While automation can increase productivity, leading to better economic performance, there are many ways that mechanization can proceed. Mechanization can call for part of the existing work force to enhance its skills, or it can leave those remaining workers with menial tasks. In either case, automation is becoming an increasingly critical issue to both management and labor. In the ICAM program, the Defense Department has backed management's vision of the future factory without equivalent consideration of labor's position. Labor has had virtually no say about the philosophy or design of the Pentagon's manufacturing technology programs. Moreover, while the ICAM prospectus lists numerous program goals — including better productivity, increased profits and greater design flexibility — the goal that industry participants consider to have the highest payoff potential is greater management control over the production process.[74]

Right now, machine tool operators are very skilled and with that skill comes a great deal of autonomy. While machinists do not choose what is to be produced, they can exert control over numerous factors, including the pace of work. The fact that their work is complex makes it more interesting. It also means that they must be paid more than less skilled workers.

There is nothing surprising about an industry seeking to increase management control over production. But Pentagon subsidies for such programs raise at least two major issues. First, should the government assist one segment of the society without hearing from those who will be affected? Our view is clear. All voices should be considered in decisions made by a representative government. The ICAM program goes forward primarily because the shroud of "national security" sometimes allows programs to proceed that would not otherwise pass the normal tests for a sound public policy. Second, is the Defense Department the best agency for nurturing new manufacturing technology? As we have seen, the Defense Department has sometimes assisted the development of new technology. However, the military's orientation toward performance rather than cost could push ICAM efforts into areas just as irrelevent to manufacturing technology as the Army's "micromodule" research was to semiconductor development.

Both ICAM and VHSIC illustrate the problems created by allowing the Department of Defense to control most of the government's impact on industry and technology. While both programs are designed to assist industry develop new technology, the final objective of these developments is to create new weapons. In sharp contrast, technological progress subsidized by the Japanese government is carefully targeted to commercial opportunities. As a result, the Japanese have dramatically expanded their technological expertise within a very short time. In this country, the least questioned reason for the government to become involved in private business is to produce weapons. Yet this may prove disastrous if we want to remain a world leader in technology. Maybe we should consider developing a civilian-oriented technology program and hope some of the results are useful to the military.

Notes

1. Simon Ramo, *America's Technology Slip* (New York: John Wiley & Sons Inc., 1980), pp. 79-80.

    G.P. Dineen and F.C. Frick, "Electronics & National Defense: A Case Study," in *Electronics: The Continuing Revolution*, P. Abelson and A. Hammond, eds., (Washington, D.C.: American Association for the Advancement of Science, 1977), pp. 82-83.

2. David Blond, "On the Adequacy and Inherent Strengths of the United States Industrial and Technological Base: Guns versus Butter in Today's Economy," Mimeograph, Office of the U.S. Secretary of Defense, Program Analysis and Evaluation, 1981.

3. James M. Utterback and Albert E. Murray, "The Influence of Defense Procurement and Sponsorship of Research and Development on the Development of the Civilian Electronics Industry," (Boston, Mass.: Center for Policy Alternatives, Massachusetts Institute of Technology, June 30, 1977), p. 3.

4. U.S. Department of Defense, Washington Headquarters Service, *Prime Contract Awards, FY 1981*, February 1982, Table 6.

5. Jacques S. Gansler, *The Defense Industry* (Cambridge, Mass.: MIT Press, 1980), p. 54, (estimates that 20 to 30 percent of all scientists and engineers work on military projects).

    Richard Dempsey and Douglas Schmude, "Occupational Impact of Defense Expenditures," *Monthly Labor Review*, December 1971, p. 12, (estimates 20 percent).

    Murray L. Weidenbaum, *Economics of Peacetime Defense* (New York: Praeger, 1974), p. 27, (estimates 50 percent).

    Ramo, *op. cit.*, p. 80, (estimates 50 percent).

6. "52 per cent of the engineers and scientists engaged in research and development work in American industry in 1963 were working on projects financed by defense or space programs," from William L. Baldwin, *The Structure of the Defense Market* (Durham, N.C.: Duke University Press, 1967), p. 146. (Hereafter, *The Structure.* . . .)

7. National Science Foundation, *Characteristices of Experienced Scientists and Engineers 1978* (Washington, D.C.: N.S.F., 1979).

8. Ira C. Magaziner and Robert Reich, *Minding America's Business: The Decline and Rise of the American Economy* (New York: Harcourt Brace Jovanovich, 1981), p. 169.

9. Electronic Industries Association, phone conversation with a public affairs officer, October 1982.

10. Andrew Pollack, "Japan's Big Lead in Memory Chips," *The New York Times*, February 28, 1982, p. F1.

11. *The American Machinist*, February 1982, p. 107.

12. National Broadcasting Corp., Inc., Transcript, *NBC Reports: Japan vs. USA, The High Tech Shootout*, (New York: NBC, August 14, 1982), p. 34.

13. Robert Ayres and Steve Miller, "Industrial Robots on the Line," *Technology Review*, May/June 1982, p. 38.

14. "Study Is Critical of U.S. Aircraft Makers," *The New York Times*, February 22, 1982.

15. Eleanor Thomas, "Recent Research on R&D and Productivity Growth: A Changing Relationship Between Input & Impact Indicators?," (Washington, D.C.: NSF, September 1980).

98

16. National Science Board, *Science Indicators 1980*, (Washington, D.C.: NSF, 1981), p. 2.

17. *Ibid.*, p. 270.

18. Tracy Dahlby, "Can the U.S. Really Guarantee Our Security in Wartime?," *Far Eastern Economic Review*, December 5, 1980, pp. 55-56.

19. Ramo, *op. cit.*, p. 251.

20. U.S. DoD, *Prime Contract Awards, op. cit.*, Chart II.

21. Richard S. Morse, "The Role of New Technological Enterprises in the U.S. Economy: A Report of the Commerce Technical Advisory Board to the Secretary of Commerce," (Washington, D.C.: Commerce Department, January 1976).

22. Floyd Kvamme of National Semiconductor, Inc., quoted by Ernest Braun and Stuart MacDonald, *Revolution in Miniature: The History & Impact of Semiconductor Electronics* (London: Cambridge University Press, 1978), p. 120.

23. Dineen and Frick, *op. cit.*, pp. 82-83.

24. Utterback and Murray, *op. cit.*, p. 25.

25. Jacques S. Gansler, *The Defense Industry* (Cambridge, Mass.: The MIT Press, 1980), Chapter 3.

26. See semiconductor industry executives' negative reaction to military contracts due to the custom nature of the Pentagon's demands in Robert Wilson, Peter Ashton and Thomas Egan, *Innovation, Competition and Government Policy in the Semiconductor Industry* (Boston: Charles Rivers Associates, March 1980), p. 6-17.

27. *Wall Street Journal*, May 6, 1963, cited in William Baldwin, *The Structure...*, *op. cit.*, p. 145.

28. Utterback and Murray, *op. cit.*, p. 24.

29. Mary Kaldor, *The Baroque Arsenal* (New York: Hill and Wang, 1981), p. 91.

30. Semiconductor executives were also reluctant to undertake government-funded R&D programs because of the government's practice of claiming title to any patents that resulted. Wilson, Ashton and Egan, *op. cit.*, pp. 6-26.

31. Braun and MacDonald, *op. cit.*, p. 142.

32. *Ibid.*, pp. 40-42.

33. *Ibid.*, p. 52.

34. *Ibid.*, pp. 55-56 and 69.

35. *Ibid.*, pp. 107-122.

36. Utterback and Murray, *op. cit.*, pp. 11-12.

37. Braun and MacDonald, *op. cit.*, p. 107.

38. *Ibid.*, pp. 107-110.

39. *Ibid.*, p. 110.

40. *Ibid.*, p. 110.

41. *Ibid.*, pp. 107-110.

42. *Ibid.*, p. 108.

43. *Ibid.*, pp. 109, 136.

44. *Ibid.*, p. 81.

45. Wilson, Ashton and Egan, *op. cit.*, pp. 2-10, 6-48, 6-65 and 6-66.

46. Braun and MacDonald, *op. cit.*, p. 154.

47. Michael Borrus, James Millstein and John Zysman, "International Competition in Advanced Industrial Sectors: Trade and Development in the Semiconductor Industry" (Washington, D.C.: U.S. Congress, Joint Economic Committee, February 1982), Table 3, pp. 30-31.

48. See analysis of the misguided custom L SI venture in Wilson, Ashton and Egan, *op. cit.*, pp. 4-16 to 4-21.

49. Borrus, Millstein and Zysman, *op. cit.*, p. 28.

50. OECD, "Gaps in Technology: Electronic Components" (Paris: Organisation of Economic Cooperaton and Development, 1968), a report excerpted in Norman Asher and Leland Strom, "The Role of the Department of Defense in the Development of Integrated Circuits" (Arlington: Institute for Defense Analysis, 1977), pp. 36-42.

Borrus, Millstein and Zysman *op. cit.*, discuss the reduced role of the Pentagon in the semiconductor market in the 1970s, pp. 32-43, 151-167.

51. Utterback and Murray, *op. cit.*, pp. 47-49.

Borrus, Millstein and Zysman, *op. cit.*, pp. 10, 151.

William L. Baldwin, *The Impact of Department of Defense Procurement on Competition in Commercial Markets: Case Studies of the Electronics & Helicopter Industries*, (Washington, D.C.: Federal Trade Commission, Office of Policy Planning, December 1980), pp. 74-77. (Hereafter, *Case Studies. . . .*)

52. Utterback and Murray, *op. cit.*, pp. 47-48.

53. Gordon Adams, Paul Murphy and William Rosenau, *Controlling Weapons Costs: Can the Pentagon Reforms Work?* (New York: Council on Economic Priorities, 1983), pp. 17-18.

54. Morse, *op. cit.*, pp. 4-7.

Utterback and Murray, *op. cit.*, pp. 47-48.

55. U.S. DoD, *Prime Contract Awards, op. cit.*, Chart II.

56. See Table 3.3 and Asher and Strom, *op. cit.*, Table 4-8.

57. William L. Baldwin, *Case Studies...*, pp. 92-93.

58. Borrus, Millstein, and Zysman, *op. cit.*, p. 151.

59. *Ibid.*, p. 1.

60. *Ibid.*, pp. 105-106.

61. "I think we've already lost out in the 256K," said W.J. Sanders 3d, chairman and president of Advanced Micro Devices of Sunnyvale, California, "The Japanese have won the dynamic RAM market," in "Japan's Big Lead in Memory Chips," *The New York Times*, February 28, 1982, p. F1.

62. Ministry of International Trade and Industry (MITI), quoted in Borrus, Millstein, and Zysman, *op. cit.*, pp. 5-6.

63. Borrus, Millstein, and Zysman, *op. cit.*, p. 80.

64. *Ibid.*, pp. 83-84.

65. *Ibid.*, pp. 98-100.

66. *Ibid.*, p. 83.

67. *Ibid.*, p. 86.

68. *Ibid.*, p. 89.

69. *Ibid.*, pp. 90-91.

70. William J. Perry, Undersecretary of Defense for Research and Engineering, testimony before the U.S. Congress, Senate Committee on Armed Services, "Department of Defense Authorization for Appropriations for the Fiscal Year 1980, Part 5," hearings, p. 2292.

71. Baldwin, *Case Studies...*, *op. cit.*, p. 94.

   Wilson, Ashton and Egan, *op. cit.*, pp. 6-4 to 6-6.

72. *Electronics Times*, December 14, 1978, quoted in Kaldor, *op. cit.*, p. 94.

73. U.S. Department of Defense, Headquarters Air Force Systems Command, "Payoff '80," Executive Report, Manufacturing Technology Investment Strategy, Andrews Air Force Base, Washington, D.C.: 1980), p. 28.

74. U.S. Air Force Materials Laboratory, "ICAM Prospectus Update B" (Wright Patterson Air Force Base, Dayton, Ohio, September 1979), p. 8.

Chart 3.1

Major Hard Goods Purchased By The DoD
As A Share Of Durable Manufactured Goods
1960 – 1981

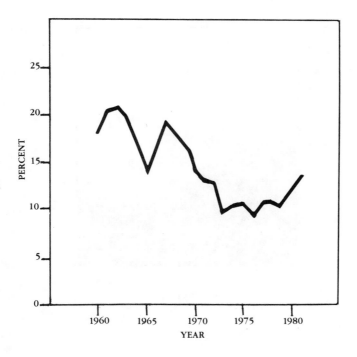

Sources: U.S. Department of Defense, Washington Headquarters Service, "Prime Contract Awards, FY 1981," Table 6. *Economic Report of the President* (Washington, D.C.: U.S. GPO, February 1982), p. 244.

102

Chart 3.2

National R & D Spending By Objective
1960 – 1983

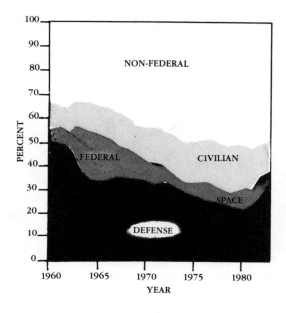

Sources: U.S. National Science Foundation, "National Patterns of Science and Technology Resources, 1981" (Washington, D.C.: U.S. GPO, April 1981). U.S. National Science Foundation, *Science Resources Series Highlights*, August 1982, Table 1, p. 3. Figures for 1982 and 1983 obtained from John Chirichiello of NSF, February 17, 1983.

Chart 3.3

Scientists And Engineers Working Primarily
On National Defense and Space Projects
1978

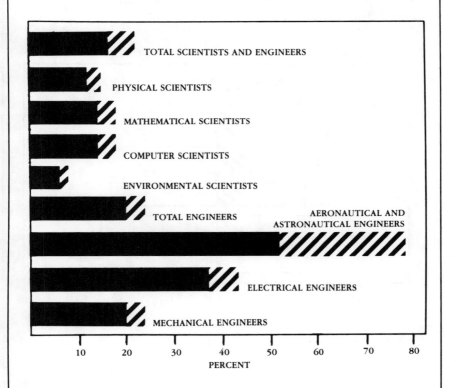

 National Defense

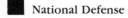 Space

Source: U.S. National Science Foundation, "Characteristics of Experienced
Scientists and Engineers, 1978, Detailed Statistical Tables," (Washington,
D.C.: U.S. GPO, 1978), Table B-13.

Chart 3.4

Average Military And Civilian R & D Expenditure
As A Share Of GDP
Vs.
Productivity Growth In Manufacturing Industries
Selected Nations
1970 – 1979

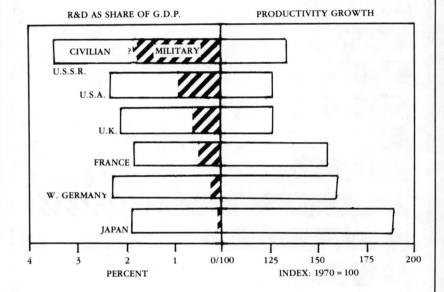

Source: U.S. National Science Board, *Science Indicators, 1980* (Washington, D.C.: NSF, March 1981), pp. 210, 212, 220.

Chart 3.5

Share Of Total Electronic Sales
Purchased by The U.S. Government
1950 – 1979

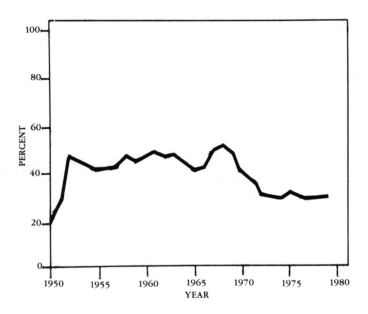

Source: Electronic Industries Association data taken from William Baldwin, *The Impact of Department of Defense Procurement on Competition in Commercial Markets: Case Studies of the Electronics and Helicopter Industries* (Washington, D.C.: Federal Trade Commission, December 1980), pp. 43-44.

Table 3.1

Key Industries Which Have Become Less
Competitive...

...In The U.S. Market

RANKED BY TOTAL SALES OF INDUSTRY
Percent of Market

	1960	1970	1980
Autos	95.9 %	82.8 %	72.9 %
Steel	95.8	85.7	83.4
Electrical Components	99.5	94.4	78.9
Farm Machinery	92.8	92.2	80.7
Consumer Electronics	94.4	68.4	53.1
Metal-Cutting Machine Tools	96.7	89.4	71.0
Metal-Forming Machine Tools	96.8	93.2	76.2
Textile Machinery	93.4	67.1	53.1

...In The World Market

RANKED BY SIZE OF U.S. EXPORTS
Percent of World Exports

	1960	1970	1980
Motor Vehicles	22.6 %	17.5 %	11.4 %
Aircraft	70.9	66.5	52.2
Telecommunications	28.5	15.2	15.0
Metal-Working Machinery	32.5	16.8	24.0
Agricultural Machinery	40.2	29.6	24.9
Hand or Machine Tools	20.5	19.1	13.5
Textile & Leather Machinery	15.5	9.9	7.2
Railway Vehicles	34.8	18.4	12.2

Source: The Business Week Team, *The Reindustrialization of America*
(New York: McGraw-Hill Book Co., 1982), p. 14.

Table 3.2

Federal Basic Research By Agency
Selected Years
(Millions of Constant 1972 Dollars)

DEPARTMENT OR AGENCY	1965	1970	1975	1980
Department of Health and Human Services*	$ 404	$ 564	$ 726	$ 995
National Science Foundation	228	269	390	463
National Aeronautics and Space Administration	NA	394	248	316
Department of Defense	351	272	189	305
Department of Energy+	344	316	251	296
Department of Agriculture	120	128	124	156
Other	101	122	108	118
TOTAL	NA	$ 2,076	$ 2,036	$ 2,649

*Data for 1965-1975 represents obligations by the Department of Health, Education and Welfare; 1980 data represents obligations of the DHHS.

+ Data for 1965 and 1970 represents obligations by the Atomic Energy Commission; 1975 data represents obligations by the Energy Research and Development Administration; 1980 represents obligations of the DoE.

Source: U.S. National Science Board, *Science Indicators, 1980* (Washington, D.C.: National Science Foundation, 1981), p. 269.

Table 3.3

Changing Distribution of Integrated Circuit Devices In
U.S. Markets

U.S. MARKETS FOR ICs BY END USE	PERCENT VALUE OF TOTAL U.S. SALES OF ICs				
	1962 [a]	1965 [b]	1969 [b]	1974 [b]	1978 [c]
Government	100 %	55 %	36 %	20 %	10 %
Computer	0	35	44	36	37.5
Industrial	0	9	16	30	37.5
Consumer	0	1	4	15	15
TOTAL U.S. DOMESTIC SHIPMENTS (Millions of Dollars)	$ 4	$ 79	$ 413	$ 1204	$ 2080

(a) The figures for 1962 are derived from John Tilton, *International Diffusion of Technology: The Case of Semiconductors* (Washington, D.C.: The Brookings Institution, 1971).

(b) The figures for 1965, 69 and 74 come from the U.S. Department of Commerce, *A Report on the U.S. Semiconductor Industry* (Washington, D.C.: U.S. GPO, 1979), p. 46, table 3.5.

(c) These figures are rough estimates based on figures found in U.S. International Trade Commission, *Competitive Factors Influencing World Trade in Integrated Circuits* (Washington, D.C.: ITC Publication No. 1013, 1979), p. 102; *Business Week*, December 3, 1979, p. 68; and "1980 Semiconductor Forum," *Rosen Electronics Letter* (New York: Rosen Research Inc., July 14, 1980), p. 150.

Source: Michael Borrus, James Millstein and John Zysman, "International Competition in Advanced Industrial Sectors: Trade and Development in the Semiconductor Industry" (Washington, D.C.: U.S. Congress, Joint Economic Committee, February 18, 1982), p. 24.

IV

The Costs of
the Current
Buildup

*. . . the economic evidence indicates that the administration's
planned defense buildup will pose no substantial economic risks,
nor provide a major inflationary impetus to the American
economy.*

William Nordhaus,
member of President Carter's
Council of Economic Advisors,
The New York Times, May 17, 1981

Concern about the economic impacts of the Reagan administration's
military buildup has been expressed since its inception.[1] The debate
heated up significantly when Lester Thurow, a prominent economist at
the Massachusetts Institute of Technology, predicted that the current
buildup "will generate the kinds of economic stress that we experienced
during the Vietnam War."[2] Thurow asserted that the Reagan administration could not cut taxes and dramatically increase the military budget
without "wrecking the economy." Moreover, he worried that the
military's demand for high technology resources could further reduce
the international competitiveness of American manufactured goods.

In response, those favoring increased military spending have taken
the position that the economy is large enough to absorb expanding arms
expenditures. Administration supporters have made four general points
in support of this assertion. First, they observe that the present buildup,
unlike those buildups during the Korean or Vietnam wars, was planned
in advance and will be spread out over a longer period of time. As a
result, they believe that defense contractors will be better prepared to
meet the new demands. Second, they maintain that the current buildup

will claim a smaller share of total economic output than was used during either Korea or Vietnam. A smaller diversion of total output presumably means less economic dislocation. Third, they contend that the administration's civilian budget reductions and the Federal Reserve Board's "tight money" policy will prevent a significant rise in inflation. Finally, they maintain that the recent recession freed up sufficient industrial capacity to meet the Pentagon's needs.[3]

Although the current buildup is not predicted to become as large as the Korean or Vietnam war expansions, the impact still could be greater. The Vietnam war increase was smaller than the Korean war buildup, yet the economic consequences were far worse. High budget deficits, an economy close to peak capacity and the lack of wartime economic controls combined during the Vietnam war to stimulate inflation. Similarly, during the current buildup we also face huge federal deficits. While revenue gaps will not hurt the economy in a deep recession, massive federal deficits during a recovery could fuel inflation or create fierce competition for money in the credit markets, depending greatly on the restrictiveness of monetary policy. Moreover, the industrial sectors serving the Pentagon can be expected to return to peak production far more quickly than the rest of the economy because a high proportion of the military buildup is slated to go for arms production. The companies that build components for weapons have less excess capacity than most other firms. The current buildup will also require many highly skilled engineers and machinists who are in short supply now. Since the government does not plan to dampen inflationary pressures with wage and price controls, the Federal Reserve Board may have to tighten monetary policy to hold down inflation. However, tight money could "crowd out" civilian investment by pushing up interest rates. It might even choke off the recovery. All things considered, there is little reason to hope that the current peacetime buildup will cause less economic dislocation than was caused by the last two wars.

Smaller Rise Does Not Mean Smaller Impact

Although as now planned, the military budget will grow more slowly than during either the Korean or Vietnam wars, the present buildup is still quite substantial. In inflation adjusted dollars, the Reagan administration's military budget started at a higher level, and is slated to grow for a longer period of time than military costs did during the other two major buildups since the Second World War (Chart 4.1). Between FY

1981 and FY 1986 the Pentagon's budget is projected to rise 50.2 percent in constant dollars. By 1985, it will exceed the peak level of expenditures during the Korean and Vietnam wars. Comparing similar periods, the present buildup is about one quarter smaller than the Vietnam expansion. Between FY 1982 and FY 1985, military expenditures are slated to grow 32.4 percent. During the Vietnam war (FY 1965 to FY 1968), the military budget rose 42.7 percent. In the Korean war (FY 1950 to FY 1953), it grew 17.9 percent.

As administration officials have also pointed out, the Reagan buildup is projected to take up a smaller share of GNP than did the Korean or Vietnam wars (Chart 4.2). In FY 1982, the military consumed 6.1 percent of GNP. By FY 1985, the Pentagon will be using an additional 1.4 percent. In comparison, at the beginning of the Vietnam war, the military spent 7.2 percent of GNP. At the height of the war in FY 1968, the Pentagon consumed an additional 2.3 percent. During the Korean war the rise was even more dramatic. The military used 4.8 percent of GNP in FY 1950. An additional nine percent of GNP was used by the military in FY 1953. The present buildup requires a smaller additional share of GNP than during the earlier periods largely because the total size of the economy has expanded. In constant dollars, the GNP in 1981 was 62 percent greater than in 1965, and 182 percent greater than in 1950.

A larger gross national product, however, does not guarantee that the present military buildup will create less economic dislocation than did the Korean or Vietnam wars. The Vietnam buildup, for example, occurred in a larger economy and required a much smaller additional share of GNP than did the Korean war. Yet military spending during the Vietnam conflict touched off the inflationary spiral that still plagues us today.[4] At the beginning of the Korean war, inflation, measured by the GNP price deflator, jumped dramatically, then fell below the pre-war level in 1952 (Table 4.1). During the Vietnam conflict, on the other hand, inflation built up steam. From 2.2 percent in 1965, inflation increased to a 5.1 percent annual rate in 1969. Interest rates also expanded more rapidly during the Vietnam war (Table 4.2). The cost of borrowing money generally rose three times as much during the Vietnam war as it did during the Korean conflict.

Three major factors have been cited to explain the harsher economic effects of the Vietnam war: First, the Vietnam conflict was financed in large measure through deficit spending. Second, the Vietnam buildup occurred when the economy was running close to peak capacity. Third, unlike the Korean war period, there were no wage and price controls during the Vietnam buildup.[5] As we will discuss in the following sections, variations of these factors might well coincide to magnify the impact of the present buildup. Moreover, the Reagan arms buildup comes at a time when America is a much more equal partner in the international economy than it was during either the Korean or Vietnam wars. During those wars, the government appropriated substantial resources without immediately endangering America's lead in product development and manufacturing technology. Today we probably cannot afford heavy arms spending without seeing American-manufactured goods further displaced by increasingly attractive imports.

Fiscal and Monetary Policy Collide

If the Reagan administration's arms buildup and economic policy proceed as planned, the country is in danger of making an economic mistake that could be worse than the one made during the Vietnam war. In that war, President Johnson expanded social spending. He did so without increasing taxes sufficiently to prevent large budget deficits and without instituting wage and price controls. During the present buildup, President Reagan's social program cuts will not compensate for both projected tax reductions and expanded arms spending. Even after the economy recovers from the current recession, budget deficits resulting from the Reagan administration's policies are projected to surpass by far the peak level, measured as a share of GNP, experienced during the Vietnam conflict. Moreover, since the Reagan administration's massive buildup is occurring during peacetime, none of the economic planning mechanisms usually instituted during war will be used to prevent dislocation. Yet heavy deficits in the next few years could have exactly the opposite effect they had during Vietnam. In the late 1960s, federal deficits stimulated inflation because they were financed by allowing the money supply to grow. Today, the Federal Reserve Board's anti-inflation policy could foreclose this option by keeping a fairly firm grip on the money supply after the economy begins to recover. "Tight money" could translate into higher interest rates, slower investment and possibly a new recession.

During both of the last two major buildups, taxes were raised to help offset increasing arms expenditures (Chart 4.3). Tax revenues during the Korean war jumped from 15.1 percent of GNP in FY 1950 to 19.5 percent in FY 1952. Individual and corporate income tax revenues, which make up the bulk of federal receipts, almost doubled between FY 1950 and FY 1952.[6] In the Vietnam conflict, tax receipts increased more slowly. Taxes as a share of GNP increased from 17.7 percent in FY 1965 to 19.2 percent in FY 1967, then dipped slightly in FY 1968 and reached a peak of 20.5 percent in FY 1969.

The Reagan administration, however, has moved in the opposite direction, reducing taxes in an attempt to stimulate investment spending. According to the administration's projections, taxes as a share of GNP will decrease from 20.9 percent in FY 1981 to 18.7 percent in FY 1983. They are predicted to rise slightly in FY 1984 and FY 1985. The administration's current budget calls for a major tax increase in 1986 that will push tax revenues above 20 percent of GNP; however, this is widely viewed as a political move designed to show smaller deficits in the later years of their projections.[7] If the Reagan administration's presently planned tax increases are not enacted, tax revenues as a share of GNP will remain just below 19 percent in FY 1986.

The administration's tax cuts and military increases will be partially counterbalanced by reductions in civilian government programs. The administration estimates that non-defense federal spending as a share of GNP will fall from 18.5 percent in FY 1983 to 16.1 percent in FY 1986 (Chart 4.4). It is unlikely, however, that the administration will receive all the social program cuts they are asking for. Therefore, if the current services of the U.S. government remain basically unchanged, non-defense federal spending as a share of GNP will not decline as the administration hopes but instead will bulge during the next few years and then decline to 17.9 percent in FY 1986. This level would be slightly higher than the percent of GNP spent on non-military spending prior to the current administration.

In contrast, civilian spending during the Korean War fell dramatically. Non-defense expenditures as a share of GNP dropped four percentage points during the first year of the buildup, from 11.6 percent in FY 1950 to 7.6 percent in FY 1951. On the other hand, civilian spending as a share of GNP rose over one percentage point during the Vietnam War, from 10.8 percent in FY 1965 to 12.0 percent in FY 1968.

The net effect of these trends shows up in the size of the federal deficit (Chart 4.5). During the Korean war, deficits did not pose a major problem. The federal deficit as a share of GNP reached a peak of 1.8 percent in FY 1953. Yet the peak came after a large surplus during the first year of the war which amounted to two percent of GNP. Indeed, the *net* amount of deficit spending during the entire Korean war was no greater than the moderate deficit experienced in the year before the war.

In the Vietnam war, deficit spending helped ignite inflation. Red ink poured steadily during the war, with deficits rising from 0.2 percent of GNP in FY 1965 to 3.0 percent of GNP in FY 1968. Deficits during that war were accommodated by allowing the money supply to expand.[8] At the same time, the economy was running at close to peak capacity and growing rapidly. As a result, additional spending did not stimulate increased production, leading to the classic inflationary condition of too many dollars chasing too few goods.

During the present buildup, administration predictions show the federal deficit as a share of GNP surpassing the Vietnam peak in every year beyond FY 1981. If President Reagan does not receive the tax increases and civilian spending cuts he has asked for, the federal deficit as a share of GNP will be more than twice the Vietnam war peak. Even after adjusting for the effects of the current recession, the Congressional Budget Office predicts that the fiscal stimulus of the federal budget between FY 1984 and FY 1988 will be as great as it was during the Vietnam war (Chart 4.6).

In the short-run, large federal deficits may help the economy climb out of the current recession by increasing demand for goods and services. However, the prospect of massive deficits during the recovery may well have a very different impact. Deficits must be financed either by allowing the money supply to grow quickly or by borrowing billions of dollars from the private credit markets. Either approach is likely to cause trouble. Increasing the money supply during the recovery could lead to another bout of high inflation. Expanded borrowing from the credit markets could reduce new investment and choke off the recovery by increasing the competition for capital and pushing up interest rates. Budget projections showing high deficits during the recovery would likely have the psychological impact of scaring investors into thinking that either inflation, or high interest rates are inevitable. Unfortunately, if enough people simply anticipate those problems, their behavior could make one or both a reality.

The economy's recent experience with deficit projections provides ample reason to fear that gloomy expectations could become reality. The current recession began in 1981 partly because the financial community worried that the Reagan administration's program would create large deficits in the future. Interest rates soared during the summer of 1981 just after the administration's tax and budget proposals were adopted by Congress. Analysts could clearly see that the civilian budget cuts would not compensate for the increase in military spending and the reduction in taxes. Moreover, most observers were not convinced that the tax cut would generate enough economic activity to prevent future deficits from growing rather than shrinking, as the administration predicted. Combined with the expectation that higher deficits would not be accommodated by growth in the money supply, investors abandoned long term bonds and stocks for the high returns of short-term instruments like treasury bills and money market funds. Interest rates on long-term loans were forced to rise to attract money. The resulting competition drove interest rates higher, choking off the weak recovery from the 1980 recession.

Since the administration did little to reduce the fear of higher deficits, interest rates remained at record levels even though the economy sunk into a deep recession and inflation cooled off. High interest rates particularly stifled new housing starts, investments in equipment like machine tools, and major consumer purchases such as automobiles.

Moreover, heavy interest payments on inventory forced numerous small businesses into bankruptcy.

Higher interest rates hurt small businesses more than corporate giants. It is harder for small firms to finance investment through stock or bond offerings. Thus, small firms must borrow a larger share of their capital from the banks. Yet bank rates for small firms tend to be about two or three points higher than for larger, preferred companies. Since small firms create a significant number of new jobs and tend to be more innovative than large firms,[9] higher interest rates damage an economy's future.

High interest rates also force businesses into short-term strategies that could adversely affect international competitiveness. When interest rates were extremely high in 1981, many investors abandoned stocks for government securities and other bonds. This shift forced businesses to show an abnormally high return on investment if they wanted to keep their stock prices from falling. Short-term corporate planning, however, only exacerbates many of the problems currently facing firms competing with foreign producers. Companies in Japan and West Germany do not have to recover their capital as quickly, allowing them to make longer-term investments in new technology and product development. In the United States, a high-rate-of-return requirement means that many companies will forgo important improvements that would not show good returns for a few years.[10] If American firms cannot make longer-term investments, U.S. industry will be hard-pressed to keep up with the fast pace of technological and productivity growth abroad, much less reverse the decline in the quality and reliability of American products.

In the summer of 1982, interest rates finally began to fall as more and more investors were convinced tight money would prevent high inflation from quickly returning to consume their earnings. As unemployment topped 10 percent last fall, the Federal Reserve Board aided the reduction in interest rates by allowing increased growth in the money supply. Now, as the economy begins to show signs of recovery, the conflict between fiscal and monetary policy will become more dangerous. Investment behavior, influenced by the fear of high deficits, could slow or abort the recovery if the Fed does not allow the money supply to grow quickly.

Military's Share of Deficit Obscured

Cutting the arms budget would be the most effective way of convincing the financial community that budget deficits are going to decrease in the long run. President Reagan claims that military spending is not to blame for higher deficits, but an analysis of the federal budget shows otherwise. The President points to the growth in entitlement programs as a major source of the government's red ink.

In FY 1981, however, 72.3 percent of all entitlement programs were actually self-funding.[11] These programs, called trust funds, are paid for by a separate tax. Trust funds, which include Social Security and Medicare, do not add to the federal deficit because they do not draw from general funds. Although the Social Security fund faces deficits in the future, changes currently under consideration in Congress will probably alleviate this problem. If we exclude trust funds from the federal budget, national defense accounted for 33.6 percent of the remainder in FY 1981, and is projected to account for 44.9 percent in FY 1986 (Table 4.3).

The military's responsibility for the deficit is also obscured by the fact that many programs in the federal budget which have a military component are not included in the national defense category. The largest military related program outside of the official category is veterans' benefits. Even though veterans' programs do not increase our present military strength, these expenditures are a cost of past wars. Parts of other agencies are also military-oriented, including: the foreign military assistance program, the National Aeronautical and Space Administration (NASA), the Coast Guard and the Merchant Marine. In addition, roughly two-thirds of all government interest payments are attributable to debt created by past wars and military spending (Appendix C).

If these expenses are included, we find that military commitments claimed 48.6 percent of the government's general revenues during FY 1981 and are projected to claim 59.2 percent in FY 1986 (Table 4.3). These figures also represent the military's share of the responsibility for the deficit if we assume that general revenues are evenly distributed among all non-trust fund federal programs.

While other options exist for reducing the deficit, they are not likely to be as effective as cutting the military budget. For example, a tax increase would probably be seen as a reduction in the amount of private funds available for investment. Social programs have already been cut substantially and further reductions face stiff opposition in Congress. Thus, if our government officials want to avoid the consequences of another collision between fiscal and monetary policy, they will probably have to cut military programs. Yet slowing the military buildup will not be easy, for expenditures are authorized far in advance of outlays. If Congress or the President want to cut the Pentagon's budget in FY 1985 and FY 1986, large cuts in expenditure authorizations will have to be made during this fiscal year.[12]

The price of failing to reduce future federal budget deficits is high.

"Crowding out" investment in the present economy could be more damaging than it was in the Vietnam era. Today, many industries need substantial modernization. Moreover, after a decade of high inflation, the economy is more susceptible to inflationary pressures than it was during the 1960s. And, as we will discuss in the next section, the deficit is not the only inflationary pressure associated with the buildup. Demand for military communications equipment, computers, semiconductors and aerospace goods could bid up the prices of skilled labor and high technology products as economic activity expands.

Supply Constraints

A major reason why the Vietnam war created more inflation than the Korean buildup was that the expansion in military spending during Vietnam occured as the economy was reaching peak capacity (Table 4.4). Since there were no wage and price controls, the increased competition for labor and manufactured goods drove up prices. While the number of people in the armed forces rose almost twice as much during the Korean war as it did in the Vietnam war, the economy had more idle manufacturing capacity in the early 1950s. Reagan administration officials point to the Korean experience to discount the possibility that the present buildup will stimulate higher prices. They argue that low factory utilization and high unemployment reduce the likelihood that the present buildup will increase inflationary pressures.

This reasoning, however, largely ignores the effect that the present buildup will have on specific industries that supply the Pentagon. As military hardware has become increasingly sophisticated, fewer industries have become responsible for the bulk of the output. In addition, almost 60 percent of the growth in military spending will come in the procurement of weapons and the development of new systems. Recent history indicates that military-related industries could experience bottlenecks and inflation long before these problems develop in other industries. As the economy recovers, the buildup could heat up the competition for economic resources, particularly skilled workers and intermediate products. This competition is likely to drive up prices in advanced technology fields such as information processing and civilian aerospace. As military needs bid up prices, American high technology products could become less competitive in that rapidly changing, international marketplace — significantly damaging a sector many economists hope will provide a stimulus for growth during the 1980s.

Concentrated Buildup: The bulk of the present buildup is focused on a weak link in the military establishment — the defense industrial base. While the buildups during the Korean and Vietnam wars were spread across all categories of military expenditures, the Reagan administration's buldup is concentrated on purchasing new arms. Instead of adding more personnel, most of the additional funds will buy highly complex weapons systems like B-1 bombers, MX missiles, Nimitz-class aircraft carriers and Abrams M-1 tanks. Thus, while the total Pentagon budget is projected to grow more slowly during the current buildup than it did during the Vietnam war, procurement growth will be faster (Chart 4.7). Authority to obligate funds for procurement will rise 50 percent between FY 1981 and FY 1983, slightly more than the 48 percent increase during the Vietnam war. During the Korean conflict, procurement authority increased almost six-fold.

During the last two wars, authority to write contracts for new equipment peaked after two years of rapid expansion. In the current buildup, however, the administration wants obligational authority for weapons to expand rapidly for at least five years. Since the actual expenditures on weapons systems lag far behind the initial obligation to buy, procurement outlays will continue to grow throughout the decade.

An examination of the administration's military buildup shows that 58 percent of the growth in outlays between FY 1982 and FY 1985 will go to procurement and research and development. In comparison, these two categories accounted for 40 percent of the growth in outlays during the Vietnam war and 43 percent during the Korean war. During past buildups a larger share of the total increase paid for soldiers and spare parts. Additional expenditures for military personnel accounted for 17.5 percent of the total budget increase in the Vietnam conflict and 27.3 percent in the Korean war. This category is slated to account for only 8.7 percent of the total growth during the Reagan buildup. Spending for operations and maintenance is also projected to make up a smaller share of the growth during the present buildup. Expansion in this category will require 20.5 percent of the total budget increase between FY 1982 and FY 1985. During the Vietnam war, growth in operations and maintenance accounted for 29.4 percent of the overall expansion. In the Korean war, the comparable figure was 23.1 percent.[13]

Since much of the money spent during the current buildup will purchase equipment and material, an analysis of the rise in the military's share of goods-producing GNP would be a better measure of the Pentagon's claim on civilian resources than is the broader measure of total defense outlays as a share of GNP. Such an analysis was performed in 1981 by Gary Wenglowski and Rosanne Cahn of the Wall Street firm of Goldman Sachs & Co. They compared the present buildup to the Vietnam War in terms of non-personnel military expenditures as a share of GNP excluding services (Chart 4.8). By this measure, they found that the growth in the share of civilian resources consumed by the Pentagon during the Reagan buildup will grow almost as quickly as during the Vietnam war. While the present buildup starts at a lower level, they also found that fast-paced growth will be sustained for a much longer period of time. By 1986, the absolute level of GNP excluding services devoted to the military will be only half a percentage point lower than at the height of the Vietnam war. Wenglowski and Cahn concluded from this comparison that "the rise in defense spending planned by the Reagan administration is likely to put more inflationary pressure on the economy than many of the conventional analyses have indicated."[14]

Weak Defense Industrial Base: Even though the recession idled over 30 percent of our manufacturing capacity, the highly specific requirements of the current arms buildup may still strain our high technology industries. The limited supply of specialized companies and skilled workers severely constrains the production of sophisticated weapons. Ever since former President Carter announced his military increases in January 1980, concern has been expressed about the ability of defense contractors to fill new Pentagon orders. "Serious bottlenecks and choke points . . . adversely affect the Defense Department's ability to procure military equipment in a timely, efficient and economic manner," reported the Defense Industrial Base Panel of the House Armed Service Committee during the fall of 1980.[15] Until the current recession depressed civilian orders, the delivery of military equipment was held up by long wait times for subsystems even though the prime contractors had plenty of capacity. According to the report of the House Armed Services Panel:

- The defense industrial base is unbalanced; while excess production capacity generally exists at the prime contractor level, there are serious deficiencies at the subcontractor levels.

- The industrial base is not capable of surging production rates in a timely fashion to meet the increased demands that could be brought on by a national emergency.

- Lead times for military equipment have increased significantly during the past three years [1977 to 1980].

- Skilled manpower shortages exist now and are projected to continue through the decade.

- The U.S. is becoming increasingly dependent on foreign sources for critical raw materials as well as for some specialized components needed in military equipment.

- Productivity growth rates for the manufacturing sector of the U.S. economy are the lowest among all free world industrialized nations; the productivity growth rate of the defense sector is lower than the overall manufacturing sector.

- The means for capital investment in new technology, facilities and machinery have been constrained by inflation, unfavorable tax policies, and management priorities.[16]

Those factors tend to bottleup production and create sectoral inflation when military spending expands rapidly. Even though the recession has reduced lead times, the basic problems that caused the long delays between 1979 and 1981 have not been alleviated. Thus, if and when the economy revives, the strain in the defense sector is likely to reappear.

Delays in the delivery of intermediate products used in military equipment became a serious problem in 1979, particularly in aerospace and electronics. New weapons systems requiring subcomponents such as titanium forgings, semiconductors, radar equipment and landing gear were forced to compete with the demands of quickly-growing civilian users. In the late 1970s, the aerospace industry, particularly Boeing Corporation, was gearing up to produce a new generation of fuel-efficient commercial aircraft. At the same time, the electronics industry was busily filling orders created by the growth in the demand for all forms of information processing equipment.

As a result, lead times for components skyrocketed. For example, the Pentagon's Defense Science Board reported that the wait time for an aircraft engine was 168 weeks in 1980. The leadtime for the same engine had been 86 weeks in 1977. Orders for large titanium forgings had to be placed 180 weeks prior to delivery in 1980, up from 70 weeks in 1978. The wait time for integrated circuits was 62 weeks in 1980, up from 25 weeks in 1978.[17]

The decline in the number of subcontractors who provide specialized parts to the major weapons manufacturers is a major reason why lead times have increased. Since the Vietnam war the number of subcontractors has fallen greatly. For example, the number of firms involved in aerospace production declined by 40 percent between 1967 and 1981, from 6,000 to 3,500.[18] There are a number of reasons for this decline, including the high cost of entry into the field and the boom and bust cycle of defense spending.[19] These factors make military business unattractive to smaller firms that lack the resources necessary to survive dry periods, such as the mid-1970's.

Since defense orders do not come at a steady pace, these subcontractors usually do not respond to increases in defense orders by increasing capacity. Instead, they find that it makes better sense, from a business point of view, to add to their backlog and thereby insure a steady flow of work. The prime contractors often cannot simply take their business elsewhere because subcontractors make highly specialized goods such as forgings, specialty semiconductors and avionics. The result, according to Marv Elkin, the vice president for material at Northrop Corporation, is that defense contractors "line up and fight" for the goods that subcontractors produce.[20]

Lead times for military-related products fell in the last half of 1981, as the recession dampened civilian economic activity. A drastic decline in the market for new, fuel-efficient aircraft significantly reduced backlogs for forgings. However, relief from long delays was less pronounced in other sectors. For example, one official from Vought Corporation commented in January 1982 that "we haven't seen a nickel's worth of improvement in lead times on avionics systems."[21] While lead times fell during 1981, they have remained surprisingly high and stable during 1982, considering the depth of the current recession (Tables 4.5 and 4.6). Indeed, wait times for some electronics equipment used by the Navy have increased. Also, the total amount of unfilled orders for defense products still continues to rise (Chart 4.9). Although there is a lull now, industry analysts are concerned that economic recovery, particularly in the commercial aircraft industry, could bring a new and perhaps tighter squeeze in 1984. As an official at Boeing explained, "If the B-1 comes on stream and starts to use up all the capacity of the titanium industry, that would be our Achilles heel."[22] The fact that unfilled orders for defense products are greater now than at the height of the Vietnam war, after adjusting for inflation, suggests that lead times could expand dramatically when the economy recovers.

A recent study by the Commerce Department's Bureau of Industrial Economics indicates that substantial capacity expansion will be required in a number of major defense-related industries if we are to avoid longer lead times and renewed inflationary pressures during the current arms buildup. The Bureau examined 58 industries important to the military. Of those industries, 14 were found to require significant additional investment to meet new military orders. The report divided the 14 industries into three groups: 1) those that will require Pentagon subsidies to meet the projected demand; 2) those that have limited slack but are presently growing quickly; and 3) those that due to limited economically-efficient slack will require expansion to prevent the cost of production from increasing. In addition, the Bureau found that in at least four other industries, new military orders would have to be filled by relying more heavily upon imports (Table 4.7).

The Commerce Department was assured by the Defense Department that the industries in the first category — guided missiles, tanks, and military aircraft — will add the necessary capacity to meet projected demand growth between 1979 and 1985. The Pentagon plans to insure that these investments are made by subsidizing expansion of firms performing this work. However, past attempts by the Defense Department to stimulate increased investment have met with limited success.[23] If these investments are not made, production rates for weapons systems will have to be slowed, raising the cost of production. To assure that the necessary investments are made, the Pentagon may have to cover a greater share of the expansion costs than it currently expects to. Thus, the simple avoidance of bottlenecks may increase the cost of weapons and the overall military budget.[24]

Analysts at the Bureau of Industrial Economics assume that the quickly-growing industries in the second category will acquire the necessary capacity because firms in these high technology industries are also serving fast-growing civilian markets. New military demand will represent only a small portion of the total increase in these high-technology sectors. While recognizing that high interest rates might slow investment, the Bureau concluded that companies in these advanced sectors would "base investment plans on the longer-term outlook."[25] Yet even if the necessary investments are made, the Bureau warned that heavy military spending could reduce American high technology exports:

> Rapid defense demand growth for products such as computers, semiconductors, and optical instruments, which are also important *exports*, could cause delay and/or curtailment of export shipments, further reducing the U.S. merchandise trade balance.[26]

Industries in the third category have sufficient slack to meet projected demand. Unless modernization takes place, however, firms in these industries will have to use older, uneconomical capacity, increasing production costs and exerting upward pressure on prices. The Commerce Department was less certain that the necessary investments would be made in these industries if interest rates stay high and the economy remains weak.

Finally, the Bureau found that the Defense Department would have to rely more heavily on foreign sources of supply for electron tubes and some metal industry products. Indeed, since the Pentagon is already very dependent on foreign sources for many of the strategic raw materials required for military production, the Commerce Department concluded that the arms buildup could substantially increase our trade deficit. The Bureau found that, on average, each million dollars of defense final demand generates direct and indirect imports totaling $120,000. In contrast, a million dollars of non-defense final demand generates only $89,000 of imports.[27]

Labor Constraints: Growth in defense-related employment during the present buildup might also create inflationary pressures. The Reagan administration's program will require significant growth in the work force employed by military contractors. In the first three years of the present buildup, defense-related industrial employment is slated to grow 41.5 percent.[28] During the Vietnam war, the private-sector work force necessary to fill the Pentagon's orders rose 49.4 percent. The Korean war required almost a five-fold increase in the number of people working on military contracts in the private sector.

On the other hand, the number of military personnel, both uniformed and civil servants working for the Pentagon, is projected to remain virtually unchanged during the current buildup. As one might expect, both of those categories grew substantially during the Vietnam and Korean wars. The number of military personnel grew dramatically during the Korean war because the force level prior to the war was low, as a result of the demobilization after World War II. The growth in military personnel was smaller during the Vietnam conflict because more than two and a half million people were kept in uniform during the Cold War.[29]

The Truman administration vastly reduced the potential inflationary impact of its rapidly expanding military employment requirements by imposing wage and price controls. The Johnson administration, on the other hand, decided not to impose wartime controls. The lack of such controls contributed to the inflationary pressures that developed during the Vietnam war. Table 4.8 shows that unemployment fell dramatically during the Korean war. While employment dropped more slowly during the Vietnam conflict, without economic controls, increased demand for workers pushed up labor costs and prices.

While the overall demand for labor is not likely to create inflationary pressures during the current buildup, the emphasis on producing highly complex weapons could cause shortages of skilled workers and engineers. As discussed in Chapter I, arms production requires a larger share of skilled employees than most other forms of manufacturing. Technically skilled employees also have a much lower unemployment rate than the rest of the population. Thus, as the economy recovers and the buildup unfolds, we could see competition for skilled employees push up salary costs. This would not be a new problem. In 1980, a Lockheed Aircraft Company executive testified that "in spite of the recession and its attendant unemployment there remains a shortage of skills needed by the defense industry. The shortage leads to competition for labor and an upward pressure on costs."[30]

The military's substantial increase in demand for skilled labor comes at a time when the supply of engineers and machinists is already stretched thin. Engineering schools are not graduating students quickly enough to fill the increased demand. In the engineering field, a National Science Foundation (NSF) survey found that over 50 percent of the firms they polled reported a shortage of new graduates in electrical, electronic and computer engineering during 1981 (Chart 4.10). Moreover, the firms surveyed by NSF hired only about 40 percent of the computer and electrical engineers that they hoped to hire during that year. Overall, NSF concluded that there was a shortage of new graduates in computer science, computer engineering, and electrical engineering. Probable shortages were found in the supply of electronics-engineering and systems-analysis graduates.[31]

Ironically, engineering schools are finding it difficult to fill the demand for more graduates because employment opportunities in industry have attracted a substantial number of faculty members away from teaching. Since the mid-1970s, it has become increasingly difficult to fill full-time engineering positions, resulting in heavier teaching loads and fewer course offerings at many universities. In the fall of 1980, NSF found that 10 percent of the faculty positions in engineering were vacant. Hardest hit were computer science and industrial engineering departments. In those two areas, faculty vacancy rates were 16 and 13 percent respectively. In addition, the proportion of post-doctorates employed by universities in these fields continues to decline, in large measure because of increased opportunities in business.[32]

The supply of skilled machinists is also limited. A survey by the National Tooling and Machining Association found that, even during the recession in 1981, job shop machining firms could have used 21 percent more journeyman machinists had fully trained applicants been available. If business conditions had been ideal, the machinist work force could have been increased by 50 percent.[33] While cautioning that industry surveys are somewhat misleading, Neal Rosenthal, chief of the Division of Occupational Outlook for the Labor Department's Bureau of Labor Statistics also found that there was a shortage of skilled machining workers during the 1970s. Even though he believes that, in general, the shortage should not get markedly worse during the 1980s, Rosenthal predicted that problems could develop in the defense industry. "If defense purchases were to rise rapidly during a short time frame and affect industries in a specified area, the shortages could become so acute that the planned increases in production could not occur."[34]

Inflation: Production bottlenecks and the shortage of skilled labor in the defense industry have inflated the cost of products purchased by the Pentagon. During the past five years, inflation in the cost of military equipment was substantially higher than in the economy in general (Table 4.9). It has stayed higher even during the recession. In key industries serving the military, such as aircraft and missiles, inflation has remained at double-digit rates.[35]

Given the defense industry's limited ability to expand production quickly, the fast pace of Reagan's military buildup is likely to trigger higher inflation in advanced technology industries. If the Pentagon does not reduce the amount of weapons purchased to adjust for cost overruns, supplemental funding needed to meet "unexpected" obligations will increased the military budget. A higher military budget means larger federal deficits. Thus, price increases in the military sector could spill over into other sectors in varying degrees, depending on how quickly the economy recovers.

A simulation of the economy's future path by Data Resources, Inc. (DRI) suggests that heavy military expenditures could result in economy-wide bottleneck problems by 1985.[36] DRI tested the effects of different levels of military spending on the economy over five years (1983 to 1987). Among the simulations they examined were a "high" scenario, consistent with the administration's ambitious plans; a "control" scenario consistent with the plans emerging from the Congressional Budget process; and a "low" scenario based on a transition to a three percent growth rate starting in 1984.

DRI's model showed that, for each of the simulations, utilization of manufacturing capacity would not rise again to 1980 levels until 1984 (Table 4.10). However, capacity utilization increases much more quickly under both the high and control simulations than in the lower military spending simulation. By 1985, utilization rates could come close to the levels attained during the last inflationary surge in 1979.

DRI's simulation also showed that inflationary pressures resulting from the buildup would peak in 1985 (Table 4.11). The wholesale price indexes for industrial commodities and intermediate products would jump from about six percent in 1983 to roughly 10 percent in 1985 in both the high and control simulations. The overall inflation rate, measured by the GNP implicit price deflator, meanwhile, trails behind. It rises about a point between 1983 and 1985 in the higher defense spending simulations.

Conclusion

Clearly, the present buildup poses numerous economic risks. While increased military spending may not trigger an inflationary surge as it did during the Vietnam war, the collision between higher government deficits and restrictive monetary policy could substantially reduce new investment and overall economic growth. Although the current buildup comes in a recession when there is plenty of unused manufacturing capacity, the highly specialized needs of defense contractors might still stimulate inflation in selected high technology industries.

The arms buildup could also increase the U.S. balance of trade deficit for two reasons. First, weapons production requires expensive metals like chromium and titanium that must be imported. Second, building arms will divert a substantial share of our engineering talent from developing civilian high technology products. As a result, the export of U.S. high technology goods could grow more slowly than if fewer weapons were being produced.

The realization that military spending poses substantial risks has grown over the past few years, even among officials of the administration. For example, we learned in the December 1981 *Atlantic Monthly* that budget director David Stockman has been concerned about the buildup since early in President Reagan's term.[37] The 1982 Annual Report of the Council of Economic Advisors warned that the increase in military spending could create sectoral bottlenecks and inflation.[38] Indeed, the conflict over the military budget seems to have played a role in Murray Weidenbaum's decision to resign from the Council. "What worries me [about the military buildup]," explained Weidenbaum, "is that these crash efforts rarely increase national security. They strain resources [and] create bottlenecks."[39]

If the military budget's growth rate is not reduced, the economy is likely to limp along, cycling between recession and weak recovery. At the same time, military procurement will create inflationary pressures in some sectors and employ resources that could be used to expand our high technology industries. If the President and Congress cannot muster the political courage to slash some of the billions of dollars in questionable military programs that even David Stockman admits exist in the Pentagon's budget, our economic future will continue to be bleak.

Notes

1. Wassily Leontieff, "Big Boosts in Defense Risk 'Economic Calamity'," *U.S. News & World Report*, March 16, 1981, p. 26.

    David Gold and Robert DeGrasse Jr., "Economic Recovery vs. Defense Spending," *The New York Times*, February 20, 1981.

2. Lester C. Thurow, "How to Wreck the Economy," *The New York Review of Books*, May 14, 1981.

    Thurow, "Beware of Reagan's Military Spending," *The New York Times*, May 31, 1981.

3. Murray L. Weidenbaum, quoted in "Spending By Military Is Defended," *The New York Times*, May 4, 1981.

    Caspar Weinberger, "Remarks to the Women's Economic Roundtable," University Club, Washington, D.C., July 28, 1981.

    William Nordhaus, "No Great Threat From Military Spending," *The New York Times*, May 17, 1981.

4. Otto Eckstein, *Tax Policy and Core Inflation* (Washington, D.C., U.S. Congress, Joint Economic Committee, 1980), p. 28.

5. Murray L. Weidenbaum, testimony, *Hearings on the Economic Effects of Vietnam Spending*, (U.S. Congress, Joint Economic Committee, April 1967), p. 203.

6. U.S. Office of Management and Budget, *Federal Government Finances* (Washington, D.C.: U.S. GPO, February 1982), p. 7.

7. In the press conference releasing the 84 budget, Secretary of the Treasury Donald Regan responded to a question about the standby tax increase in 1986 by saying: "Nineteen eighty-four is an election year. Do I have to say more?," quoted in Hedrick Smith, "Reagan Seeks Rise in Arms Spending in Budget Message," *The New York Times*, February 1, 1983, pp. 1, 16.

8. *Economic Report of the President* (Washington, D.C.: U.S. GPO, February 1983), p. 233.

9. Richard Morse, "The Role of New Technological Enterprises in the U.S. Economy: A Report of the Commerce Technical Advisory Board to the Secretary of Commerce," (Washington, D.C.: Commerce Department, 1976).

10. Lee B. Thomas, Jr., "The Economic Implications of the Arms Race," Plenary Address to the Woodlands Conference, November 9, 1982.

11. *Budget of the U.S. Government, FY 1984* (Washington, D.C.: U.S. GPO, 1983), pp. 3-9, 9-48. (Hereafter, *U.S. Budget....*)

12. About 55 percent of procurement authority is paid out two years beyond the year that it is authorized. See "Defense Spending Increases and Inflation," U.S. Congressional Budget Office, March 24, 1980.

13. U.S. Department of Defense, Office of the Assistant Secretary of Defense (Comptroller), unpublished data breaking down Pentagon outlays by program back to FY 1945.

    U.S. Budget..., *op. cit.*, p. 5-8.

14. Gary M. Wenglowski and Rosanne Cahn, "Impact of Defense Buildup Underestimated," *Pocket Chartroom*, (New York: Goldman Sachs Economics, June/July 1981).

15. U.S. Congress, House Armed Services Committee, Report of the Defense Industrial Base Panel, *The Ailing Defense Industrial Base: Unready for Crisis*, December 31, 1980, p. 13. (Hereafter, *The Ailing....*)

128

16. *Ibid.*, p. 11.

17. U.S. Department of Defense, Office of the Under Secretary of Defense for Research and Engineering, Summer Study Panel on Industrial Responsiveness, *Report of the Defense Science Board 1980*, January 1981, p. 31.

18. "Pluckett Says Years, Not Months Needed for Industry 'Surge'," *Aerospace Daily*, July 15, 1981, p. 74.

19. Jacques S. Gansler, *The Defense Industry* (Cambridge, Mass.: MIT Press, 1980), Chapter 6.

20. "In Military Buildup, Big Contractors Face Supplier Bottlenecks," *Wall Street Journal*, August 21, 1981, p. 1.

21. "Industrial Lead Times: Manufacturers Facing Surpluses in Materials," *Aviation Week & Space Technology*, January 11, 1982, p. 62.

22. "Industrial Lead Times: Materials, Supply Shortages Ease," Special Report, *Aviation Week & Space Technology*, January 4, 1982, p. 38.

23. U.S. Congress, Senate Committee on Banking, Housing and Urban Affairs, jointly with the Subcommittee on Priorities and Economy in Government of the Joint Economic Committee, "Department of Defense Contract Profit Policy" (Washington, D.C.: U.S. GPO, March 21, 1979). p. 2.

24. Charles Mohr, "Air Force Study Says Budgets, Uncut, Still Won't Buy Arms in 5-Year Plan, *The New York Times*, February 4, 1983, p. B5.

25. U.S. Department of Commerce, Bureau of Industrial Economics, "Sectoral Implications of Defense Expenditures," August 1982, p. 7.

26. *Ibid.*, p. 8.

27. *Ibid.*, p. 7.

28. U.S. Department of Defense, Office of the Assistant Secretary of Defense, (Comptroller), "National Defense Budget Estimates for FY 1983," p. 82.

29. *Ibid.*, p. 82

30. *The Ailing...*, *op. cit.*, p. 14.

31. National Science Foundation, "Labor Markets for New Science & Engineering Graduates in Private Industry," *Science Resources Studies Highlights*, June 9, 1982.

32. National Science Foundation, "Engineering Colleges Report 10% of Faculty Positions Vacant in Fall 1980," *Science Resources Studies Highlights*, November 2, 1981.

33. The National Tooling & Machining Association, "Tooling & Machining Industry Manpower Survey," Special Report to the Membership, (Washington, D.C.: NTMA, September, 1981).

34. Neal H. Rosenthal, "Shortages of Machinists: An Evaluation of the Information," *Monthly Labor Review*, July 1982, p. 31.

35. U.S. Congressional Budget Office, Barbara Hollinshead, "Memorandum on Defense Inflation and Leadtimes," October 27, 1982, Table 4.

36. Data Resources, Inc., *Defense Economics Research Report*, August 1982, p. 6.

37. William Grieder, "The Education of David Stockman," *The Atlantic*, December, 1981.

38. *Economic Report of the President*, (Washington, D.C.: U.S. GPO, February 1982), p. 86.

39. Owen Ullman, "Weidenbaum Attacks Reagan Arms Outlays," *Newsday*, August 27, 1982.

Chart 4.1

Department Of Defense Outlays
Constant 1983 Dollars

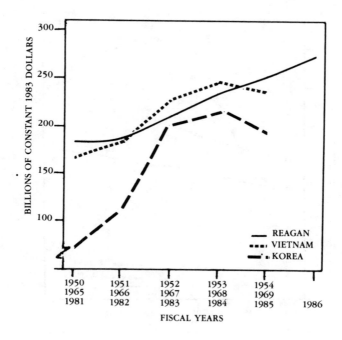

Sources: U.S. Department of Defense, Office of Assistant Secretary of Defense (Comptroller), unpublished data. Estimates for 1982 to 1986 from U.S. Department of Defense, Office of Assistant Secretary of Defense (Public Affairs), "FY 1984 Department of Defense Budget," January 31, 1983.

Chart 4.2

National Defense Outlays As A Share Of GNP

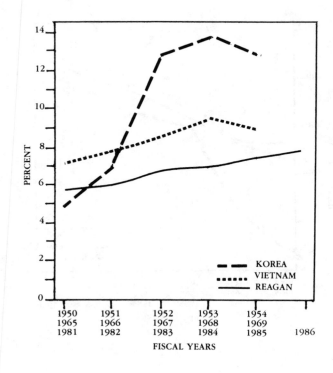

KOREA
VIETNAM
REAGAN

1950	1951	1952	1953	1954	
1965	1966	1967	1968	1969	
1981	1982	1983	1984	1985	1986

FISCAL YEARS

Sources: U.S. Office of Management and Budget, Budget Review Division, "Federal Government Finance," February 1982, pp. 72-73. Estimates for 1982 to 1986 from *Budget of the United States Government, FY 1984* (Washington, D.C.: U.S. GPO, January 1983), pp. 9-4, 9-53.

Chart 4.3

Tax Receipts As A Share Of GNP

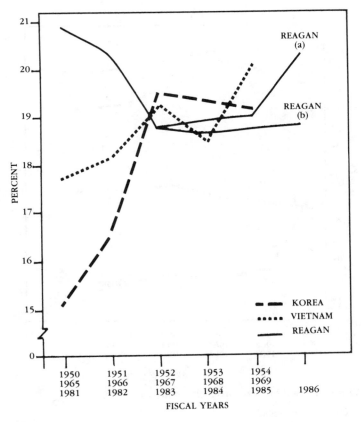

(a) With proposed tax increases.

(b) Without tax increases.

Sources: U.S. Office of Management and Budget, Budget Review Division, "Federal Government Finance," February 1982, pp. 72-73. Estimates for 1982 to 1986 from *Budget of the United States Government, FY 1984* (Washington, D.C.: U.S. GPO, January 1983), pp. 3-17, 9-4, 9-53.

Chart 4.4

Non-Defense Federal Spending As A Share of GNP

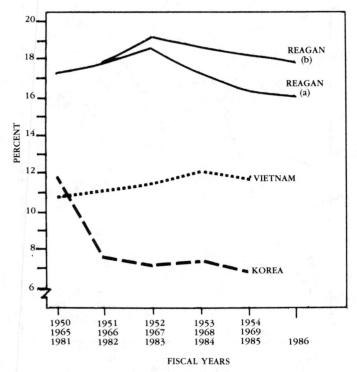

(a) With proposed civilian program reductions.

(b) At current services.

Sources: U.S. Office of Management and Budget, Budget Review Division, "Federal Government Finance," February 1982, pp. 4, 5, 18, 19. Estimates for 1982 to 1986 from *Budget of the United States Government, FY 1984* (Washington, D.C.: U.S. GPO, January 1983), pp. 3-17, 9-4, 9-53.

Chart 4.5

Unified Budget Deficits As A Share Of GNP

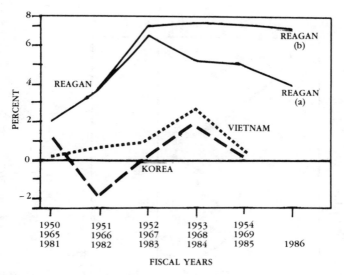

FISCAL YEARS

(a) With proposed tax increases and service reductions.

(b) Without tax increase or service reductions.

Sources: Office of Management and Budget, Budget Review Division, "Federal Government Finance," February 1982, pp. 72-73. Estimates for 1982 to 1986 from *Budget of the United States Government, FY 1984* (Washington, D.C.: U.S. GPO, January 1983), pp. 3-17, 9-4, 9-53.

134

Chart 4.6

Standard-Employment Deficit As A Share Of Standardized GNP*

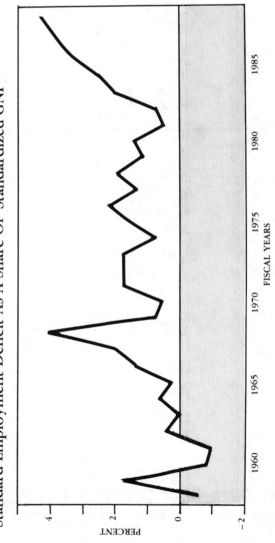

*The federal deficit and GNP are both adjusted in each year to the level that they would have been (or will be) if the unemployment rate was (or will be), 6 percent.

Sources: U.S. Congressional Budget Office, *The Outlook for Economic Recovery, A Report to the Senate and House Committees on the Budget, Part I* (Washington, D.C.: U.S. GPO, February 3, 1983), p. 66.

Chart 4.7

Total Obligational Authority For Procurement
Constant 1983 Dollars

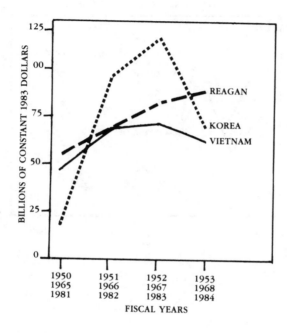

Sources: U.S. Department of Defense, Office of Assistant Secretary of Defense (Comptroller), "National Budget Estimates for FY 1983," pp. 53-54. Estimates for 1982 to 1986 from U.S. Department of Defense, Office of Assistant Secretary of Defense (Public Affairs), "FY 1984 Department of Defense Budget," January 31, 1983.

Chart 4.8

Defense As A Share Of GNP

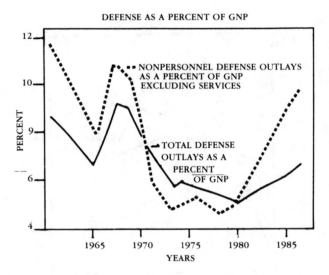

DEFENSE AS A PERCENT OF GNP

Source: Gary M. Wenglowski and Rosanne Cahn, "Impact of Defense Buildup Underestimated," *Pocket Chartroom*, Goldman Sachs Economics, June/July 1981.

Chart 4.9

Manufacturers' Unfilled Orders, Defense Products
Monthly Average
(Constant 1972 Dollars)

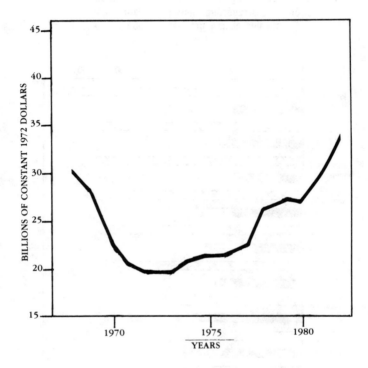

Source: U.S. Department of Commerce, Bureau of Economic Analysis, *Business Conditions Digest* (Washington, D.C.: U.S. GPO, various issues), statistical series 561. Data for 1968 to 1971 adjusted to 1972 dollars using the implicit price deflator for federal government purchases, *Economic Report of the President* (Washington, D.C.: U.S. GPO, February 1982), p. 237. Data for 1973 to 1981 was adjusted using the BEA implicit price deflator for national defense purchase less compensation, unpublished data.

Chart 4.10

Labor Markets for New Science and Engineering Graduates in Private Industry

Science and engineering fields by proportion of employers reporting shortage, balance, and surplus of new graduates: 1981

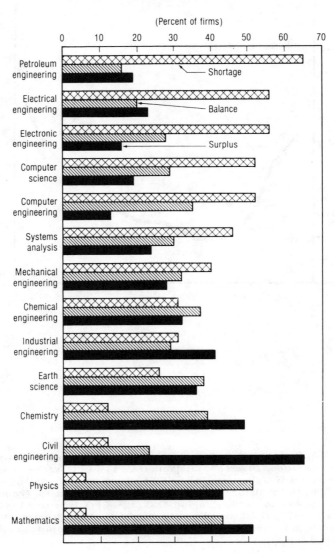

(Percent of firms)

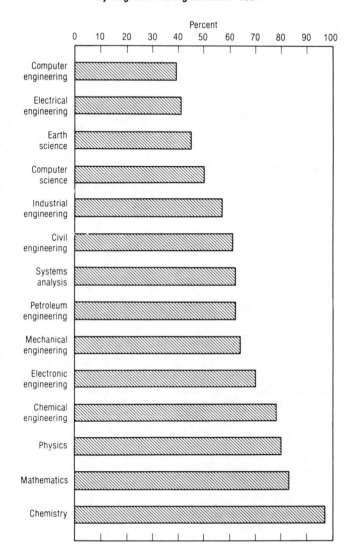

**Science and engineering fields
by degree of hiring success: 1981**

Source: U.S. National Science Foundation, "Labor Markets for New Science and Engineering Graduates," *Science Resources Studies Highlights*, June 9, 1982, Charts 2 and 3.

Table 4.1

Inflation Rate
Annual Percent

YEARS					
Vietnam	1965	1966	1967	1968	1969
Korea	1950	1951	1952	1953	1954

GNP IMPLICIT PRICE DEFLATOR					
Vietnam	2.2 %	3.2	3.0	4.4	5.1
Korea	2.1 %	6.6	1.4	1.6	1.2

INDUSTRIAL COMMODITIES					
Vietnam	1.3 %	2.2	1.5	2.5	3.4
Korea	3.6 %	10.4	-2.3	0.8	0.2

INTERMEDIATE MATERIALS					
Vietnam	1.4 %	2.5	0.8	2.3	3.4
Korea	4.5 %	12.1	-3.0	0.6	0.6

Source: *Economic Report of the President* (Washington, D.C.: U.S. GPO, February 1982), p. 300.

Table 4.2

Interest Rates
Average Annual Percent

YEARS					
Vietnam	1965	1966	1967	1968	1969
Korea	1950	1951	1952	1953	1954

Prime Rate					
Vietnam	4.54 %	5.63	5.61	6.30	7.96
Korea	2.07 %	2.56	3.00	3.17	3.05

U.S Treasury Bills					
Vietnam	3.954 %	4.881	4.321	5.339	6.677
Korea	1.218 %	1.552	1.766	1.931	0.953

Corporate Bonds					
Vietnam	4.49 %	5.13	5.51	6.18	7.03
Korea	2.62 %	2.86	2.96	3.20	2.90

Source: *Economic Report of the President* (Washington, D.C.: U.S. GPO, February 1982), p. 308.

Table 4.3

Total Military Spending Budget
FY 1981 and 1986
(Millions of Dollars)

AGENCY OR PROGRAM	1981 OUTLAYS	PERCENT OF FED. FUNDS	1986 OUTLAYS	PERCENT OF FED. FUNDS
National Defense Function	$ 159,765	33.6 %	$ 323,035	44.9 %
Military-Related Programs				
Veterans' Benefits	22,988	4.8	27,159	3.8
Foreign Military Assistance	793	.2	949	.1
National Aeronuatics and Space Admin.	1,084	.2	1,526	.2
Coast Guard	341	.1	517	.1
Merchant Marine	13	*	8	*
Aid to Federally Impacted Areas	172	*	215	*
Interest Payments on Military-Related Debt	45,565	9.6	72,388	10.1
Subtotal of Additions	70,956	14.9	102,762	14.3
TOTAL MILITARY BUDGET	$ 230,721	48.6 %	$ 425,797	59.2 %
TOTAL FEDERAL FUNDS	$ 475,171	100.0 %	$ 719,266	100.0 %

* Less than .1 percent.

Source: Appendix C.

Table 4.4

Production Capacity in Manufacturing
Percent

YEARS					
Vietnam	1965	1966	1967	1968	1969
Korea	1950	1951	1952	1953	1954

TOTAL MANUFACTURING

Vietnam	89.6 %	91.1	86.9	87.1	86.2
Korea	82.8 %	85.8	85.4	89.2	80.3

PRIMARY PROCESSING

Vietnam	91.1 %	91.4	85.7	87.7	88.5
Korea	88.5 %	90.2	84.9	89.4	80.6

ADVANCED PROCESSING

Vietnam	88.9 %	91.2	87.6	86.8	85.0
Korea	79.8 %	83.4	85.9	89.3	80.1

Source: *Economic Report of the President* (Washington, D.C.: U.S. GPO, February 1982), p. 218.

Table 4.5

Defense Material Lead Times
Multi-Contractor Base
(Index: October 1980 = 1.000)

	OCT. '81	OCT. '82	JAN. '83
Steel Plate (Stainless)	.826	.783	.783
Large Steel Forgings (over 50 lbs)	.742	.597	.565
Aluminum Sheet	.630	.704	.667
Titanium Rod	.709	.527	.455
Titanium Forgings (over 50 lbs)	.737	.505	.463
Integrated Circuits	1.000	1.000	1.000
Fasteners (Titanium)	.962	.769	.750
Fasteners (Non-Titanium)	.970	.788	.849
Non-Standard Bearings	.870	.944	.944

Source: U.S. Department of Defense, Joint Aeronautical Materials Activity, cited in Barbara Hollinshead, "Monthly Tracking of Defense Inflation and Leadtimes," Congressional Budget Office, September 9, 1982, Table 5 and phone conversation, March 23, 1983.

Table 4.6

Manufacturers' Lead Times for Ship Components
Index: January 1979 = 1.000

	JAN. '80	JAN. '81	JAN. '82	JAN. '83
Steel Plate (Carbon, Military Specifications)	1.000	0.917	1.083	.833
Aluminum Plate (Heat-Treatable)	1.833	1.583	1.000	.833
Aluminum Shapes (Structural)	1.500	1.333	1.167	1.000
Steel Alloy Castings (Large)	1.000	.625	.625	.542
Main Boilers	1.059	1.000	1.000	.941
Propellers (Controllable Pitch)	1.063	1.000	1.000	.938
Electronic Countermeasure System*	1.000	1.000	1.000	1.143
Air Search Radar System**	1.000	1.000	1.000	.918
Sonar System*	1.000	1.333	1.333	1.222

*Data for these systems are based in January 1980, the first period of data availability.

Source: U.S. Department of Defense, NAVSHIPSO, cited in Barbara Hollins-head, "Monthly Tracking of Defense Inflation and Leadtimes," Congressional Budget Office," September 9, 1982, Table 3 and phone conversation, March 23, 1983.

Table 4.7

Industries Affected by Buildup

INDUSTRY	OUTPUT USED BY DOD 1979	GROWTH IN DOD OUTPUT 1979-1985	GROWTH IN TOTAL OUTPUT 1973-1979	1979-1985	ECONOMICALLY EFFIC CAPACITY [a] Slack	Expansion
REQUIRING DOD SUBSIDIES						
Guided Missiles	71.0 %	127 %	-15 %	86 %	20 %	66 % [b]
Tanks	78.1	104	65	83	28	55 [b]
Military Aircraft	84.1	49	NA	67	67	13 [b]
FAST GROWING						
Nonferrous Forgings	18.0	68	33	25	1	35
Electronic Computing Equipment	3.6	422	188	83	19	87
Semiconductors & Related Devices	9.5	75	196	76	10	96
Engineering & Scientific Equipment	23.5	44	11	52	15	[c]
Radio & TV Communication Equipment	44.8	65	52	33	22	[c]
LIMITED ECONOMICAL SLACK						
Small Arms Ammunition	25.4 %	226 %	-19 %	82 %	72 %	0 %
Machine Tools, Metal Cutting	6.1	81	21	35	27	44
Instruments to Measure Electricity	5.6	76	56	34	18	[c]
Carbon & Graphite Products	6.1	68	52	20	5	26
Aircraft & Missile Engines & Parts	42.3	49	7	33	41	0
Optical Instruments & Lenses	21.6	118	186	53	19	[c]

RY	OUTPUT USED BY DOD 1979	GROWTH IN DOD OUTPUT 1979-1985	GROWTH IN TOTAL OUTPUT 1973-1979	1979-1985	ECONOMICALLY EFFICIENT CAPACITY [a] Slack	Expansion	Total
O IMPORT							
ometallurgical ucts	4.9 %	24 %	-10 %	-19 %	5 %	-32 %	-27 %
melting & ning	6.2	83	-22	12	10	-14	-4
melting & ning	9.0	45	-24	-5	49	-49	0
on tubes	8.3	84	-8	17	2	0	2

(a) Change in potential supply derived from information on slack capacity, actual, and expected expansion (contraction) of capacity between 1979 and 1985.

(b) The mix of products made by this industry is so diverse that an overall measure of supply growth is of little significance. Further disaggregation is needed to evaluate the demand and supply balance.

(c) Supply expansion depends less upon physical capacity than upon the availability of specialized minerals, materials, or components and skilled labor.

Source: U.S. Department of Commerce, Bureau of Industrial Economics, "Sectoral Implications of Defense Expenditures," August 1982, Tables 3 and 4.

Table 4.8

Unemployment
Percent

YEARS					
Vietnam	1965	1966	1967	1968	1969
Korea	1950	1951	1952	1953	1954
Vietnam	4.5 %	3.8	3.8	3.6	3.5
Korea	5.3 %	3.3	3.0	2.9	5.5

Source: *Economic Report of the President* (Washington, D.C.: U.S. GPO, February 1982), p. 269.

Table 4.9

Implicit Price Deflators
Percent Change

YEAR	ALL GNP	NATIONAL DEFENSE PURCHASES LESS COMPENSATION
1978	7.4 %	8.3 %
1979	8.6	10.3
1980	9.3	15.6
1981	9.4	11.9
1982	6.0	8.3

Sources: Price deflator for all GNP from: *Economic Report of the President* (Washington, D.C.: U.S. GPO, February 1983), p. 169. National defense price deflator for 1978 to 1980 from: U.S. Department of Commerce, Bureau of Economic Analysis, unpublished data. Data for 1981 and 1982 from: Barbara Hollinshead, "Monthly Tracking of Defense Inflation and Leadtimes," U.S. Congressional Budget Office, December 29, 1982, Table 1.

Table 4.10

Projected Capacity Utilization Rates
Percent

YEAR	1983	1984	1985	1986	1987
TOTAL MANUFACTURING					
High	76.0 %	80.9	83.6	84.9	84.7
Control	75.6 %	80.1	82.0	83.3	83.2
Low	74.9 %	78.6	80.1	80.4	79.8
PRIMARY PROCESSING					
High	74.7 %	80.8	83.6	84.5	83.9
Control	74.2 %	80.0	82.0	82.7	82.2
Low	73.8 %	79.1	81.1	81.0	80.0
ADVANCED PROCESSING					
High	76.7 %	80.9	83.5	85.2	85.3
Control	76.4 %	80.1	82.0	83.7	83.9
Low	75.4 %	78.3	79.6	80.1	79.8

Source: Data Resources, Inc., *Defense Economics Research Report*, August
1982, Table 6.

Table 4.11

Projected Inflation Rates
Percent Change

YEAR	1983	1984	1985	1986	1987
GNP IMPLICIT PRICE DEFLATOR					
High	6.3 %	6.4	7.4	7.3	7.0
Control	6.3 %	6.4	7.2	7.1	6.8
Low	6.2 %	6.3	7.0	6.8	6.4
WHOLESALE PRICE INDEX, INDUSTRIAL COMMODITIES					
High	6.2 %	8.7	10.0	8.9	8.1
Control	6.1 %	8.6	9.8	8.5	7.6
Low	6.1 %	8.4	9.5	7.9	6.9
WHOLESALE PRICE INDEX, INTERMEDIATE MATERIALS					
High	6.1 %	8.9	10.4	8.8	7.9
Control	6.1 %	8.8	10.2	8.4	7.4
Low	6.0 %	8.6	9.8	7.9	6.6

Source: Data Resources, Inc., *Defense Economics Research Report*, August 1982, Table 5.

Summary of Findings

Since economics significantly affect national security decisions, and politicians have often claimed that building weapons provides numerous economic benefits, CEP undertook a two-year study of the impact of military spending on the U.S. economy. CEP assessed the costs as well as the benefits associated with Pentagon programs. In particular, we analyzed the claims that military spending creates new employment, stimulates economic growth and nurtures technological progress.

Our report is divided into four chapters. In the first, we assess the role of military spending in the overall economy and compare military employment with the jobs that would be created by other uses of the money. The second chapter contains a comparative analysis of the impact that military spending has had on the economic performance of 17 industrial nations during the Cold War. In the third chapter, we evaluate the affects of military programs on U.S. technological progress. This chapter includes a case study of the semiconductor industry. Chapter four contains a comparison of the present military buildup to the increases that occurred during the Vietnam and Korean wars.

Chapter I

The Defense Department's budget has remained high and relatively stable during the last three decades, except for substantial increases during the Korean and Vietnam wars. It has fallen as a share of the entire gross national product (GNP) because the economy has grown. Pentagon spending is the largest federal mechanism for directly stimulating the economy with purchases. Military purchases of goods and services represented almost 70 percent of the federal government's total purchases in 1981. As a result, military expenditures play an important role in "pork barrel" politics.

Military spending has strong regional and industrial constituencies in the few areas where the bulk of the work is done and the bases are located. In FY 1981, about 65 percent of all prime contracts were let to companies in 10 states. During the same year, 10 states received 56 percent of non-procurement military spending. In 1979, five industries accounted for 55 percent of all the Defense Department's purchases from the private sector. In four of those five industries, the Pentagon purchases comprised over 50 percent of the industry's total production.

Although military expenditures are politically powerful, they are far from the most effective way to create employment. Seven of the 11 manufacturing industries selling the greatest volume of goods to the Pentagon create fewer jobs per dollar spent than the median manufacturing industry. About 28,000 direct and indirect jobs are created for every billion dollars (constant 1981 dollars) spent by the Pentagon in the private sector. But the same billion dollars would create 32,000 jobs if spent for new public transit, 57,000 jobs if used for personal consumption, or 71,000 jobs if spent on education.

The employment created by military procurement is also concentrated in highly skilled occupations. Eleven of the 15 principal manufacturing industries producing for the Pentagon employ a smaller percentage of production workers than the average. In four of the five industries producing the most military output, the percentage of professional and technical workers is significantly greater than in the average manufacturing industry.

Since professional and technical workers have the lowest unemployment rate of any occupational category, it follows that military spending creates fewer jobs in occupations with high unemployment. In December 1982, when the overall unemployment was 10.8 percent, the rate for professional and technical workers was only 3.7 percent. Unemployment among laborers and machine operators was above 20 percent.

Chapter II

Falling competitiveness in the price and quality of many of America's manufactured goods is largely responsible for our declining standard of living relative to other industrial nations. This decline began in the mid-1960s and accelerated after the oil crisis. In 1964, the United States exported almost 90 percent more manufactured goods than it imported. By the late 1960s, the percentage fell to below 20. During the 1970s, America's balance of trade in manufactured goods was negative in three years.

CEP performed cross-national statistical analysis on data from 17 noncommunist, advanced industrial nations over two decades, to examine the reasons for this decline. Our analysis indicates that America's higher share of gross domestic product (GDP) spent on the military has contributed to the decline in manufacturing competence. Nations with higher military burdens tend to have lower levels of investment and lower productivity growth (prior to the energy crisis). Indeed, of the 17 nations compared, the United States had among the lowest levels of both investment and productivity growth along with the heaviest military burden. That finding was consistent over each of several time periods we studied.

We found that higher levels of investment generally resulted in faster overall economic growth. Prior to the energy crisis, investment also correlated with lower unemployment. Higher productivity also seemed to lower unemployment. It also tended to increase overall growth in the period before the oil crisis.

The dramatic rise in energy prices in 1973 hurt economic performance in all countries we studied. New investments were needed simply to maintain the then-current level of output per employee because increased oil prices made many energy-intensive production processes unprofitable. It also seems that new investment had a less positive economic effect in some nations than others, probably because the plants and machinery in some nations were on average less energy-efficient than in others.

Another factor that seems to have influenced economic performance was the relative level of industrialization among the nations we studied. Those nations with less mature industrial economies, measured by a relatively higher amount of GDP accounted for by agriculture, tended to have higher rates of investment and quicker economic and productivity growth rates in the years prior to the oil crisis. After 1973, this measure of less mature industrialization was still associated with higher investment. Since the United States ranked as one of the most mature industrial nations, that characteristic may explain a large part of our poorer economic performance.

Three of the factors we tested did not seem to hinder economic performance. We found no evidence that a higher civilian government burden reduced U.S. investment or productivity growth. The United States ranked 13 among the 17 nations in the share of GDP spent on civilian government consumption and second to last among 14 nations in the share of GDP devoted to transfer payments.

Labor costs also did not seem to play a significant role in comparative economic performance. Nations with higher labor-costs tended to offset this disadvantage with higher output-per-employee rates. Moreover, manufacturing labor-costs among most of the nations we studied have converged over the last two decades; indeed, by 1980 four European nations had higher labor costs than did the United States. Japan, however, still continues to enjoy lower labor expenses than many other nations.

In addition, the growth in America's labor force was not the reason for the decrease in manufacturing productivity growth. Some economists have suggested that the growth in the work force diminished the growth in capital per worker, leading to lower productivity growth during the 1970s. However, CEP found that the manufacturing labor force actually grew more slowly after 1973 than it had during the 1960s.

Some might think that the evidence we found linking higher military spending to poorer economic performance could be explained by the notion that more mature nations, which tend to grow more slowly, depend on military spending as a source of demand. While our evidence indicates that the more developed nations in our study had larger military establishments, it seems likely that far from helping those nations, higher arms spending instead magnifies the difficulties their economies face. The main impact of military spending probably is to divert labor and capital from emerging industries and to decrease the incentives to take financial risks. In our statistical analysis, the military burden explained a larger amount of the variation in economic performance among industrial nations than did our measure of economic maturity.

Chapter III

The military exerts a significant influence on our technological development, given the amount of manufactured goods purchased and research projects supported by the Defense Department. Between 1960 and 1973, the Department of Defense purchased 16.9 percent of the durable manufactured goods produced in the United States. This figure dropped to about 10.9 percent between 1973 and 1981. These figures are understated because they do not count the government's purchases of atomic weapons and part of the space program with military purposes.

The Pentagon further influenced our technological development by funding 38.1 percent of all public and private research and development (R&D) between 1960 and 1973. In the post-Vietnam period, this figure fell to 25.6 percent. Space-related R&D, at least 20 percent of which had direct military applications, averaged 11.8 percent of all R&D between 1960 and 1973, and 7.2 percent thereafter.

Military R&D has been by far the federal government's largest mechanism for influencing technological growth. Defense Department R&D averaged 61.4 percent of federal R&D between 1960 and 1973, and 52.7 percent since then.

We estimate that military procurement and R&D employed between 25 and 35 percent of the nation's scientists and engineers during the 1960s and between 15 and 25 percent during the 1970s.

If the economic benefits of military research and procurement outweighed the costs, we would expect that American firms in industries closely allied with the military would have maintained or expanded their overall market shares. But the contrary is true in the electronics, aircraft and machine tool industries. The Japanese have significantly penetrated markets for electronic memory chips and computer-controlled machine tools. America's dominance in the commercial airline market is being challenged by Airbus Industrie, a European consortium.

CEP also found a rough, negative relationship between the share of GDP spent on military R&D and the rate of productivity growth among major industrial nations. One possible reason for this finding is that virtually all military research is focused on specific applications of technology for warfare. Throughout the last two decades, only about three percent has gone for basic research.

Our case study of the electronics industry yielded four key observations:

1. The end-products developed for military use have few commercial applications. Those that do usually must be significantly redesigned for the commercial market.

2. Military research has not often supported projects that have led to significant innovation. Military personnel have difficulty judging promising projects and the Pentagon tends to support more established firms over younger firms that tend to be more innovative.

3. The military's role as "first user" has become increasingly irrelevant given the rapid expansion of commercial applications for semiconductor technology.

4. The Pentagon's current attempts to guide development of semiconductor and machine tool technology raise serious economic and political issues. Military subsidies for new semiconductor technology during the 1980s may hinder development of new civilian products. Moreover, Defense Department programs designed to increase factory automation have gone forward without full input from the unions likely to be affected.

Chapter IV

The Reagan administration's proposed military buildup is the largest in America's peacetime history. It calls for an expansion only somewhat smaller than that which took place during the Vietnam war and significantly smaller than the Korean war increase. Between FY 1982 and FY 1985, military expenditures are slated to grow 32.4 percent in constant dollars. During a comparable three-year period of the Vietnam war (FY 1965 to FY 1968), the military budget rose 42.7 percent. During the Korean conflict (FY 1950 to FY 1953), the budget grew 179.2

percent.

The present increase will require a smaller additional share of GNP than in past buildups. In FY 1982, the military consumed 6.1 percent of GNP; by FY 1985, it will use an additional 1.4 percent. In FY 1965, the military consumed 7.2 percent of GNP; and at the height of the Vietnam war in FY 1968, it required an additional 2.3 percent. The Korean war increase was the most dramatic: In FY 1950, the military used 4.8 percent of GNP, but by FY 1953, an additional nine percent of our national product was consumed.

While the buildup planned by the Reagan administration is smaller than those we experienced during Korea and Vietnam, there is little reason to believe that its economic impact will be less. While the Vietnam conflict required a smaller amount of new resources than the Korean war, the economic problems caused by the Vietnam war were greater. That war triggered the cycle of price and wage increases that still plagues the economy. The different economic impacts of the Korean and Vietnam wars can largely be explained by three features unique to the latter: 1) the Vietnam war was financed by deficit spending; 2) those deficits occurred when the economy was functioning at peak capacity; and 3) there were no wartime economic controls during the Vietnam war to prevent inflation from rising.

The Reagan administration's fiscal policy will also result in large federal deficits. Measured as a share of GNP, the deficits projected by the present administration will exceed the Vietnam-war peak in every one of the next five years (i.e., through FY 1988). Moreover, if the administration does not get all the tax increases and civilian spending reductions it has requested from Congress, then the budget deficit will be more than twice as large measured as a share of GNP during each of the next five years as it was at the peak of the Vietnam war. Even after adjusting for the effects of the recession, the Congressional Budget Office predicts that the fiscal stimulus of the federal budget between FY 1984 and FY 1988 will be as great as it was during the Vietnam War.

While this fiscal stimulus will probably help push us out of the current recession, massive federal deficits during the recovery could fuel inflation or create acute competition for money in the credit markets, depending mostly upon the nation's monetary policy. Since we are not at war, the government does not plan to institute wage and price controls to prevent a new outbreak of inflation. If the Federal Reserve Board moves to hold off inflation by slowing the growth of the money supply, the government's borrowing needs could push interest rates higher and choke off the recovery.

Military spending is largely responsible for the massive deficits we face. After subtracting self-funding programs from the federal budget and adding all military-related costs to the national defense function, we find that 48.6 percent of the federal government's general funds were spent on the military in FY 1981. In FY 1986, the Pentagon is expected to use 59.2 percent of the government's general funds.

Supply constraints in military-related industries could add to the inflationary pressure created by the administration's expansive fiscal policy. The bulk of the current buildup is focused on a weak link in the military establishment — the defense industrial base. Between FY 1982 and FY 1985, fully 58 percent of the growth in military outlays will be devoted to procurement and R&D. By contrast, procurement and R&D accounted for 40 percent of the growth during the Vietnam war, and 43 percent during the Korean war. During past buildups, a larger share of the defense-budget increase paid for soldiers and spare parts than is currently the case.

The defense industrial base may not be able to produce the additional output required by the Pentagon without creating sectoral inflation. While the wait times for subsystems and components have fallen from the record levels of 1980, they remain high. The value of unfilled orders for defense products has continued to rise and is now greater (in constant dollars) than at the height of the Vietnam war. The Commerce Department has identified 14 key military-related industries that will require more expansion than currently planned if bottlenecks and cost-overruns are to be avoided. Analysts at Commerce also found that the current buildup might slow the export of high technology goods, thereby contributing to an increase in our trade deficit.

In addition, the supply of skilled labor may be inadequate to meet the Pentagon's needs. Between FY 1981 and FY 1983, industrial employment created by the Pentagon is slated to grow 41.5 percent. During the Vietnam war, the private sector work force filling the Pentagon's orders rose 49.4 percent; the Korean war required a five-fold increase.

The military's increased demand for skilled labor comes at a time when the supply of engineers and machinists is already stretched thin. A National Science Foundation (NSF) survey found that over 50 percent of the firms they polled reported a shortage of new graduates in electrical, electronic and computer engineering during 1981. Those shortages could become worse in the future, since employment opportunities in industry have attracted a substantial number of faculty members away from teaching.

The supply of skilled machinists is also limited. A survey by the National Tooling and Machining Association found that in 1981 job shop machining firms could have used 21 percent more journeyman machinists if fully trained applicants had been available. While somewhat more cautious, a Labor Department official also reports that there is a shortage of skilled machine workers. He believes that "If defense purchases were to rise rapidly during a short time frame and affect industries in specified areas, the shortages could become so acute that the planned increases in production could not occur."

Production bottlenecks and the shortage of skilled labor in the defense sector have inflated the cost of products purchased by the Pentagon. During the past five years, inflation in the cost of military equipment has been substantially higher than in the economy as a whole.

A simulation of the economy performed by Data Resources, Inc. suggests that the present buildup could result in economy-wide bottleneck problems by 1985. In that scenario, the wholesale price indexes for industrial commodities and intermediate products could jump from about six percent in 1983 to roughly 10 percent in 1985.

Conclusion

The U.S. surely can afford to pay whatever it costs to provide for its security. At the same time, like all countries, America must set limits on military and non-military forms of current consumption. The reason, simply, is to assure that we have enough left to invest in our economic future.

Economics thus is not central but it is essential to take into account when it comes to military spending. Too often arguments that tout various economic benefits of peacetime arms expansion neglect to clarify the net costs.

We have found that a diversion to the military of government resources on a scale planned by the Reagan administration will seriously weaken the nation's ability to meet the challenges of unemployment, foreign market losses, diminishing technological leadership and antiquated industrial plants.

We have also found that those same resources would strengthen the economy if spent directly on solving our economic problems.

Appendix A

State by State Breakdown Of Military Spending

This appendix provides the reader with the background data and methodology for our analysis of the state by state impact of military expenditures.

Two types of Defense Department data were used for this analysis: prime contract awards above $10,000[1] and estimated expenditures excluding major procurement awards.[2] Table A.1 lists the amount of contract awards and non-procurement expenditures that each state and the District of Columbia received in FY 1981. By adding these data together, we created an estimate of the total amount of Pentagon funds that each state received in FY 1981. These data-sets were adjusted for the size of each state's work force.[3]

We calculated a "military tax" — the amount of taxes each state paid to cover military expenditures (Table A.2). The military tax burden was derived using the following methodology: First, we identified the amount of federal tax revenues paid by each state.[4] Second, we determined the share of those taxes that were devoted to military programs.[5] Third, we adjusted the military tax burden for the size of the work force in each state.

With these data we were able to determine the net amount of economic stimulation from military expenditures that each state received per worker (Table A.3). This was done by subtracting the military tax that each state paid per worker from the amount of funds that each state received from the Pentagon per worker.

We then ranked the states based on the net level of Pentagon expenditures per worker (Table A.4). States were grouped into four categories of net military stimulation: 1) those that gained $1000 or more per worker; 2) those that gained between $500 and $1000 per worker; 3) those that received between $0 and $500; and 4) those that experienced a net loss of revenue to the Pentagon.

Table A.5 groups the states into four major regions: the northeast, the midwest, the south, and the west.[6] It shows, for each region, the number of states that fall into the four (above listed) categories of net stimulation.

Notes

1. U.S. Department of Defense, Washington Headquarters Services, "Prime Contract Awards by Region and State, FY 1981," January 1982, pp. 13-14.

2. U.S. Department of Defense, Washington Headquarters Services, "Estimated Expenditures for States and Selected Areas, FY 1981."

3. U.S. Department of Labor, Bureau of Labor Statistics, "States: Labor Force status of the civilian noninstitutional population 16 years and over by sex, age, race, Hispanic origin, and marital status, 1981 annual averages," unpublished data.

4. Total federal revenues for FY 1981 were distributed by state using the percentage of federal revenues collected from each state in FY 1980. *Facts and Figures on Government Finance* (Tax Foundation, Inc., 1981), p. 144.

5. The "military tax" for each state was calculated in two steps: First, we determined the percentage of total federal outlays that went for the two types of Pentagon expenditures. Second, we applied these percentages to the taxes that each state paid to derive the military-related tax. Note that, since the overall federal budget was in deficit during 1981, the total amount of taxes paid by the states did not cover the total cost of the military programs. Thus even though the overall impact of the military was stimulative during that year, the data show that only a few states gained a significant amount of net stimulation.

6. Regional breakdown follows the form established by Virginia Mayer and Margaret Downs, "The Pentagon Tilt: Regional Biases in Defense Spending and Strategy" (Washington, D.C.: Northeast-Midwest Institute, January 1981), Table 1.

Key to Tables A.1 through A.4

Abbreviation	Precise Name
STCONT	Value of Prime Contracts above $10,000 in FY 1981.
STEXP	Estimated value of non-procurement Defense Department expenditures in FY 1981.
STME	Total of contract awards and non-procurement expenditures.
WKFORCE	Civilian work force.
ADJSC	Contract awards adjusted for the size of the work force.
ADJSE	Non-procurement expenditures adjusted for the size of the work force.
ADJST	Total military spending adjusted for the size of the work force.
ST	State tax burden.
SCT	Prime contract tax burden.
SET	Non-procurement tax burden.
ASCT	Contract tax burden adjusted for the work force.
ASET	Non-procurement tax burden adjusted for the work force.
ASMT	Total military tax burden adjusted for the work force.
NCS	Net impact per worker of prime contract awards.
NES	Net impact per worker of non-procurement expenditures.
NMS	Net impact of military spending per worker.

Table A.1

State Distribution of Defense Department Spending

FY 1981

(Thousands of Dollars)

STATE	STCONT	STEXP	STME	WKFORCE	ADJSC	ADJSE	ADJST
ALABAMA	847752	1808244	2655996	1665	509.16	1086.03	1595.19
ALASKA	349423	718854	1068277	192	1819.91	3744.03	5563.94
ARIZONA	1141807	1176025	2317832	1265	902.61	929.66	1832.28
ARKANSAS	218485	451450	669935	1029	212.33	438.73	651.05
CALIF	16699825	11290539	27989364	11781	1417.44	958.37	2375.81
COLORADO	938074	1618191	2556265	1529	613.52	1058.33	1671.85
CONN	494258	443883	4938141	1589	2828.36	279.35	3107.70
DELAWARE	237837	207653	445490	288	825.82	721.02	1546.84
FLORIDA	3169443	3643437	6812880	4513	702.29	807.32	1509.61
GEORGIA	1334188	2840364	4174552	2596	513.94	1094.13	1608.07
HAWAII	590746	1548257	2139003	449	1315.69	3448.23	4763.93
IDAHO	40770	202477	243247	427	95.48	474.19	569.67
ILLINOIS	1216715	2125465	3342180	5577	218.17	381.11	599.28
INDIANA	1717644	629069	2346713	2617	656.34	240.38	896.72
IOWA	333217	238800	572017	1418	234.99	168.41	403.40
KANSAS	983087	770528	1753615	1188	827.51	648.59	1476.11
KENTUCKY	407226	1139756	1546982	1662	245.02	685.77	930.80
LOUISIAN	3045133	913718	3958851	1857	1639.81	492.04	2131.85
MAINE	476407	283564	759971	509	935.97	557.10	1493.07
MARYLAND	2280571	2258111	4749782	2164	1104.75	1090.16	2194.91

MINN	1188463	298147	1486610	2143	554.58	139.13	693.71
MISS	1442704	848912	2291616	1052	1371.39	806.95	2178.34
MISSOURI	4411471	1241126	5652597	2317	1903.96	535.66	2439.62
MONTANA	43466	184388	227854	382	113.79	482.69	596.48
NEBRASKA	109664	476193	585857	773	141.87	616.03	757.90
NEVADA	78381	430833	509214	463	169.29	930.52	1099.81
NEWHAMP	393075	411390	804465	480	818.91	857.06	1675.97
NEWJERSE	2313258	1513129	3826387	3578	646.52	422.90	1069.42
NEWMEX	385770	853097	1238867	575	670.90	1483.65	2154.55
NEWYORK	6520511	1584897	8105408	8016	813.44	197.72	1011.15
NOCAR	860018	2143380	3003398	2916	294.93	735.04	1029.97
NODAK	106938	302194	409132	309	346.08	977.97	1324.05
OHIO	2471545	2109111	4580656	5085	486.05	414.77	900.82
OKLAHOMA	656978	1967115	2624093	1442	455.60	1364.16	1819.76
OREGON	171328	207081	378409	1330	128.82	155.70	284.52
PENN	2405647	2120283	4525930	5476	439.31	387.20	826.50
RHODEIS	235959	310349	546308	478	493.64	649.27	1142.90
SOCAR	481974	1680247	2162221	1417	340.14	1185.78	1525.91
SODAK	56583	191599	248182	333	169.92	575.37	745.29
TENN	521071	733330	1254401	2110	246.95	347.55	594.50
TEXAS	7503964	6012662	13516626	7075	1060.63	849.85	1910.48
UTAH	404457	1098899	1503356	646	626.09	1701.08	2327.18
VERMONT	167603	52136	219739	260	644.63	200.52	845.15
VIRGINIA	3611821	6709611	10321432	2600	1389.16	2580.62	3969.78
WASHING	2792891	1871403	4664294	1987	1405.58	941.82	2347.41
WVIRGINI	114440	105347	219787	786	145.60	134.03	279.63
WISCONSI	606661	225154	831815	2371	255.87	94.96	350.83
WYOMING	64030	143990	208020	250	256.12	575.96	832.08
DC	626594	1759143	2385737	312	2008.31	5638.28	7646.59

Table A.2

State Distribution of Defense Department Taxes

FY 1981

(Thousands of Dollars)

STATE	ST	SCT	SET	SMT	ASCT	ASET	ASMT
ALABAMA	7790536	1040327	878044	1918371	624.82	527.35	1152.17
ALASKA	1737889	232073	195871	427944	1208.71	1020.16	2228.88
ARIZONA	5932793	792249	668664	1460913	626.28	528.59	1154.87
ARKANSAS	4134977	552173	466039	1018212	536.61	452.90	989.52
CALIF	69575479	9290918	7841606	17132526	788.64	665.61	1454.25
COLORADO	7610754	1016319	857781	1874101	664.70	561.01	1225.70
CONN	10487260	1400440	1181982	2582422	881.33	743.85	1625.19
DELAWARE	1797816	240075	202626	442701	833.60	703.56	1537.16
FLORIDA	22952118	3064963	2586852	5651815	679.14	573.20	1252.34
GEORGIA	11326241	1512475	1276541	2789016	582.62	491.73	1074.35
HAWAII	2636797	352111	297184	649295	784.21	661.88	1446.09
IDAHO	1977598	264083	222888	486971	618.46	521.99	1140.45
ILLINOIS	36915155	4923548	4160577	9090126	883.91	746.02	1629.93
INDIANA	14682164	1960616	1654775	3615391	749.18	632.32	1381.50
IOWA	7910390	1056332	891552	1947884	744.94	628.74	1373.68
KANSAS	6412210	856269	722698	1578967	720.77	608.33	1329.10
KENTUCKY	7670682	1024322	864536	1888857	616.32	520.18	1136.50
LOUISIAN	9228789	1232387	1040144	2272531	663.64	560.12	1223.76
MAINE	2217306	296093	249905	545998	581.72	490.97	1072.69
MARYLAND	12764494	1704535	1438641	3143177	787.68	664.81	1452.48

MISSOURI	12345003	1648518	1391362	3039880	711.49	600.50	1311.99
MONTANA	1917670	256080	216134	472214	670.37	565.80	1236.16
NEBRASKA	4075050	544171	459285	1003455	703.97	594.16	1298.13
NEVADA	2337161	312098	263413	575511	674.08	568.93	1243.00
NEWHAMP	2337161	312098	263413	575511	650.20	548.78	1198.98
NEWJERSE	23611317	3152990	2661148	5814139	881.22	743.75	1624.97
NEWMEX	2636797	352111	297184	649295	612.37	516.84	1129.21
NEWYORK	50338848	6722111	5673515	12395626	838.59	707.77	1546.36
NOCAR	12045367	1608505	1357591	2966096	551.61	465.57	1017.18
NODAK	1558107	208065	175609	383674	673.35	568.31	1241.66
OHIO	30203309	4033267	3404109	7437376	793.17	669.44	1462.61
OKLAHOMA	7011482	936294	790240	1726534	649.30	548.02	1197.32
OREGON	7131337	952299	803748	1756047	716.01	604.32	1320.34
PENN	31581634	4217325	3559455	7776780	770.15	650.01	1420.16
RHODEIS	2397088	320101	270167	590268	669.67	565.20	1234.87
SOCAR	5992720	800251	675418	1475670	564.75	476.65	1041.40
SODAK	1438253	192060	162100	354161	576.76	486.79	1063.55
TENN	9708206	1296407	1094178	2390585	614.41	518.57	1132.98
TEXAS	36675446	4897538	4133561	9031099	692.23	584.25	1276.48
UTAH	2876506	384121	324201	708321	594.61	501.86	1096.47
VERMONT	1018762	136043	114821	250864	523.24	441.62	964.86
VIRGINIA	13843183	1848581	1560217	3408797	710.99	600.08	1311.08
WASHING	11685804	1560490	1317066	2877556	785.35	662.84	1448.19
WVIRGINI	4134977	552173	466039	1018212	702.51	592.92	1295.44
WISCONSI	11925513	1592500	1344083	2936583	671.66	566.88	1238.54
WYOMING	1378326	184058	155346	339404	736.23	621.38	1357.62
DC	2337161	312098	263413	575511	1000.31	844.27	1844.59

Table A.3

Net Defense Department Spending Per Worker by State
FY 1981

STATE	NCS	NES	NMS
ALABAMA	-115.66	558.68	443.0
ALASKA	611.20	2723.87	3335.1
ARIZONA	276.33	401.08	677.4
ARKANSAS	-324.28	-14.18	-338.5
CALIF	628.80	292.75	921.6
COLORADO	-51.17	497.32	446.2
CONN	1947.02	-464.51	1482.5
DELAWARE	-7.77	17.46	9.7
FLORIDA	23.15	234.12	257.3
GEORGIA	-68.68	602.40	533.7
HAWAII	531.48	2786.35	3317.8
IDAHO	-522.98	-47.80	-570.8
ILLINOIS	-665.74	-364.91	-1030.7
INDIANA	-92.84	-391.94	-484.8
IOWA	-509.95	-460.33	-970.3
KANSAS	106.75	40.26	147.0
KENTUCKY	-371.30	165.60	-205.7
LOUISIAN	976.17	-68.08	908.1
MAINE	354.25	66.13	420.4

ʌ133	846.31	363.33	1210.3
MISSOURI	1192.47	-64.84	1127.6
MONTANA	-556.58	-83.10	-639.7
NEBRASKA	-562.10	21.87	-540.2
NEVADA	-504.79	361.60	-143.2
NEWHAMP	168.70	308.29	477.0
NEWJERSE	-234.69	-320.86	-555.5
NEWMEX	58.54	966.81	1025.3
NEWYORK	-25.15	-510.06	-535.2
NOCAR	-256.68	269.47	12.8
NODAK	-327.27	409.66	82.4
OHIO	-307.12	-254.67	-561.8
OKLAHOMA	-193.70	816.14	622.4
OREGON	-587.20	-448.62	-1035.8
PENN	-330.84	-262.81	-593.7
RHODEIS	-176.03	84.06	-92.0
SOCAR	-224.61	709.12	484.5
SODAK	-406.84	88.58	-318.3
TENN	-367.46	-171.02	-538.5
TEXAS	368.40	265.60	634.0
UTAH	31.48	1199.22	1230.7
VERMONT	121.39	-241.10	-119.7
VIRGINIA	678.17	1980.54	2658.7
WASHING	620.23	278.98	899.2
WVIRGINI	-556.91	-458.90	-1015.8
WISCONSI	-415.79	-471.92	-887.7
WYOMING	-480.11	-45.42	-525.5
DC	1008.00	4794.01	5802.0

Table A.4

Ranking by State of Net Defense Department Spending Per Worker
FY 1981

STATE	NCS	NES	NMS
DC	3	1	1
ALASKA	10	3	2
HAWAII	11	2	3
VIRGINIA	7	4	4
CONN	1	48	5
UTAH	20	5	6
MISS	6	15	7
MISSOURI	2	33	8
NEWMEX	19	6	9
CALIF	8	18	10
LOUISIAN	4	34	11
WASHING	9	19	12
MARYLAND	14	12	13
ARIZONA	15	14	14
MASS	5	37	15
TEXAS	12	21	16
OKLAHOMA	30	7	17
GEORGIA	25	9	18
SOCAR	31	8	19

ALABAMA	27	10	27	22
MAINE	13	26	13	23
FLORIDA	21	22	21	24
KANSAS	18	27	18	25
NODAK	36	13	36	26
NOCAR	33	20	33	27
DELAWARE	22	29	22	28
RHODEIS	29	25	29	29
VERMONT	17	38	17	30
NEVADA	44	16	44	31
KENTUCKY	39	23	39	32
SODAK	40	24	40	33
ARKANSAS	35	30	35	34
INDIANA	26	43	26	35
WYOMING	43	31	43	36
NEWYORK	23	50	23	37
TENN	38	36	38	38
NEBRASKA	49	28	49	39
NEWJERSE	32	41	32	40
OHIO	34	39	34	41
IDAHO	46	32	46	42
MINN	28	44	28	43
PENN	37	40	37	44
MONTANA	47	35	47	45
WISCONSI	41	49	41	46
IOWA	45	47	45	47
MICHIGAN	42	51	42	48
WVIRGINI	48	46	48	49
ILLINOIS	51	42	51	50
OREGON	50	45	50	51

Table A.5

Regional Breakdown of Net Defense Department
Spending Per Worker
FY 1981

	Over $1000	$500 to $1000	$0 to $500	Net Loss
NORTHEAST				
Connecticut	X			
Maine			X	
Massashusetts		X		
New Hampshire			X	
Rhode Island				X
Vermont				X
Delaware			X	
Maryland		X		
New Jersey				X
New York				X
Pennsylvania				X
TOTAL	1	2	3	5

MIDWEST

Illinois	X			
Indiana	X			
Iowa	X			
Michigan	X			
Minnesota	X			
Ohio	X			
Wisconsin	X			
TOTAL	7	0	0	0
SOUTH				
Alabama		X		
Arkansas	X			
D.C.				X
Florida		X		
Georgia			X	
Kentucky	X			
Louisiana			X	
Mississippi				X
North Carolina		X		
Oklahoma			X	

TABLE A.5
(cont'd)

	Over $1000	$500 to $1000	$0 to $500	Net Loss
South Carolina			X	
Tennessee				X
Texas		X		
Virginia	X			
West Virginia				X
TOTAL	3	4	4	4
WEST				
Alaska	X			
Arizona		X		
California		X		
Colorado			X	
Hawaii	X			
Idaho				X

Kansas				
Missouri	X			X
Montana				X
Nebraska				X
Nevada				
New Mexico	X			
North Dakota			X	X
Oregon				X
South Dakota	X			
Utah				
Washington		X		
Wyoming				X
TOTAL	5	3	3	7

Appendix B

Cross-National Analysis of the Economic Impact of Military Spending

This appendix provides the reader with a detailed discussion of our methodology for examining the cross-national impacts of military spending. It also presents the data we collected and the results of our statistical tests.

The development of our cross-national analysis was based on the premise that we could not adequately assess the opportunity cost of military spending by examining its effects on just one nation's performance over time. While there is evidence that investment declined when military spending rose during the last four decades in the United States,[1] we wanted to see if this relationship held true among industrial nations.[2] Moreover, we wanted to examine the impact of military spending on other aspects of economic performance during the Cold War.

In addition to our central hypothesis that higher military spending damages economic performance, we examined four alternative hypotheses to see if they had stronger explanatory power: One, nations with higher civilian government spending experienced less investment or economic growth. Two, nations with higher wage costs had poorer economic performance. Three, expansion of the U.S. work force reduced productivity growth. Finally, more heavily industrialized nations grew more slowly. All four of these hypotheses were drawn from the current literature on the causes of America's economic problems.

We tested each hypothesis using data from industrialized nations averaged over the last two decades. We attempted to isolate the effects of the oil crisis by breaking the data into two sub-periods: 1960 to 1973 and 1973 to 1980. In this way, we were also able to test each hypothesis before and after the major economic changes created by the dramatic rise in energy prices.

We wanted to test our hypotheses using as large a sample of countries as possible. Three factors determined which nations were included. First, we gathered data only on nations in which market mechanisms largely determined the distribution of economic resources. This test excluded centrally planned economies such as the Soviet Union and China. Second, we included only those countries with large and diverse industrial capabilities. This test excluded less developed nations in Latin America, Asia and Africa. Finally, we included only those nations for which we could obtain data consistent with the majority of other countries in our study. As it turned out, 17 nations conformed to these standards. They were: Australia, Austria, Belgium, Canada, Denmark, Finland, France, West Germany, Italy, Japan, the Netherlands, New Zealand, Norway, Sweden, Switzerland, the United Kingdom, and the United States.

For each of the 17 nations, we gathered two sets of variables, those that measure and those that might determine economic performance. While this distinction is not hard and fast (for example, investment was both a measure and determinant of economic performance), this breakdown provided a framework for our analysis. We used the most reliable and consistent data that could be obtained. The four basic sources of data were the Stockholm International Peace Research Institute, the Organisation for Economic Cooperation and Development, the United Nations, and the U.S. Labor Department's Bureau of Labor Statistics. The variables examined are listed below. Unfortunately, we could not find data on all variables for all the countries in the study. The list includes a short description of the variable, the hypothesis it was used to test, and the number of nations for which we could obtain data.

We collected data on three variables that reflect a primary aspect of economic health:

- Real growth in gross domestic product (GDP) — measures the inflation-adjusted increase in the purchases of goods and services from year to year. We obtained data for all 17 nations.[3]

- Unemployment rate — measures the share of the work force that is not utilized in the economy. We obtained data for nine nations.[4]

- Growth in the consumer price index — measures the inflation rate for consumer goods. We obtained data for 14 nations.[5]

We examined five other variables to develop a fuller view of economic performance:

- Growth in output per hour worked in manufacturing (otherwise known as manufacturing productivity) — measures the increase in the labor efficiency of the manufacturing sector. We assumed that higher productivity growth would result in better economic performance by reducing the cost of production.

Data were available for 11 nations.[6]

- Gross fixed capital formation as a share of GDP — measures the portion of a nation's GDP spent on capital improvements each year. This variable was used to test the theory that higher investment improves productivity and overall economic performance. Data were obtained for all 17 nations.[7]

- Growth in total manufacturing capital — measures the inflation-adjusted increase in total capital equipment. As a more specific measure of investment, it was also used to examine the impact of investment on performance. We obtained data on this variable for 10 nations.[8]

- Growth in the ratio of total manufacturing capital to manufacturing employment — derived by subtracting the growth in manufacturing labor from the growth in manufacturing capital,[9] this variable measures the average increase in the amount of capital per worker. Data were available for nine nations.[10]

- Personal consumption as a share of GDP — measures the amount of GDP spent on consumption by individuals. Data were available for all 17 countries we studied.[11]

We collected data on eight factors that might inhibit economic performance:

- Military spending as a share of GDP — measures the portion of a nation's GDP spent for military purposes. This variable was used to test our central hypothesis. Data were available for all 17 nations.[12]

- Civilian government consumption as a share of GDP — the share of GDP spent for non-military government purposes; derived by subtracting the share of GDP spent on the military from the share spent on all government. It was used to examine the possibility that civilian government is the reason for our poorer performance. Data were available for all 17 nations.[13]

- Government transfer payments as a share of GDP — measures the share of GDP transferred from one group of individuals to another through the government. This variable was also used to test the impact of civilian government programs on economic performance. Data were available for 15 nations.[14]

- Compensation in manufacturing — average cost of labor per hour in the manufacturing sector, measured in U.S. dollars. Used to assess the impact of higher labor costs on economic performance. Data were available for 10 nations.[15]

- Growth in compensation in the manufacturing sector — average increase in labor costs. We obtained data for 11 nations.[16]

- Growth in total hours worked in the manufacturing sector — increase in the employed work force. This variable was used to test the theory that growth in the work force reduced productivity growth. Data were available for 11 nations.[17]

- GDP per employed person — overall measure of output per employee. It was used to examine the hypothesis that more developed industrial nations grow more slowly. We could only obtain data for nine countries.[18]

- Agriculture as a share of GDP — measures the dependence of an economy on agricultural output. This measure gives an indication of how industrialized a nation is. It was used to test our "maturity" hypothesis. Data were obtained on 16 nations.[19]

Tables B.1 through B.3 list the value and relative ranking of each variable for all the countries studied over each time period.

Our data analysis proceeded in three steps: First, we examined the effects of productivity growth and investment on economic growth, unemployment and inflation. Second, we tested our central hypothesis along with the four alternatives. Third, we examined the possibility that disguised relationships explained the results.

We used correlation analysis for most of our work. Correlation analysis is used to discover whether two factors vary together. For example, imagine two sets of numbers, the heights of a group of fathers and the heights of their daughters. If, as we might expect, the taller men were the fathers of the taller daughters, we would say that the heights of fathers and of their daughters are positively correlated. We can determine the strength of this relationship by computing the correlation coefficient. The stronger the association the closer the correlation coefficient gets to one; the weaker and more random the relationship, the closer a correlation coefficient gets to zero. Similarly, with negative relationships (for example, as between smoking and lung capacity), the correlation coefficient approaches negative one.

Correlations can be caused by statistical coincidence and not by any actual association between the two sets of numbers. To test this possibility, one uses a significance test.* A significance test measures the probability that the relationship shown by the correlation coefficient indeed exists. In this study, we assumed that if the significance test indicated that the probability of a correlation not being real was below five percent, then it was "strong" evidence. If the chance of a correlation being random was between 10 and five percent, then it was labeled

---

* Referred to in the charts as: Prob > [R] Under Ho: RHo = 0.

"moderate" evidence of a correlation. If the chance was between 20 and 10 percent, then we labeled it "weak" evidence. We assumed that any correlation with a 20 percent or greater probability of being random was insignificant.

It is important to understand that correlation analysis measures association: it does not prove causation. For example, there is probably a high correlation between the amount of beer consumed and the number of trips to the beach made on any given day. However it would be foolish to say that drinking beer causes trips to the beach or vice versa. Instead, increases in these two factors are caused by a third, unmentioned factor — hot weather. Thus, one must remember that statistical analysis simply provides a means of testing a logical theory.

For our purposes, we employed a type of correlation analysis called the Spearman Rank Order Correlation Test. Along with being simple to calculate, the Spearman test has the added advantage of not requiring the sample to be random. The Spearman coefficient is derived by comparing the relative ranking of the two variables for each nation being studied. We calculated the correlation coefficients and their significance levels using the Statistical Analysis System (SAS) loaded on Columbia University's IBM 370 computer. The results of the three sets of correlations are contained in Tables B.4 through B.6.

We also tested to see if any one nation was responsible for the associations we found by excluding nations that most dramatically exemplified those results from the calculation of the correlation coefficients. For example, Japan had the highest level of investment and the lowest level of military spending. We excluded Japan from the calculation of the Spearman coefficients to see if a significant relationship existed between these two variables without the influence of the Japanese data. We also excluded two other nations that we suspected might have undue influence on certain correlations — the United Kingdom and the United States.

The results of these tests, which were performed on the 1960 to 1980 averages, are displayed in Tables B.7 through B.9. They indicate that our basic findings regarding military spending and economic performance were not determined by the strength of data from any one nation. However, some of the relationships we identified, including the association between manufacturing productivity growth and economic growth, disappear when Japan is excluded from the calculation. Though one nation may indeed be responsible for some of the correlations we found, the size of the sample may be another possible reason that these associations deteriorate when a nation is excluded from our analysis. In the case of productivity growth, we could find consistent data for only 11 nations. When one nation is excluded, the statistical test for significance becomes harder to meet.

Sample size was an even more destructive factor in our attempts to find a multi-variable model that explained economic performance. We tested the possibility that a series of factors, working in different ways, explained the differences in economic performance among nations. This was done using multiple regression analysis. Regression analysis calculates the most likely means of predicting the behavior of one variable (called the dependent variable), using a series of other variables (called independent variables). There are four types of statistics produced by regression analysis that are used to evaluate a given test. First, the r-square tells how much of the variation of the dependent variables can be explained by the group of independent variables. Second, the significance level of r-square* tells us if the model is statistically significant. Third, parameters are calculated for each of the variables in the model. The parameters tell how much change we can expect in the dependent variable if any one of the independent variables changes. Parameters also indicate if the changes are positive or negative. Finally, the significance level of each parameter† is also calculated.

We performed multiple regression analysis on six different models. Our choice of models was severely limited by the sample size of certain variables. Regression requires data on each variable in a given sample. Thus, when we included productivity growth in a model, the six nations for which we could not get data were excluded from the sample. As a result, when we examined investment and overall economic growth, we developed two models: one with as large a sample of nations as possible and one with a greater diversity of explanatory variables.

We attempted to explain the variation of four of our economic performance variables — investment, productivity growth, unemployment and overall growth — with multiple variable models. In the first test of investment behavior (Table B.10), we included three independent variables: military spending, civilian government spending and the share of GDP accounted for by agricultural production. This model predicted less than 60 percent of the overall variation. However, the model had a high significance level. The parameters indicated that in this model, all three factors had a negative influence on investment. Military spending had the greatest negative influence. More importantly, the variable used to test economic maturity acted in the opposite way that we predicted. In this model, less industrialized nations tended to have lower investment. In our second test of investment (Table B.11), we added the labor compensation rate in manufacturing and the growth in the labor force. This model had a higher r-square value but a lower significance level. Military spending still showed the strongest influence and the maturity variable still acted opposite to our prediction.

Our regression analysis on manufacturing productivity included all the variables mentioned above plus investment (Table B.12). The

---

* Referred to in charts as: PR > F.
† Referred to in charts as: PR > [T].

r-square value of this model was very high and the significance level was strong, even though the sample only included nine nations. In this model, nations with faster growth in the work force tended to have lower productivity growth. Surprisingly, nations with higher labor costs experienced faster productivity growth. Growth in capital stocks increased productivity. Higher military spending and higher civilian spending tended to slow productivity growth. Finally, more highly industrialized nations tended to have slower productivity growth. However, the validity of these findings is questionable given the low significance levels of the parameters.

Our attempt to explain unemployment was unsuccessful (Table B.13). Given the fact that only eight nations could be included in the sample, the significance levels for r-square and the parameters were very low.

Our first attempt to explain GDP growth included only investment, military spending, civilian government spending and agriculture (Table B.14). The r-square and its significance level for this model were both high. Each of the variables performed as predicted, except for agriculture. This model suggested that more mature nations grew more quickly. As in the case of our investment models, it also indicated that nations with higher civilian government burdens had poorer economic performance. Military spending had the greatest negative impact on performance. In our second test of overall economic growth (Table B.15), we added productivity growth and the growth in the manufacturing labor force. The r-square and its significance level were very high even though the regression only included nine nations. The parameters indicated that investment, productivity growth and growth in the labor force were the only statistically significant factors in economic growth. Each had a positive influence in this model.

Overall, our attempts to develop a more sophisticated model of economic performance were stymied by a lack of data. However, the models reviewed here suggest that the maturity hypothesis needs to be tested more carefully before we accept it as valid. Moreover, we cannot reject the possibility that civilian government expenditures reduced economic performance. However, this fact still would not explain America's poorer performance since the United States had a smaller civilian government burden over the past two decades than most other industrialized nations. Finally, we did not uncover any evidence that contradicts our central hypothesis: Military spending tended to reduce investment and productivity growth.

Notes

1. Bruce Russett, *What Price Vigilance?* (New Haven: Yale University Press, 1970), pp. 137-146.

2. Some work on this question has already been performed. In particular, see:

   Ronald P. Smith, "Military Expenditure and Capitalism," *Cambridge Journal of Economics*, No. 1, 1977, pp. 61-76.

   Ronald P. Smith, "Military Expenditure and Investment in OECD Countries, 1954-1973," *Journal of Comparative Economics*, No. 4, 1980, pp. 19-32.

3. Organisation for Economic Cooperation and Development, *National Accounts of OECD Countries, 1950-1980, Volume I* (Paris: OECD, 1982). (Hereafter, *National Accounts....*)

4. U.S. Department of Labor, Bureau of Labor Statistics, "Statistical Supplement to International Comparisons of Unemployment, Bulletin 1979," unpublished, June 1982, Supplement to Table 3, p. 10.

5. U.S. Department of Labor, Bureau of Labor Statistics, "Consumer Price Indexes, Fifteen Countries, 1950-1981," June 1982.

6. U.S. Department of Labor, Bureau of Labor Statistics, "International Comparisons of Manufacturing Productivity and Labor Cost Trends, Preliminary Measures for 1981," June 2, 1982, Table 1. (Hereafter, "International Comparisons....")

7. United Nations, *Yearbook of National Accounts Statistics, 1979* (New York: U.N., 1980) and OECD, *National Accounts...*, op. cit.

8. Organisation for Economic Cooperation and Development, unpublished data.

9. While this is not the precise method for deriving the growth in the ratio of capital to labor, it is widely used as an accurate estimate. See "Growth Accounting Analysis," Background Paper Prepared for NYSE Study, *U.S. Economic Performance in a Global Perspective*, February 1981, pp. 2-3.

10. Organisation for Economic Cooperation and Development, unpublished data. U.S. Department of Labor, Bureau of Labor Statistics, "International Comparisons...," op. cit., Table 1.

11. United Nations, op. cit., and OECD, *National Accounts...*, op. cit.

12. Stockholm International Peace Research Institute, *World Armaments and Disarmament, SIPRI Yearbook 1982* (London: Taylor & Francis Ltd., 1982), pp. 150-151. (Hereafter, *SIPRI Yearbook 1982.*) SIPRI, *Yearbook 1975* (Cambridge, Mass.: MIT Press, 1975), pp. 122-123, 126-127, 132-133. (Hereafter, *SIPRI Yearbook 1975.*)

13. OECD, *National Accounts...*, op. cit. SIPRI, *SIPRI Yearbook 1982*, op. cit., and *SIPRI Yearbook 1975*, op. cit.

14. Organisation for Economic Cooperation and Development, *National Accounts of OECD Countries, 1961-1978, Volume II* (Paris: OECD, 1980).

15. U.S. Department of Labor, Bureau of Labor Statistics, "Hourly Compensation Costs and Direct Pay for Production Workers in Manufacturing, Ten Countries, 1960-1981," unpublished data, April 1982, p. 7.

16. U.S. Department of Labor, Bureau of Labor Statistics, "International Comparisons...," op. cit.

17. *Ibid.*

18. U.S. Department of Labor, Bureau of Labor Statistics, "Comparative Real Gross Domestic Product, Real GDP Per Capita, and Real GDP Per Employed Person, 1950-1981," unpublished data, April 1982, p. 7.

19. Organisation for Economic Cooperation and Development, *National Accounts of OECD Countries, 1950-1979, Volume I* (Paris: OECD, 1981).

Key to Tables B.1 through B.15

Abbreviation	Precise Name
GDPRG	Real growth in gross domestic product (GDP).
UNEMP	Unemployment rate.
I	Rate of increase in the consumer price index.
MANPROD	Growth in output per hour worked in manufacturing (otherwise known as manufacturing productivity growth).
GFK	Gross fixed capital formation as a share of GDP.
KG	Growth in manufacturing capital stocks.
GKLR	Growth in the ratio of manufacturing capital stocks to manufacturing labor.
C	Personal consumption as a share of GDP.
GM	Military spending as a share of GDP.
CGC	Civilian government consumption as a share of GDP.
GT	Government transfer payments as a share of GDP.
HE	Compensation per hour in manufacturing.
GHE	Growth in compensation per hour in the manufacturing sector.
GHRS	Growth in total hours worked in the manufacturing sector.
GDPPE	GDP per employed person (overall productivity).
AGR	Agricultural output as a share of GDP.

KEY TO ACTUAL YEARS COVERED BY CROSS-NATIONAL DATA

	GDPRG	UNEMPL	I	MANPROD	GFK	KG	GKLR	C	GM	CGC	GT	HE	GHE	GHRS	GDPPE	AGR
Australia	a	a	b	·	a	·	·	a	a	a	c	·	·	·	·	i
Austria	a	·	·	·	a	·	·	a	a	a	e	·	·	·	·	e
Belgium	a	·	b	b	a	a	·	a	a	a	c	b	a	b	b	c
Canada	a	a	b	b	a	c	·	a	a	a	c	b	a	b	b	c
Denmark	a	·	b	b	a	·	·	a	a	a	·	·	a	b	·	c
Finland	a	·	·	·	a	c	·	a	a	a	f	·	·	·	·	j
France	a	a	b	b	a	c	·	a	a	a	c	b	a	b	b	g
Germany	a	a	b	b	a	c	·	a	a	a	c	b	a	b	b	k
Italy	a	a	b	b	a	c	·	a	a	a	c	b	b	b	b	c
Japan	a	a	b	b	a	c	·	a	d	a	g	b	a	b	b	c
Netherlands	a	a	b	b	a	·	·	a	a	a	h	b	a	b	b	l
New Zealand	a	·	·	·	a	·	·	a	a	a	·	·	·	·	·	m
Norway	a	·	b	b	a	c	·	a	a	a	c	b	a	b	·	n
Sweden	a	a	b	b	a	·	·	a	a	a	c	·	·	b	·	o
Switzerland	a	·	b	·	a	·	·	·	a	a	c	b	a	·	·	·
UK	a	a	b	b	a	c	·	a	a	a	c	b	a	b	b	c
US	a	a	b	b	a	c	·	a	a	a	c	b	a	b	b	c

(a) 1960 – 1980
(b) 1960 – 1981
(c) 1961 – 1978
(d) 1960 – 1979
(e) 1964 – 1977
(f) 1975 – 1978
(g) 1970 – 1978
(h) 1968 – 1978
(i) 1961 – 1976
(j) 1966 – 1974
(k) 1970 – 1977
(l) 1969 – 1976
(m) 1971 – 1977
(n) 1962 – 1978
(o) 1963 – 1978

Table B.1

Cross-National Data
1960 – 1980

COUNTRY	GDPRG	UNEMPLOY	I	MANPROD	GFK	KG	GKLR	C	GM	CGC	GT	HE	GHE	GHRS	GDPPE	AGR
AUSTRAIL	4.3	3.1	6.6	.	24.8	.	.	61.3	3.1	10.0	10.3	.	.	.	.	8.22
AUSTRIA	4.4	.	.	.	26.6	.	.	57.0	1.2	13.9	19.2	.	.	.	.	6.65
BELGIUM	4.2	.	5.1	7.4	21.6	4.9	6.8	63.1	3.2	11.2	19.7	4.15	12.7	-1.9	76.99	4.28
CANADA	4.5	5.9	5.5	3.7	22.3	5.3	4.2	58.8	2.6	15.0	13.1	4.35	8.7	1.1	92.46	3.88
DENMARK	3.7	.	7.8	6.3	22.3	.	.	59.0	2.5	17.1	.	.	13.3	-2.0	.	6.37
FINLAND	4.5	.	.	.	26.3	7.8	.	56.6	1.6	13.8	16.2	.	.	.	.	9.75
FRANCE	4.7	2.9	7.0	5.5	22.6	5.3	5.5	61.5	4.6	9.1	22.0	2.99	11.9	-0.2	71.04	5.73
GERMANY	4.0	1.5	4.1	5.3	24.0	6.0	7.3	55.5	3.8	13.4	17.0	4.07	10.2	-1.3	73.97	3.49
ITALY	4.5	3.3	9.2	5.8	20.7	5.4	5.7	62.6	2.9	11.8	18.9	2.81	16.2	-0.3	57.23	8.67
JAPAN	8.3	1.5	7.2	9.2	32.7	11.9	11.2	55.6	0.9	7.8	9.4	1.93	14.8	0.7	48.70	7.42
NETH	4.3	.	5.7	7.2	23.6	.	.	58.6	3.7	12.1	28.0	4.03	13.2	-2.2	83.27	5.15
NZEALAND	3.3	.	.	.	22.3	.	.	61.2	1.9	12.4	.	.	.	.	.	11.74
NORWAY	4.5	.	6.4	.	29.5	.	.	54.4	3.3	13.6	20.8	.	.	.	.	6.42
SWEDEN	3.3	1.9	4.6	5.0	22.2	4.8	6.5	55.3	3.7	18.0	17.0	4.60	12.0	-1.7	.	4.00
SWITZ	3.2	.	4.1	.	26.3	.	.	60.9	2.4	8.7	11.8	.	.	.	.	.
UK	2.5	3.8	8.7	3.5	18.3	3.3	5.2	62.7	5.4	13.1	16.2	2.27	13.1	-1.9	56.77	2.72
US	3.4	5.6	5.4	2.6	18.0	2.6	1.7	63.0	7.3	10.9	11.0	4.97	6.9	0.9	100.00	3.17

Ranks
1960–1980

COUNTRY	GDPRG	UNEMPLOY	I	MANPROD	GFK	KG	GKLR	C	GM	CGC	GT	HE	GHE	GHRS	GDPPE	AGR
JAPAN	1.0	8.5	4.0	1	1.0	1.0	1	14	17.0	17	15.0	10	2	3.0	9	5
FRANCE	2.0	6.0	5.0	6	9.0	5.5	6	5	3.0	15	2.0	7	8	4.0	6	9
CANADA	4.5	1.0	9.0	9	11.0	5.5	8	10	11.0	3	11.0	3	10	1.0	2	13
FINLAND	4.5	.	.	.	4.5	2.0	.	13	15.0	5	9.5	.	.	.	.	2
ITALY	4.5	4.0	1.0	5	15.0	4.0	5	4	10.0	11	6.0	8	1	5.0	7	3
NORWAY	4.5	.	7.0	.	2.0	.	.	17	7.0	6	3.0	.	.	.	.	7
AUSTRIA	7.0	.	.	.	3.0	.	.	12	16.0	4	5.0	.	.	.	.	6
AUSTRAIL	8.5	5.0	6.0	.	6.0	.	.	6	9.0	14	14.0	.	.	.	.	4
NETH	8.5	.	8.0	3	8.0	.	3	11	5.5	10	1.0	6	4	11.0	3	10
BELGIUM	10.0	.	11.0	2	14.0	7.0	2	1	8.0	12	4.0	4	6	8.5	4	11
GERMANY	11.0	8.5	13.5	7	7.0	3.0	.	15	4.0	7	7.5	5	9	6.0	5	14
DENMARK	12.0	.	3.0	4	11.0	.	.	9	12.0	2	.	.	3	10.0	.	8
US	13.0	2.0	10.0	11	17.0	10.0	9	2	1.0	13	13.0	1	11	2.0	1	15
NZEALAND	14.5	.	.	.	11.0	.	.	7	14.0	9	.	.	.	.	.	1
SWEDEN	14.5	7.0	12.0	8	13.0	8.0	4	16	5.5	1	7.5	2	7	7.0	.	12
SWITZ	16.0	.	13.5	.	4.5	.	.	8	13.0	16	12.0	.	.	.	.	.
UK	17.0	3.0	2.0	10	16.0	9.0	7	3	2.0	8	9.5	9	5	8.5	8	16

Table B.2

Cross-National Data
1960–1973

COUNTRY	GDPRG	UNEMPLOY	I	MANPROD	GFK	KG	GKLR	C	GM	CGC	GT	HE	GHE	GDPPE	AGR
AUSTRAIL	5.2	1.9	3.1	.	25.9	.	.	62.2	3.3	8.1	9.8	.	.	.	8.96
AUSTRIA	5.2	.	.	.	26.6	.	.	58.0	1.2	12.6	18.5	.	.	.	7.47
BELGIUM	4.9	.	3.1	7.0	21.5	6.5	7.0	64.0	3.2	10.0	17.5	1.55	10.7	67.71	4.90
CANADA	5.2	5.3	2.8	4.5	21.9	5.3	3.6	60.2	3.1	13.3	11.6	2.73	6.4	89.86	3.75
DENMARK	4.7	.	5.6	6.4	22.6	.	.	60.9	2.7	14.0	.	.	11.8	.	6.48
FINLAND	5.2	.	.	.	25.8	8.2	.	57.3	1.7	12.4	.	.	.	.	10.96
FRANCE	5.7	1.9	4.3	6.0	22.7	5.4	4.8	61.3	5.1	8.1	20.7	1.39	9.2	64.95	6.34
GERMANY	4.8	0.7	3.1	5.5	25.0	6.9	7.1	55.8	4.0	11.5	15.5	1.68	9.4	64.74	4.23
ITALY	5.3	3.2	4.0	6.9	21.0	6.0	6.1	62.7	3.1	11.1	17.0	1.28	12.3	50.61	9.32
JAPAN	10.6	1.3	5.6	10.7	32.8	14.5	12.4	55.0	0.9	7.3	6.7	0.66	14.6	37.44	8.50
NETH	5.3	.	4.6	7.6	25.2	.	.	58.3	3.9	11.0	23.6	1.53	12.8	73.08	5.50
NZEALAND	4.0	.	.	.	22.3	.	.	61.5	2.0	11.6	.	.	.	.	13.51
NORWAY	4.4	.	4.5	.	28.3	.	.	56.4	3.5	11.9	18.0	.	.	.	6.83
SWEDEN	4.1	1.8	4.5	6.7	23.1	5.1	6.6	56.8	3.9	15.1	13.8	2.18	10.4	.	4.81
SWITZ	4.8	.	3.7	.	27.9	.	.	60.0	2.5	7.8	9.8	.	.	.	.
UK	2.9	2.9	4.5	4.3	17.9	3.7	4.9	63.9	5.7	11.6	14.8	1.23	8.6	54.35	2.85
US	3.8	4.9	2.8	3.0	18.0	2.7	1.1	62.7	8.4	9.8	9.6	3.48	5.0	100.00	3.14

Ranks
1960–1973

COUNTRY	GDPRG	UNEMPLOY	I	MANPROD	GFK	KG	GKLR	C	GM	CGC	GT	HE	GHE	GHRS	GDPPE	AGR
JAPAN	1.0	8.0	1.5	1	1	1	1	17.0	17.0	17.0	14.0	10	1	1.0	9	5
FRANCE	2.0	5.5	7.0	7	10	6	7	7.0	3.0	14.5	2.0	7	8	4.0	5	9
ITALY	3.5	3.0	8.0	4	15	5	5	3.5	10.5	10.0	6.0	8	3	5.0	8	3
NETH	3.5	.	3.0	2	7	.	.	11.0	5.5	11.0	1.0	6	2	8.5	3	10
AUSTRAIL	6.5	5.5	11.0	.	5	.	.	5.0	8.0	14.5	11.5	.	.	.	.	4
AUSTRIA	6.5	.	.	.	4	.	.	12.0	16.0	4.0	3.0	2	10	2.0	.	6
CANADA	6.5	1.0	13.5	9	13	7	8	9.0	10.5	3.0	10.0	2	.	.	2	14
FINLAND	6.5	.	.	.	6	2	.	13.0	15.0	5.0	.	.	.	.	.	2
BELGIUM	9.0	.	11.0	3	14	4	3	1.0	9.0	12.0	5.0	5	5	7.0	4	11
GERMANY	10.5	9.0	11.0	8	8	3	2	16.0	4.0	9.0	7.0	4	7	6.0	6	13
SWITZ	10.5	.	9.0	.	3	.	.	10.0	13.0	16.0	11.5	.	.	.	.	.
DENMARK	12.0	.	1.5	6	11	.	.	8.0	12.0	2.0	.	.	4	8.5	.	8
NORWAY	13.0	.	5.0	.	2	.	.	15.0	7.0	6.0	4.0	3	6	.	.	7
SWEDEN	14.0	7.0	5.0	5	9	8	4	14.0	5.5	1.0	9.0	.	.	11.0	.	12
NZEALAND	15.0	.	.	.	12	.	.	6.0	14.0	7.5	.	1	11	.	.	1
US	16.0	2.0	13.5	11	16	10	9	3.5	1.0	13.0	13.0	9	9	3.0	1	15
UK	17.0	4.0	5.0	10	17	9	6	2.0	2.0	7.5	8.0	.	.	10.0	7	16

Table B.3

Cross-National Data
1973–1980

COUNTRY	GDPRG	UNEMPLOY	I	MANPROD	GFK	KG	GKLR	C	GM	CGC	GT	HE	GHE	GHRS	GDPPE	AGR
AUSTRAIL	2.9	4.9	11.6	.	23.0	.	.	60.0	2.9	13.0	11.8	.	.	.	.	5.95
AUSTRIA	3.2	.	.	.	26.6	.	.	55.5	1.2	16.0	20.5	.	.	.	.	5.18
BELGIUM	2.9	.	8.0	6.7	21.9	1.8	6.3	61.8	3.1	13.4	24.5	8.37	12.8	-4.5	86.26	3.03
CANADA	3.4	7.0	9.5	1.6	22.9	5.3	4.9	56.5	1.9	17.7	16.0	6.98	11.2	0.4	94.97	4.14
DENMARK	2.0	.	10.9	4.8	21.9	7.0	.	56.0	2.3	22.0	16.0	.	12.6	-2.3	.	6.00
FINLAND	3.3	.	.	.	27.0	.	.	55.4	1.4	16.3	16.2	.	.	.	.	9.15
FRANCE	3.2	4.7	10.9	4.6	22.5	4.9	7.1	61.8	3.9	10.6	24.5	5.50	15.1	-2.2	77.12	5.37
GERMANY	2.7	2.8	5.1	4.5	22.3	4.0	6.5	55.0	3.4	16.5	19.8	7.95	9.4	-2.5	63.19	2.65
ITALY	3.4	3.5	16.6	3.6	20.3	4.2	4.5	62.4	2.5	13.0	22.7	5.30	19.6	-0.3	63.66	7.35
JAPAN	4.5	1.9	9.4	6.8	32.4	6.8	7.1	56.6	0.9	8.7	10.7	3.99	5.7	-0.3	61.56	5.27
NETH.	2.6	4.9	7.2	5.3	21.1	.	.	59.0	3.3	13.5	31.6	8.11	10.5	-3.4	59.47	4.80
NZEALAND	2.1	.	.	.	22.4	.	.	60.6	1.6	13.7	.	.	.	.	.	11.04
NORWAY	4.6	.	9.1	.	31.5	.	.	51.3	3.1	16.3	25.9	.	.	.	.	5.65
SWEDEN	2.1	2.0	10.1	2.0	20.8	4.3	6.7	52.9	3.3	22.7	23.4	6.54	12.8	-2.4	.	4.24
SWITZ	0.7	.	4.8	.	23.8	.	.	62.3	2.1	10.4	15.8	.	.	.	.	.
UK	1.8	5.3	14.8	2.1	18.9	2.5	6.3	60.5	4.9	15.6	19.0	3.97	19.1	-3.8	55.20	2.47
US	2.7	6.6	9.1	1.7	18.1	2.5	1.9	63.6	5.6	12.4	13.7	7.41	9.5	0.6	100.00	3.22

Ranks
1973–1980

COUNTRY	GDPRG	UNEMPLOY	I	MANPROD	GFK	KG	GKLR	C	GM	CGC	GT	HE	GHE	GHRS	GDPPE	AGR
NORWAY	1.0	.	9.5	.	2.0	.	.	17.0	7.5	5.5	2.0	.	.	.	.	6
JAPAN	2.0	10.0	8.0	1	1.0	2.0	1.5	10.0	17.0	17.0	15.0	9	9.0	3.5	8	8
CANADA	3.5	1.0	7.0	11	7.0	3.0	7.0	11.0	13.0	3.0	11.0	6	7.0	2.0	2	12
ITALY	3.5	7.0	1.0	7	15.0	6.0	8.0	2.0	10.0	12.5	6.0	8	1.0	3.5	7	3
FINLAND	5.0	.	.	.	3.0	1.0	.	14.0	15.0	5.5	10.0	.	.	.	.	2
AUSTRIA	6.5	.	4.5	5	4.0	4.0	1.5	13.0	16.0	7.0	7.0	7	3.0	5.0	6	9
FRANCE	6.5	6.0	3.0	.	8.0	.	.	4.5	3.0	15.0	3.5	.	.	.	.	7
AUSTRAIL	8.5	4.5	11.0	2	6.0	10.0	5.5	8.0	9.0	12.5	14.0	2	4.5	11.0	4	5
BELGIUM	8.5	.	13.0	6	11.5	7.0	4.0	4.5	7.5	11.0	3.5	4	11.0	8.0	5	14
GERMANY	10.5	8.0	9.5	10	10.0	8.5	9.0	15.0	4.0	4.0	6.0	5	10.0	1.0	1	15
US	10.5	2.0	.	.	17.0	.	.	1.0	1.0	14.0	13.0	3	8.0	9.0	3	13
METH.	12.0	4.5	12.0	3	13.0	.	.	9.0	5.5	9.0	1.0	.	.	.	.	10
NZEALAND	13.5	.	.	.	9.0	5.0	3.0	6.5	14.0	10.0	.	1	4.5	7.0	.	1
SWEDEN	13.5	9.0	6.0	9	14.0	.	.	16.0	5.5	1.0	5.0	.	6.0	6.0	.	11
DENMARK	15.0	.	4.5	4	11.5	8.5	5.5	12.0	11.0	2.0	.	.	2.0	10.0	9	4
UK	16.0	3.0	2.0	8	16.0	.	.	6.5	2.0	8.0	9.0	10	.	.	.	16
SWITZ	17.0	.	14.0	.	5.0	.	.	3.0	12.0	16.0	12.0	.	.	.	.	.

Table B.4

Spearman Correlation Coefficients
1960-1980

SPEARMAN CORRELATION COEFFICIENTS / PROB > |R| UNDER HO:RHO=0 / NUMBER OF OBSERVATIONS

	GDPRG	UNEMPLOY	I		MANPROD
GDPRG	1.00000 0.0000 17			GDPRG	0.57403 0.0648 11
UNEMPLOY	-0.23529 0.5422 9	1.00000 0.0000 9		UNEMPLOY	-0.68265 0.0621 8
I	0.36505 0.1994 14	0.20084 0.6044 9	1.00000 0.0000 14	I	0.17273 0.6115 11

	GFK	KG	GKLR	C
GDPRG	0.47121 0.0562 17	0.74465 0.0135 10	0.30953 0.4175 9	-0.25927 0.3150 17
MANPROD	0.56037 0.0730 11	0.72804 0.0262 9	0.80000 0.0098 9	-0.12727 0.7052 11
UNEMPLOY	-0.66946 0.0486 9	-0.66265 0.0733 8	-0.94612 0.0004 8	0.67783 0.0448 9
I	-0.14758 0.6146 14	0.12552 0.7476 9	-0.23333 0.5457 9	0.23762 0.4133 14

	GM	CGC	GT	HE	GHE	GHRS	GDPPE	AGR
GDPRG	-0.29525	-0.14445	0.14725	-0.42553	0.25057	0.41553	-0.30963	0.41545
	0.2499	0.5802	0.6005	0.2202	0.4574	0.2037	0.4175	0.1095
	17	17	15	10	11	11	9	16
MANPROD	-0.66059	-0.32727	0.37690	-0.49091	0.68182	-0.36447	-0.40000	0.77273
	0.0269	0.3259	0.2830	0.1497	0.0208	0.2705	0.2861	0.0053
	11	11	10	10	11	11	9	11
GFK	-0.55458	-0.10940	-0.06535	-0.32121	0.15034	-0.02283	-0.28333	0.48378
	0.0182	0.6760	0.8170	0.3655	0.6590	0.9469	0.4600	0.0576
	17	17	15	10	11	11	9	16
KG	-0.77812	-0.09726	-0.07339	-0.56067	0.35147	0.22689	-0.51498	0.70517
	0.0080	0.7892	0.8403	0.1163	0.3537	0.5572	0.1915	0.0227
	10	10	10	9	9	9	8	10
GKLR	-0.50000	-0.13333	0.13389	-0.43333	0.50000	-0.36820	-0.57143	0.48333
	0.1705	0.7324	0.7313	0.2440	0.1705	0.3296	0.1390	0.1875
	9	9	9	9	9	9	8	9
C	0.29552	-0.46324	-0.07335	0.03030	-0.03636	0.00911	0.21667	-0.16176
	0.2495	0.0611	0.7950	0.9338	0.9155	0.9768	0.5755	0.5495
	17	17	15	10	11	11	9	16
UNEMPLOY	0.20921	0.21758	-0.08824	0.35925	-0.40719	0.39522	0.54056	-0.30126
	0.5890	0.5739	0.8214	0.3821	0.3187	0.3325	0.2103	0.4308
	9	9	9	8	8	8	7	9
I	-0.11894	-0.06381	0.02617	-0.76970	0.70000	-0.05567	-0.66667	0.50549
	0.6855	0.8284	0.9324	0.0092	0.0185	0.7796	0.0499	0.0780
	14	14	13	10	11	11	9	13

194

Table B.4 (cont'd)

	GM	CGC	GT	HE	GHE	GHRS	GDPPE	AGR
GM	1.00000							
	0.0000							
	17							
CGC	-0.05273	1.00000						
	0.8407	0.0000						
	17	17						
GT	0.27663	0.28980	1.00000					
	0.3182	0.2948	0.0000					
	15	15	15					
HE	0.24924	0.40606	-0.04863	1.00000				
	0.4874	0.2443	0.8939	0.0000				
	10	10	10	10				
GHE	-0.56848	-0.10909	0.24924	-0.75758	1.00000			
	0.0674	0.7495	0.4874	0.0111	0.0000			
	11	11	10	10	11			
GHRS	-0.00457	-0.35991	-0.63415	0.18237	-0.46014	1.00000		
	0.9894	0.2769	0.0489	0.6141	0.1544	0.0000		
	11	11	10	10	11	11		
GDPPE	0.25000	0.30000	0.10000	0.95000	-0.71667	0.20084	1.00000	
	0.5165	0.4328	0.7980	0.0001	0.0238	0.6044	0.0000	
	9	9	10	9	9	9	9	
AGR	-0.74172	-0.13824	0.02203	-0.45455	0.73536	-0.07745	-0.38333	1.00000
	0.0010	0.6097	0.9404	0.1869	0.0098	0.8209	0.3085	0.0000
	16	16	14	10	11	11	9	16

Table B.5

Spearman Correlation Coefficients
1973-1980

SPEARMAN CORRELATION COEFFICIENTS / PROB > |R| UNDER H0:RHO=0 / NUMBER OF OBSERVATIONS

	GDPRG	UNEMPLOY	I	MANPROD
GDPRG	1.00000			0.15525
	0.0000			0.6485
	17			11
UNEMPLOY	-0.17125	1.00000		-0.60000
	0.6352	0.0000		0.0876
	10	10		9
I	0.14475	0.06657	1.00000	-0.26879
	0.6215	0.8544	0.0000	0.4242
	14	10	14	11

	GFK	KG	GKLR	C
GDPRG	0.51476	0.63915	0.09322	-0.22082
	0.0345	0.0466	0.8115	0.3942
	17	10	9	17
MANPROD	0.41002	0.05021	0.62187	0.00455
	0.2104	0.8979	0.0738	0.9894
	11	9	9	11
UNEMPLOY	-0.28572	-0.32336	-0.64672	0.40122
	0.4236	0.4346	0.0831	0.2505
	10	8	6	10
I	-0.28556	0.24288	-0.04202	0.10254
	0.3223	0.5292	0.9145	0.7272
	14	9	9	14

Table B.5 (cont'd)

	GM	CGC	GT	HE	GHE	GHRS	GDPPE	AGR
GDPRG	-0.32862	-0.08231	0.00717	-0.35357	-0.08895	0.54691	-0.10925	0.25388
	0.1978	0.7246	0.5798	0.3151	0.7993	0.0817	0.7796	0.3427
	17	17	15	10	11	11	9	16
MANPROD	-0.34624	-0.39091	0.33435	-0.01818	-0.07745	-0.42825	-0.33333	0.27273
	0.2969	0.2345	0.3450	0.9602	0.8209	0.1886	0.3807	0.4171
	11	11	10	10	11	11	9	11
GFK	-0.68938	-0.10927	-0.20375	-0.06667	-0.28539	0.12329	-0.11667	0.40324
	0.0022	0.6763	0.4664	0.8548	0.3949	0.7180	0.7650	0.1214
	17	17	15	10	11	11	9	16
KG	-0.69301	0.02432	-0.35366	-0.27615	-0.07563	0.49580	-0.22755	0.74164
	0.0263	0.9468	0.3161	0.4720	0.8467	0.1747	0.5878	0.0141
	10	10	10	9	9	9	8	10
GKLR	-0.18488	-0.16807	0.23629	-0.02521	-0.04641	-0.36709	-0.49401	0.19328
	0.6339	0.6656	0.5405	0.9487	0.9056	0.3311	0.2134	0.6183
	9	9	9	9	9	9	8	9
C	0.22420	-0.76290	-0.22004	-0.30355	0.29909	0.21461	0.08368	-0.04124
	0.3870	0.0004	0.4307	0.3932	0.3716	0.5263	0.8305	0.8795
	17	17	15	10	11	11	9	16
UNEMPLOY	0.32012	0.14329	-0.11550	-0.06667	0.08333	0.20921	0.54762	-0.32827
	0.3672	0.6929	0.7507	0.8647	0.8312	0.5890	0.1600	0.3544
	10	10	10	9	9	9	8	10
I	0.00773	0.09923	-0.13499	-0.57576	0.81735	0.20548	-0.51667	0.46006
	0.9791	0.7357	0.6602	0.0816	0.0021	0.5444	0.1544	0.1137
	14	14	13	10	11	11	9	13

	GM	CGC	GT	HE	GHE	GHRS	GDPPE	AGR
GM	1.00000 0.0000 17							
CGC	0.01658 0.9496 17	1.00000 0.0000 17						
GT	0.32498 0.2373 15	0.33662 0.2195 15	1.00000 0.0000 15					
HE	0.04255 0.9071 10	0.46667 0.1739 10	0.53496 0.1111 10	1.00000 0.0000 10				
GHE	0.02055 0.9522 11	0.01822 0.9576 11	0.35671 0.3116 10	-0.31611 0.3736 10	1.00000 0.0000 11			
GHRS	-0.20548 0.5444 11	-0.29613 0.3766 11	-0.61585 0.0580 10	-0.27964 0.4339 11	-0.22831 0.4995 11	1.00000 0.0000 11		
GDPPE	0.13333 0.7324 9	0.25000 0.5165 9	0.06695 0.8641 9	0.73333 0.0246 9	-0.48333 0.1875 9	0.35964 0.3415 .9	1.00000 0.0000 9	
AGR	-0.58174 0.0181 16	-0.10898 0.6879 16	-0.00440 0.9881 14	-0.16364 0.6515 10	0.27791 0.4080 11	0.42369 0.1941 11	-0.08333 0.8312 9	1.00000 0.0000 16

Table B.6

Spearman Correlation Coefficients
1960-1973

SPEARMAN CORRELATION COEFFICIENTS / PROB > |R| UNDER H0:RHO=0 / NUMBER OF OBSERVATIONS

	GDPRG	UNEMPLOY	I	MANPROD
GDPRG	1.00000 / 0.0000 / 17			
UNEMPLOY	-0.21429 / 0.5798 / 9	1.00000 / 0.0000 / 9		
I	0.10591 / 0.7186 / 14	-0.55510 / 0.1208 / 9	1.00000 / 0.0000 / 14	

	MANPROD
GDPRG	0.65604 / 0.0284 / 11
UNEMPLOY	-0.50000 / 0.2070 / 8
I	0.56424 / 0.0706 / 11

	GFK	KG	GKLR	C
GDPRG	0.37902 / 0.1335 / 17	0.66870 / 0.0345 / 10	0.30000 / 0.4328 / 9	-0.22916 / 0.3763 / 17
MANPROD	0.60909 / 0.0467 / 11	0.76667 / 0.0159 / 9	0.75000 / 0.0199 / 9	-0.31435 / 0.3465 / 11
UNEMPLOY	-0.74478 / 0.0213 / 9	-0.59524 / 0.1195 / 8	-0.85714 / 0.0065 / 8	0.67227 / 0.0473 / 9
I	0.34669 / 0.2246 / 14	0.22787 / 0.5554 / 9	0.52325 / 0.1483 / 9	-0.38155 / 0.1783 / 14

	GM	CGC	GT	HE	GHE	GHRS	GDPPE	AGR
GDPRG	-0.35786	-0.37269	0.22481	-0.46809	0.58948	0.55936	-0.34310	0.39586
	0.1584	0.1407	0.4397	0.1725	0.0674	0.0736	0.3660	0.1291
	17	17	14	10	11	11	9	16
MANPROD	-0.64841	-0.27273	0.29697	-0.50303	0.93636	-0.03645	-0.43333	0.76364
	0.0309	0.4171	0.4047	0.1383	0.0001	0.9153	0.2440	0.0062
	11	11	10	10	11	11	9	11
GFK	-0.47362	-0.18160	-0.03740	-0.13939	0.58182	0.09112	-0.18333	0.47059
	0.0548	0.4855	0.8990	0.7009	0.0604	0.7855	0.6368	0.0658
	17	17	14	10	11	11	9	16
KG	-0.75988	-0.26061	0.18333	-0.48333	0.76667	0.25000	-0.59524	0.74545
	0.0108	0.4671	0.6368	0.1875	0.0159	0.5165	0.1195	0.0133
	10	10	9	9	9	9	8	10
GXLR	-0.51046	-0.13333	0.03333	-0.51667	0.83333	-0.18333	-0.73810	0.48333
	0.1603	0.7324	0.9322	0.1544	0.0053	0.6368	0.0366	0.1875
	9	9	9	9	9	9	8	9
C	0.30510	-0.18785	0.01982	0.01216	-0.35535	-0.16438	0.19247	-0.15305
	0.2337	0.4703	0.9464	0.9734	0.2835	0.6291	0.6198	0.5715
	17	17	14	10	11	11	9	16
UNEMPLOY	0.12605	0.22689	-0.05021	0.45238	-0.64286	0.28571	0.53571	-0.28452
	0.7466	0.5572	0.8979	0.2604	0.0856	0.4927	0.2152	0.4581
	9	9	9	8	8	8	7	9
I	-0.22829	0.13794	0.27021	-0.72786	0.70186	-0.36553	-0.64708	0.35379
	0.4324	0.6382	0.3719	0.0170	0.0161	0.2690	0.0596	0.2356
	14	14	13	10	11	11	9	13

Table B.6

	GM	CGC	GT	HE	GHE	GHRS	GDPPE	AGR
GM	1.00000							
	0.0000							
	17							
CGC	-0.08845	1.00000						
	0.7357	0.0000						
	17	17						
GT	0.16097	0.32709	1.00000					
	0.5825	0.2537	0.0000					
	14	14	14					
HE	0.28049	0.35758	-0.18788	1.00000				
	0.4325	0.3104	0.6032	0.0000				
	10	10	10	10				
GHE	-0.68037	-0.17273	0.27273	-0.58788	1.00000			
	0.0212	0.6115	0.4458	0.0739	0.0000			
	11	11	10	10	11			
GHRS	-0.23112	-0.62415	-0.46667	0.00606	-0.10023	1.00000		
	0.4941	0.0401	0.1739	0.9867	0.7694	0.0000		
	11	11	10	10	11	11		
GDPPE	0.40168	0.13333	0.11667	0.86667	-0.60000	0.03333	1.00000	
	0.2839	0.7324	0.7650	0.0025	0.0876	0.9322	0.0000	
	9	9	9	9	9	9	9	
AGR	-0.71723	-0.08837	0.16484	-0.52727	0.81818	0.18223	-0.51667	1.00000
	0.0018	0.7449	0.5905	0.1173	0.0021	0.5918	0.1544	0.0000
	16	16	13	10	11	11	9	16

Table B.7

Correlations Excluding Japan

	GDPRG	UNEMPLOY	I	MANPROD
GDPRG	1.00000 0.0000 16			
UNEMPLOY	0.03593 0.9327 8	1.00000 0.0000 8		
I	0.34350 0.2505 13	0.38095 0.3518 8	1.00000 0.0000 13	
GDPRG				0.43161 0.2129 10
UNEMPLOY				-0.57143 0.1802 7
I				0.09091 0.8028 10

	GFK	KG	GKLR	C
GDPRG	0.36412 0.1656 16	0.64696 0.0597 9	0.01198 0.5775 8	-0.18952 0.4811 16
MANPROD	0.41338 0.2351 10	0.61078 0.1077 8	0.71429 0.0465 8	0.00608 0.9887 10
UNEMPLOY	-0.54762 0.1600 8	-0.50452 0.2482 7	-0.82857 0.0025 7	0.59524 0.1195 8
I	-0.26722 0.3775 13	-0.03583 0.9327 8	-0.52381 0.1627 8	0.26611 0.3433 13

Table B.7

	GM	CGC	GT	HE	GHE	GHRS	GDPPE	AGR
GDPRG	-0.15294	0.02819	0.41585	-0.20921	0.03040	0.34756	-0.01198	0.38991
	0.5718	0.5175	0.1392	0.5850	0.9336	0.3251	0.9775	0.1508
	16	16	14	9	10	10	8	15
MANPROD	-0.54711	-0.10303	0.89541	-0.30000	0.62424	-0.60183	-0.14286	0.74545
	0.1017	0.7770	0.0011	0.4328	0.0537	0.0655	0.7358	0.0133
	10	10	9	9	10	10	8	10
GFK	-0.47711	0.06937	0.15105	-0.06667	-0.03647	-0.18902	0.02381	0.47671
	0.0617	0.7985	0.6062	0.8647	0.5203	0.6010	0.5554	0.0724
	16	16	14	9	10	10	8	15
KG	-0.69457	0.24288	0.27848	-0.37126	0.11976	0.16867	-0.27028	0.66109
	0.0379	0.5292	0.4681	0.3652	0.7776	0.6897	0.5577	0.0525
	9	9	9	9	8	8	7	9
GKLR	-0.28571	0.23810	0.62277	-0.19048	0.38095	-0.59881	-0.35714	0.35714
	0.4527	0.5702	0.0991	0.6514	0.3518	0.1168	0.4316	0.3851
	8	8	8	8	8	8	7	8
C	0.25607	-0.64706	-0.20284	-0.11667	0.05455	0.10334	-0.02381	-0.17143
	0.3384	0.0067	0.4872	0.7650	0.8810	0.7763	0.5554	0.5413
	16	16	14	9	10	10	8	15
UNEMPLOY	-0.07143	-0.04762	-0.49103	0.10714	-0.32143	0.57143	0.37143	-0.26190
	0.8665	0.9108	0.2166	0.8192	0.4821	0.1802	0.4685	0.5305
	8	8	8	7	7	7	6	8
I	0.00275	0.02751	0.21579	-0.73333	0.64848	-0.12766	-0.59524	0.48252
	0.9929	0.9289	0.5006	0.0246	0.0425	0.7253	0.1195	0.1121
	13	13	12	9	10	10	8	12

	GM	CGC	GT	HE	GHE	GHRS	GDPPE	AGR
GM	1.00000							
	0.0000							
	16							
CGC	-0.26343	1.00000						
	0.3242	0.0000						
	16	16						
GT	0.10915	0.12555	1.00000					
	0.7103	0.6689	0.0000					
	14	14	14					
HE	-0.03347	0.18333	-0.44352	1.00000				
	0.9319	0.6368	0.2316	0.0000				
	9	9	9	9				
GHE	-0.46201	0.13539	0.61925	-0.70000	1.00000			
	0.1789	0.7009	0.0753	0.0358	0.0000			
	10	10	9	9	10			
GHRS	0.18293	-0.26746	-0.54622	0.35984	-0.69301	1.00000		
	0.6130	0.4550	0.1281	0.3415	0.0253	0.0000		
	10	10	9	9	10	10		
GDPPE	-0.07143	0.00000	-0.26571	0.92857	-0.64266	0.35525	1.00000	
	0.8665	1.0000	0.4527	0.0009	0.0656	0.3521	0.0000	
	8	8	8	8	8	8	8	
AGR	-0.75067	-0.04286	0.20386	-0.28333	0.64848	-0.21885	-0.16667	1.00000
	0.0013	0.8795	0.5041	0.4600	0.0425	0.5436	0.6932	0.0000
	15	15	13	9	10	10	8	15

Table B.8

Correlations Excluding the United Kingdom

	GDPRG	UNEMPLOY	I	MANPROD
GDPRG	1.00000			
	0.0000			
	16			
UNEMPLOY	-0.08434	1.00000		
	0.8426	0.0000		
	8	8		
I	0.65375	0.14372	1.00000	
	0.0154	0.7342	0.0000	
	13	8	13	

		MANPROD
GDPRG		0.45593
		0.1854
		10
UNEMPLOY		-0.59462
		0.1551
		7
I		0.41818
		0.2291
		10

	GFK	KG	GKLR	C
GDPRG	0.37603	0.68051	0.19162	-0.14244
	0.1512	0.0435	0.6464	0.5587
	16	9	8	16
MANPROD	0.41338	0.61079	0.73610	0.05455
	0.2351	0.1077	0.0366	0.8810
	10	8	8	10
UNEMPLOY	-0.52277	-0.61818	-0.91858	0.65855
	0.0551	0.1350	0.0034	0.0757
	8	7	7	8
I	0.01102	0.37126	-0.16657	0.15661
	0.9715	0.3652	0.6932	0.6085
	13	6	8	13

	GM	CGC	GT	HE	GHE	GHRS	GDPPE	AGR
GDPRG	-0.16482 0.5419 16	-0.15282 0.5720 16	0.12696 0.6654 14	-0.81172 0.0079 9	0.34651 0.3257 10	0.35856 0.3088 10	-0.68255 0.0621 8	0.28883 0.2965 15
MANPROD	-0.54711 0.1017 10	-0.34545 0.3282 10	0.30963 0.4175 9	-0.76667 0.0159 9	0.79394 0.0061 10	-0.50303 0.1363 10	-0.64286 0.0856 8	0.70905 0.0217 10
GFK	-0.47711 0.0617 16	-0.14465 0.5930 16	-0.12996 0.6579 14	-0.53333 0.1392 9	0.15198 0.6751 10	-0.10334 0.7763 10	-0.47619 0.2329 8	0.37635 0.1668 15
KG	-0.69457 0.0379 9	-0.16737 0.6669 9	-0.21008 0.5875 9	-0.87427 0.0045 8	0.45510 0.2572 8	0.08383 0.8435 8	-0.81064 0.0269 7	0.61088 0.0805 9
GKLR	-0.42857 0.2894 8	-0.11905 0.7789 8	-0.04791 0.9103 8	-0.57143 0.1390 8	0.59524 0.1195 8	-0.54762 0.1600 8	-0.71429 0.0713 7	0.35714 0.3851 8
C	0.17513 0.5165 16	-0.47941 0.0602 16	-0.02640 0.9286 14	0.08333 0.8312 9	-0.01818 0.9602 10	0.11515 0.7514 10	0.30952 0.4556 8	-0.00357 0.9859 15
UNEMPLOY	0.03593 0.9327 8	0.22755 0.5878 8	0.03012 0.9436 8	0.45047 0.3104 7	-0.45047 0.3104 7	0.53066 0.1289 7	0.63775 0.1731 6	-0.09581 0.8215 8
I	-0.30579 0.3096 13	-0.10179 0.7407 13	0.05789 0.8582 12	-0.73333 0.0246 8	0.68485 0.0289 10	0.03030 0.9338 10	-0.59524 0.1195 8	0.83217 0.0008 12

Table B.8

	GM	CGC	GT	HE	GHE	GHRS	GDPPE	AGR
GM	1.00000							
	0.0000							
	16							
CGC	-0.06181	1.00000						
	0.8201	0.0000						
	16	16						
GT	0.36674	0.29923	1.00000					
	0.1971	0.2987	0.0000					
	14	14	14					
HE	0.43515	0.50000	-0.20921	1.00000				
	0.2418	0.1705	0.5880	0.0000				
	9	9	9	9				
GHE	-0.65046	-0.09091	0.30125	-0.75000	1.00000			
	0.0417	0.8028	0.4308	0.0199	0.0000			
	10	10	9	9	10			
GHRS	0.04663	-0.35394	-0.71130	0.08333	-0.45455	1.00000		
	0.8939	0.2600	0.0317	0.8312	0.1888	0.0000		
	10	10	9	9	10	10		
GDPPE	0.42857	0.45238	0.02381	0.52857	-0.76190	0.16667	1.00000	
	0.2654	0.2604	0.9554	0.0009	0.0280	0.8532	0.0000	
	8	8	8	8	8	8	8	
AGR	-0.68990	-0.13214	-0.04952	-0.86667	0.91515	-0.23636	-0.80952	1.00000
	0.0044	0.6387	0.8724	0.0025	0.0002	0.5109	0.0149	0.0000
	15	15	13	9	10	10	8	15

Table B.9

Correlations Excluding the United States

SPEARMAN CORRELATION COEFFICIENTS / PROB > IRI UNDER H0:RHO=0 / NUMBER OF OBSERVATIONS

	GDPRG	UNEMPLOY	I	MANPROD
GDPRG	1.00000			0.48025
	0.0000			0.1501
	16			10
UNEMPLOY	-0.18072	1.00000		-0.59462
	0.6685	0.0000		0.1551
	8	8		7
I	0.30748	0.37126	1.00000	0.05051
	0.3068	0.3652	0.0000	0.8028
	13	8	13	10

	GFK	KG	SKLR	C
GDPRG	0.43411	0.69795	0.17964	-0.20772
	0.0929	0.0366	0.6703	0.4401
	16	9	8	16
MANPROD	0.41338	0.61079	0.71429	0.05455
	0.2351	0.1077	0.0465	0.8810
	10	8	8	10
UNEMPLOY	-0.62277	-0.61818	-0.95499	0.65865
	0.0991	0.1350	0.0008	0.0757
	8	7	7	8
I	-0.28650	0.03553	-0.33333	0.38750
	0.3426	0.5327	0.4198	0.1903
	13	8	8	13

Table B.9

	GM	CGC	GT	HE	GHE	GHRS	GDPPE	AGR
GDPRG	-0.24351 0.3634 16	-0.19882 0.4604 16	0.08362 0.7763 14	-0.35984 0.3415 9	0.12158 0.7379 10	0.65854 0.0384 10	-0.17564 0.6703 8	0.35020 0.2007 15
MANPROD	-0.54711 0.1017 10	0.0739 10	0.22289 0.4444 9	-0.30000 0.4328 9	0.57576 0.0616 10	-0.17623 0.6261 10	-0.14286 0.7358 8	0.70905 0.0217 10
GFK	-0.47711 0.0617 16	-0.19188 0.4765 16	-0.21058 0.4633 14	-0.06667 0.8647 9	-0.13374 0.7126 10	0.23780 0.5062 10	0.02381 0.9554 8	0.37635 0.1668 15
KG	-0.69457 0.0379 9	-0.28452 0.4581 9	-0.32512 0.3871 9	-0.37126 0.3652 8	0.07165 0.8657 8	0.65060 0.0806 8	-0.27028 0.5577 7	0.61058 0.0805 9
GKLR	-0.28571 0.4927 8	-0.35714 0.3851 8	-0.04791 0.9103 8	-0.19048 0.6514 8	0.28571 0.4927 8	-0.11976 0.7776 8	-0.35714 0.4316 7	0.30952 0.4556 8
C	0.17513 0.5165 16	-0.44412 0.0848 16	0.03084 0.9167 14	-0.28333 0.4600 9	0.22424 0.5334 10	-0.17021 0.6363 10	-0.04762 0.9108 8	-0.00357 0.9899 15
UNEMPLOY	0.03593 0.9327 8	0.25150 0.5479 8	0.00602 0.9887 8	0.10811 0.8175 7	-0.14415 0.7578 7	0.05005 0.8477 7	0.31887 0.5379 6	-0.09581 0.8215 8
I	-0.04408 0.8863 13	-0.10729 0.7272 13	0.00526 0.9870 12	-0.81667 0.0072 9	0.73333 0.0158 10	-0.03040 0.9336 10	-0.69048 0.0580 8	0.50350 0.0952 12

	GM	CGC	GT	HE	GHE	GHRS	GDPPE	AGR
GM	1.00000							
	0.0000							
	16							
CGC	0.02502	1.00000						
	0.9267	0.0000						
	16	16						
GT	0.47519	0.18723	1.00000					
	0.0859	0.5216	0.0000					
	14	14	14					
HE	-0.03347	0.66333	0.15900	1.00000				
	0.9319	0.0424	0.6828	0.0000				
	9	9	9	9				
GHE	-0.42553	-0.33333	0.10042	-0.66637	1.00000			
	0.2202	0.3466	0.7971	0.0499	0.0000			
	10	10	9	9	9			
GHRS	-0.24390	-0.27534	-0.54622	-0.09205	-0.26179	1.00000		
	0.4971	0.4339	0.1281	0.6136	0.4133	0.0000		
	10	10	9	9	10	10		
GDPPE	-0.07143	0.54762	0.38095	0.92857	-0.59524	-0.11976	1.00000	
	0.8655	0.1600	0.3518	0.0008	0.1195	0.7776	0.0000	
	8	8	8	8	8	8	8	
AGR	-0.68990	-0.25714	-0.09366	-0.38333	0.72121	0.11550	-0.28571	1.00000
	0.0044	0.3549	0.7609	0.3085	0.0186	0.7507	0.4927	0.0000
	15	15	13	9	10	10	8	15

Table B.10

Regression on Investment

S T A T I S T I C A L   A N A L Y S I S   S Y S T E M

GENERAL LINEAR MODELS PROCEDURE

DEPENDENT VARIABLE INFORMATION

NUMBER OF OBSERVATIONS IN DATA SET = 17

NOTE: ALL DEPENDENT VARIABLES ARE CONSISTENT WITH RESPECT TO THE PRESENCE OR ABSENCE OF MISSING VALUES. HOWEVER, ONLY 16 OBSERVATIONS IN DATA SET CAN BE USED IN THIS ANALYSIS.

GENERAL LINEAR MODELS PROCEDURE

DEPENDENT VARIABLE: GFK

SOURCE	DF	SUM OF SQUARES	MEAN SQUARE	F VALUE	PR > F	R-SQUARE	C.V.
MODEL	3	125.68386800	41.89462267	5.60	0.0123	0.583497	11.5797
ERROR	12	89.71363200	7.47613600		STD DEV		GFK MEAN
CORRECTED TOTAL	15	215.39750000			2.73425237		23.61250000

PARAMETER	ESTIMATE	T FOR H0: PARAMETER=0	PR > |T|	STD ERROR OF ESTIMATE
INTERCEPT	38.59510068	6.35	0.0001	6.07849873
GM	-2.05713516	-3.45	0.0048	0.59652833
CGC	-0.48089784	-1.73	0.1097	0.27835665
AGR	-0.36503462	-0.96	0.3557	0.37996745

Table B.11

Regression on Investment

S T A T I S T I C A L   A N A L Y S I S   S Y S T E M

GENERAL LINEAR MODELS PROCEDURE

DEPENDENT VARIABLE INFORMATION

NUMBER OF OBSERVATIONS IN DATA SET = 17

NOTE: ALL DEPENDENT VARIABLES ARE CONSISTENT WITH RESPECT TO THE PRESENCE OR ABSENCE OF MISSING VALUES. HOWEVER, ONLY 9
OBSERVATIONS IN DATA SET CAN BE USED IN THIS ANALYSIS.

GENERAL LINEAR MODELS PROCEDURE

DEPENDENT VARIABLE: KG

SOURCE	DF	SUM OF SQUARES	MEAN SQUARE	F VALUE	PR > F	R-SQUARE	C.V.
MODEL	5	46.81340227	9.36268045	3.27	0.1791	0.845007	30.7601
ERROR	3	8.58659773	2.86219924		STD DEV		KG MEAN
CORRECTED TOTAL	8	55.40000000			1.69180355		5.50000000

PARAMETER	ESTIMATE	T FOR H0: PARAMETER=0	PR > |T|	STD ERROR OF ESTIMATE
INTERCEPT	15.91153430	2.88	0.0637	5.53232366
GM	-1.20606811	-2.72	0.0723	0.44265269
CGC	-0.28484940	-1.02	0.3831	0.27947817
HE	-0.30401456	-0.38	0.7286	0.79807109
GHRS	0.30591332	0.53	0.6342	0.57954819
AGR	-0.22181613	-0.49	0.6595	0.45529019

Table B.12

Regression on Productivity Growth

S T A T I S T I C A L   A N A L Y S I S   S Y S T E M

GENERAL LINEAR MODELS PROCEDURE

DEPENDENT VARIABLE INFORMATION

NUMBER OF OBSERVATIONS IN DATA SET = 17

NOTE: ALL DEPENDENT VARIABLES ARE CONSISTENT WITH RESPECT TO THE PRESENCE OR ABSENCE OF MISSING VALUES. HOWEVER, ONLY 9 OBSERVATIONS IN DATA SET CAN BE USED IN THIS ANALYSIS.

GENERAL LINEAR MODELS PROCEDURE

DEPENDENT VARIABLE: MANPROD

SOURCE	DF	SUM OF SQUARES	MEAN SQUARE	F VALUE	PR > F	R-SQUARE	C.V.
MODEL	6	32.52926254	5.42154376	19.69	0.0491	0.983351	9.8392
ERROR	2	0.55073746	0.27536873		STD DEV		MANPROD MEAN
CORRECTED TOTAL	8	33.08000000			0.52475588		5.33333333

PARAMETER	ESTIMATE	T FOR HO: PARAMETER=0	PR > |T|	STD ERROR OF ESTIMATE
INTERCEPT	5.06665607	1.52	0.2672	3.32624509
KG	0.40237511	2.25	0.1537	0.17907986
GM	-0.41936667	-1.64	0.2430	0.25592915
CGC	-0.33780647	-3.36	0.0784	0.10058221
HE	0.65630269	2.59	0.1224	0.25345825
GHRS	-0.87980902	-4.68	0.0427	0.18792393
AGR	0.20821276	1.42	0.2916	0.14670017

Table B.13

Regression on Unemployment

S T A T I S T I C A L   A N A L Y S I S   S Y S T E M

GENERAL LINEAR MODELS PROCEDURE

DEPENDENT VARIABLE INFORMATION

NUMBER OF OBSERVATIONS IN DATA SET = 17

NOTE: ALL DEPENDENT VARIABLES ARE CONSISTENT WITH RESPECT TO THE PRESENCE OR ABSENCE OF MISSING VALUES. HOWEVER, ONLY 8 OBSERVATIONS IN DATA SET CAN BE USED IN THIS ANALYSIS.

GENERAL LINEAR MODELS PROCEDURE

DEPENDENT VARIABLE: UNEMPLOY

SOURCE	DF	SUM OF SQUARES	MEAN SQUARE	F VALUE	PR > F	R-SQUARE	C.V.
MODEL	6	20.12058847	3.35343141	4.30	0.3532	0.962708	26.7528
ERROR	1	0.77941153	0.77941153		STD DEV		UNEMPLOY MEAN
CORRECTED TOTAL	7	20.90000000			0.88284287		3.30000000

PARAMETER	ESTIMATE	T FOR H0: PARAMETER=0	PR > |T|	STD ERROR OF ESTIMATE
INTERCEPT	9.75084017	0.98	0.5081	10.00081138
MANPROD	-2.14865417	-1.02	0.4923	2.09746190
KG	0.74198605	0.45	0.7308	1.64867469
GM	-0.13065759	-0.15	0.9068	0.88610768
CGC	-0.09846873	-0.38	0.7661	0.25584449
GHRS	0.22835125	0.26	0.8377	0.87642015
AGR	0.43468210	0.55	0.6787	0.78698342

Table B.14

Regression on GDP Growth

S T A T I S T I C A L   A N A L Y S I S   S Y S T E M

GENERAL LINEAR MODELS PROCEDURE

DEPENDENT VARIABLE INFORMATION

NUMBER OF OBSERVATIONS IN DATA SET = 17

NOTE: ALL DEPENDENT VARIABLES ARE CONSISTENT WITH RESPECT TO THE PRESENCE OR ABSENCE OF MISSING VALUES. HOWEVER, ONLY 16
OBSERVATIONS IN DATA SET CAN BE USED IN THIS ANALYSIS.

GENERAL LINEAR MODELS PROCEDURE

DEPENDENT VARIABLE: GDPRG

SOURCE	DF	SUM OF SQUARES	MEAN SQUARE	F VALUE	PR > F	R-SQUARE	C.V.
MODEL	4	18.98168783	4.74542196	13.56	0.0003	0.831436	13.8357
ERROR	11	3.84831217	0.34984656		STD DEV		GDPRG MEAN
CORRECTED TOTAL	15	22.83000000			0.59147828		4.27500000

PARAMETER	ESTIMATE	T FOR H0: PARAMETER=0	PR > |T|	STD ERROR OF ESTIMATE
INTERCEPT	5.82989806	2.12	0.0572	2.74549697
GFK	0.15572675	2.49	0.0298	0.06244671
GM	-0.35187257	-1.93	0.0795	0.18208285
CGC	-0.24653282	-3.66	0.0037	0.06728765
AGR	-0.15794241	-1.85	0.0911	0.08529758

Table B.15

Regression on GDP Growth

S T A T I S T I C A L   A N A L Y S I S   S Y S T E M

GENERAL LINEAR MODELS PROCEDURE

DEPENDENT VARIABLE INFORMATION

NUMBER OF OBSERVATIONS IN DATA SET = 17

NOTE: ALL DEPENDENT VARIABLES ARE CONSISTENT WITH RESPECT TO THE PRESENCE OR ABSENCE OF MISSING VALUES. HOWEVER, ONLY 9 OBSERVATIONS IN DATA SET CAN BE USED IN THIS ANALYSIS.

GENERAL LINEAR MODELS PROCEDURE

DEPENDENT VARIABLE: GDPRG

SOURCE	DF	SUM OF SQUARES	MEAN SQUARE	F VALUE	PR > F	R-SQUARE	C.V.
MODEL	6	21.31224506	3.55204084	304.76	0.0033	0.998907	2.4661
ERROR	2	0.02331049	0.01165525		STD DEV		GDPRG MEAN
CORRECTED TOTAL	8	21.33555556			0.10795947		4.37777778

PARAMETER	ESTIMATE	T FOR H0: PARAMETER=0	PR > |T|	STD ERROR OF ESTIMATE
INTERCEPT	1.80325399	2.13	0.1663	0.84462755
KG	0.30956747	7.42	0.0177	0.04171899
MANPROD	0.31444963	4.51	0.0458	0.06973010
GM	0.00796825	0.13	0.9087	0.06145525
CGC	-0.04074810	-1.55	0.2616	0.02631836
GHRS	0.49036573	8.42	0.0138	0.05823548
AGR	-0.01776678	-0.60	0.6084	0.02951736

Appendix C

Total Military Spending Budget*

Analysts have long recognized that the official Defense Department budget excludes the cost of many military-related activities conducted by the federal government. The purpose of this appendix is to present a comprehensive listing of federally funded military activities and to create a more comprehensive measure of military spending for the years 1940 to 1988.

Contrary to recent statements by administration officials, the military is the single most important recipient of general government revenues. Official estimates of military spending are low because the Office of Management and Budget's (OMB) definition of defense only includes those programs that directly support the U.S. armed forces. Actually, a substantial portion of every federal budget since World War II has financed the continuing cost of prior military activities through debt interest and veterans' benefits, while several other military-related programs have been funded through civilian budget categories.

Furthermore, by adding self-funding trust fund accounts like Social Security to the federal budget in 1969, the government enlarged the budget pie, thereby lessening the military's apparent share of both the federal budget and the budget deficit. Measuring military costs as a percentage of federal funds, which are the monies available to all non-trust federal programs, provides a clearer picture of the government's actual spending priorities.

By assessing the total cost of past and present military activities for each year since 1940, and by measuring military spending as a percentage of federal funds, we found that military outlays represented 48.6 percent of available budget dollars in 1981. This percentage is expected to rise to 59.2 percent in 1986.

*Developed by Paul Murphy and David Gold, with assistance from Robert DeGrasse Jr.

What Is Military Spending?

The first step in determining the true costs of federally funded military activities is to clarify the meaning of the term "military spending." The OMB, which exercises administrative control over the federal budget, defines the national defense function broadly as the cost of programs that are "directly related to the common defense and security of the United States."[1] In practice, however, the OMB limits the scope of the national defense budget to those programs directly supporting the U.S. armed forces. Specifically, the OMB includes in its defense budget only the costs of raising, equipping and maintaining the U.S. armed forces (including civilian supporting activities); the development, procurement and maintenance of weapons systems (including nuclear weapons); and other, directly related costs.[2] These programs, however, do not represent all of the government's military-related expenditures.

The official defense budget ignores the substantial ongoing costs of past military activities, particularly military-related interest on the federal debt and veterans' benefits. When the government borrows money to cover budget deficits, a portion of those borrowed funds finances military programs. The interest on that portion of the federal debt is a military expense. In addition, veterens' benefits also represent contracts that the government made with members of the armed forces and should therefore be considered military expenses.

Furthermore, several smaller but nonetheless significant military programs are classified within civilian budget categories. Foreign Military Assistance, the Maritime Administration and the Coast Guard were part of the military budget during World War II. They were gradually shifted into civilian budget categories following the war as their missions changed. However, many of their functions are still military-related. The National Aeronautics and Space Administration (NASA) is considered a civilian agency, yet many of its activities support the military. Likewise, School Assistance to Federally Affected Areas (SAFAA), which reimburses school districts for the cost of educating children of military personnel, is part of the Department of Education's budget.

We define military spending as the current cost of all past and present activities in support of the U.S. armed forces and our military allies. On this basis, we identified the following eight programs as military spending:

1. The defense function, as defined by OMB, including the Department of Defense, the Department of Energy nuclear weapons activities, and defense-related activities;

2. Interest on the federal debt attributable to military spending;

3. Veterans' benefits and services;

4. A portion of NASA;

5. Foreign military assistance grants;

6. A portion of the Coast Guard;

7. A portion of the Impact Aid for Education program (P.L.874); and

8. A portion of the Maritime Administration.

Methodology &
Program Justification

1. The Defense Function: The OMB's defense function is the primary component of our total military spending budget. The OMB has used functions, or groups of related programs, for classifying data since the 1940s. Past defense functions have included the military components of up to 13 government agencies in addition to the armed services.[3] However with the passage of the Budget Impoundment and Control Act in 1974, the use of stricter criteria for establishing a budget function has narrowed the defense function to only three spending categories. These are the Department of Defense (established in 1948), atomic energy defense activities (Department of Energy), and other, directly related costs (the Federal Emergency Management Agency and the Selective Service).[4]

We employ two different defense functions in our calculations. The first is the current OMB version, which we use for fiscal years 1940 and 1947-1982. We use a second one for the fiscal years 1941-1946, taken from the FY 1947/48 *Budget of the U.S. Government*, which presents the most inclusive summary of wartime expenditures available. We compensate these figures for offsetting receipts, a special category first incorporated in federal budgets in the early 1970s, using seperate data supplied by OMB.[5]

Because of restrictions on data concerning nuclear weapons development, construction and maintenance, we rely on official figures for atomic energy defense activities as the best estimate of actual expenditures on nuclear weapons.

2. Military-Related Interest on the Federal Debt: When the government borrows funds to finance a budget deficit, a percentage of the borrowed money and of the interest on that money will finance the military's share of the federal budget. Since World War II, these borrowing costs have increased substantially. The government has balanced the budget only eight times since 1940. Not only is interest compounded on unpaid debt, but interest rates themselves have increased dramatically, render-' ing all government programs more expensive than original estimates.

Tables C.1 and C.2 list the data we used for estimating military-related deficits and surpluses, and for estimating the military portion of federal interest payments. Virtually all military spending comes from federal funds, one of two large pools of money in the federal budget. These tax dollars are annually available for the general purposes of government, as opposed to trust funds, which can only be spent by the trust for which they were collected. Since budget deficits and surpluses are defined by expenditures in relation to federal funds, we assume a direct proportion between the military's annual share of federal funds and the annual military-related deficit or surplus. We simply add annual military expenditures and measure this sum as a percentage of federal funds. This figure then becomes the annual military-related deficit (or surplus) percentage, which we multiply by the annual federal deficit (or surplus), giving us a dollar amount for the military-related deficit (or surplus).

To determine the military-related share of annual interest payments, we use running totals of the annual military-related deficit (or surplus). When the government runs deficits in successive years, some of the current year's interest is for debt from prior years. We therefore measure the accumulated military-related deficit, divide by the accumulated total deficit and multiply this fraction by the following year's interest outlay. This gives an estimate of the military-related portion of the interest costs. We enter this into the following year's total military spending budget and begin the cycle of calculations once again. Because FY 1940 is the base year, military-related interest first appears in the FY 1941 budget.

3. Veterans' Benefits: Veterans' benefits represent current expenditures for the government's past military activities. The armed services use them as a means of attracting and keeping enlisted personnel, while many individuals depend on them to fund medical and other costs incurred as a direct result of their military service. Since these benefits are available exclusively to past and current members of the armed services and their dependents, we include their total cost in our military spending budget.

4. National Aeronautics and Space Administration: NASA is one of the Pentagon's most important sources of aeronautical research, development and construction. NASA provides the Defense Department with scientific, technical and management assistance on projects ranging from design of the B-1B bomber to the space shuttle launchings. In a letter to NASA Chief Administrator James Beggs expressing support for NASA's fight against cuts in its 1983 research budget, Secretary of Defense Caspar Weinberger stated:

> NASA aeronautics research facilities and technical capabilities have been and will continue to be critical to the development of military aircraft.[6]

NASA also provides the Pentagon with indirect support by helping to sustain the aerospace industrial base through research and manufacture of civilian aircraft.[7]

The military component of NASA is difficult to determine. Much data is classified and NASA's own published estimate of military-related work is misleading. In an April 1982 report, NASA officials claimed that only one-tenth of one percent of their FY 1983 budget request supported Defense Department programs.[8] In response to these low estimates, the investigative arm of Congress, the General Accounting Office (GAO), conducted a detailed analysis of NASA military programs. After reviewing back-up budget documentation and discussions with individual program managers at NASA, GAO analysts concluded that 20.5 percent of NASA's 1983 research and development budget request was directed exclusively to military programs and that another 7.7 percent benefited both military and civilian programs.[9]

We apply the GAO's estimate that 20 percent of NASA's FY 1983 R&D costs are military-related to all NASA budget categories, beginning with their first budget in FY 1959. We recognize that the military components of an agency's programs can fluctuate from year to year. Lacking the resources for in-depth studies of NASA's budgets, we rely on 20 percent as a conservative estimate of NASA's annual military-related expenditures.

5. Foreign Military Assistance Grants: The Mutual Defense Assistance Program (MDAP) is one of the major means the United States has used to carry out its military and foreign policies in the post-war period. As the Cold War unfolded, Congress established MDAP in FY 1949 to enlarge the military component of U.S. aid. MDAP authorized agencies of the Pentagon, under the direction of the State Department, to provide direct grants of weapons, loans for weapons purchases and military training to foreign governments.

Since the U.S. government only gives foreign assistance funds to countries that share its strategic objectives, many argue that all foreign assistance should be considered a form of military expenditures. In keeping with our cautious definition of military spending however, we include only categories that are specifically earmarked for military assistance. The three major categories are: Military Assistance Program Deliveries (MAP), International Military Education and Training (IMET), and loans for weapons purchases and military construction that have been waived (FMS Financing Waived). Additionally, for the fiscal years 1977 to 1981, we include funds for the Peacekeeping Operations Program (POP), air base construction in Israel and Waived Administrative Surcharges (WAS), as reported in a study of U.S. security assistance programs.[10]

When the OMB transferred military assistance out of the Defense Department into the international affairs category in 1979, it transferred historical budget data only back to FY 1962. To avoid double-counting we include separate military assistance figures only from FY 1962 to the present.

6. Coast Guard: In both wartime and peacetime, the Coast Guard devotes substantial resources to U.S. naval posture and war fighting capability. According to the Transportation Department's recently released study, *Coast Guard Roles and Missions*, the Coast Guard is a "branch of the armed forces within the Department of Transportation except when operating as part of the Navy." It has a constant mission to "maintain a state of readiness to function as a specialized service in the Navy in time of war."[11]

Since 1940, the extent of the Coast Guard's military-related activities has varied widely. As a branch of the Navy during World War II, the Coast Guard's entire program supported the war effort. Today, however, various sources place the Coast Guard's military component at between four and 16 percent of its annual budget.[12]

Department of Transportation Budget Director William Fitzgerald states that the military component of the Coast Guard in non-war years includes four categories: reserve training; the military readiness component of Coast Guard operating expenses; a portion of the acquisition budget (for meeting Navy construction specifications); and a small portion of research, development, testing and evaluation. Fitzgerald does not mention retired pay, which is defined in the OMB *Budget Appendix* as being exclusively for retired military personnel, nor radio navigation and polar ice-breaking activities, both of which contain active military components according to the *Roles and Missions* study.[13]

We include all Coast Guard expenditures for fiscal years 1941-1946, as reported in the Navy Department budget for those years. For all other annual figures, we cumulate only the three most direct and significant military-related Coast Guard budget components: retired pay; the military readiness component of operating expenses; and reserve training. While other military activities exist, the relatively small amount of money involved does not justify the additional work required to track them down.

7. Impact Aid For Education: Since its inception in 1951, a significant portion of the funds for School Assistance in Federally Affected Areas (SAFAA) has gone to school districts to pay for the education of the children of enlisted military personnel and civilian Defense Department employees who either live or work on non-taxable federal property. SAFAA supports the armed services because it reimburses school districts for taxes that would normally be paid by the individuals themselves. We therefore include the cost of the military-related portions of SAFAA as part of the total military budget.[14]

According to Department of Education Budget Examiner, Bayla White, four program categories in the SAFAA budget are military-related: "payments for 'a' children," "payments for 'b' children," "payments to other federal agencies," and "construction."[15] We estimate the military-related portion of SAFAA based upon the percentage of military-related employment in the "a" and "b" classifications each year, while taking all of the payments to other federal agencies' budgets. Since it is very difficult to isolate military-related school construction costs and there is relatively little money involved, we ignore the SAFAA "construction" category.

8. Maritime Administration: Another hidden military cost is the Maritime Administration (MARAD). The Maritime Administration is the Navy's chief auxiliary force for supplying U.S. and foreign armed forces in times of international crisis. Established as part of the 1934 Merchant Marine Act, MARAD directed the shipment of troops and supplies to Europe and the Pacific along with the War Shipping Administration (WSA) during World War II. Following the war, Congress gave MARAD administrative control of the National Defense Reserve Fleet (NDRF), initially a fleet of 250 commercial ships kept in constant readiness in ports on the East and West coasts. After reaching peaks of nearly 2300 ships during the Korean War, and 1700 ships during the Vietnam War, the NDRF has gradually shrunk in size to its current level of approximately 250 ships.[16]

For our definition of military spending, we include the total Maritime Commission and War Shipping Administration budgets for the fiscal years 1941-46 (as reported in the defense function for those years) and the cost of the NDRF for all years following FY 1946. Because the Maritime Commission budget was so small in pre-war FY 1940, before the NDRF had been established, we do not include a military component for MARAD that year.

Others might have adopted a broader definition. Many government officials recognize MARAD's significant military role. MARAD administers military-related activities in addition to NDRF, such as the War-Risk Insurance Program (providing compensation to ship operators and seamen for war-related losses), the Merchant Marine Reserve and military-related construction subsidies. The existence of substantial shipbuilding facilities constitutes a kind of military deterrence as well.

Notes

1. U.S. Office of Management and Budget, "The Functional Classification In The Budget (1979 Revision)," Technical Paper Series BRD/FAB 79-1 (Washington, D.C.: OMB, February 22, 1979), p. 3.

2. *Ibid.*, p. 3.

3. *Budget of the United States Government For The FY Ending June 30, 1947* Washington, D.C.: U.S. GPO, 1946) pp. A-14 to A-16. The 13 additional categories include: the Executive Office of the President; Emergency Funds Appropriated to the President; Independent Establishments; the Federal Security Agency; the Federal Works Agency; the National Housing Agency; and the Departments of Agriculture, Commerce, Interior, Justice, Labor, State, and Treasury.

4. *The Budget of the United States Government FY 1983* (Washington, D.C.: U.S. GPO, 1982), pp. 5-10 and 9-30.

5. Offsetting receipts result from business-type transactions with the public or from a payment from one government account to another. They are treated as deductions from spending (negative outlays) in determining annual budget outlay totals. The defense function figures from FY 1941 to 1946 do not include offsetting receipts, which were only calculated after federal funds and trust funds were combined into one budget in 1969. In a letter, Thomas Cuny, an OMB economist, supplied us with DoD offsetting receipt figures for those years. They are:

    Offsetting Receipts
    Fiscal Year
    (in millions of dollars)

1941	$ 8
1942	36
1943	686
1944	2,920
1945	2,983
1946	2,850

6. Secretary of Defense, Caspar Weinberger, in a letter to NASA Chief Administrator James Beggs, cited this as one of NASA's key contributions to national security. *Aerospace Daily*, December 10, 1981, p. 206.

7. U.S. General Accounting Office, "Analysis of NASA's FY 1983 Budget Request for Research and Development to Determine the Amount That Supports DoD's Programs" (Washington, D.C.: GAO, April 26, 1982), p. 1.

8. U.S. National Research Council, *NASA's Role In Aeronautics: A Workshop, Volume 1*, Summary (Washington, D.C.: NRC, 1981) p. 9.

9. U.S. General Accounting Office, *op. cit.*, p. 1.

10. U.S. Department of Defense, Data Management Division, Comptroller-Defense Security Assistance Agency, *FY Series As of September 1981* (back-up document to a Congressional Presentation) (Washington, D.C.: DoD-Comptroller, 1982), pp. 2-3.

11. U.S. Department of Transportation, *Coast Guard Roles and Missions* (Washington, D.C.: Department of Transportation, March 1982), p. 131.

12. For instance, Capt. Robert G. Moore implies that at least 16 percent of Coast Guard activities are military-related in his article "Hip Boots or Blue Water? An Examination of the U.S. Coast Guard and its Future," *Proceedings* (Annapolis, Md: May 1982), p. 196. John B. Hayes, U.S. Coast Guard, states in an interview that "...the taxpayer gets one of the best bangs for the buck from the Coast Guard. For a very modest investment which amounts to about 10 percent of our total budget, the nation gets an organization immediately prepared to go to war with the Navy [sic]...," "The Desperate Straits We're In," *Proceedings* (Annapolis, Md: U.S. Naval Institute, October 1980), p. 24. On page 9 of its *Coast Guard Roles and Missions* study, the Department of Transportation estimates only 4.4 percent of the fiscal 1982 Coast Guard budget to be represented by the Military Operations/Military Preparedness category.

13. W.H. Fitzgerald, Director of the Budget, Department of Transportation, in a letter to CEP dated July 19, 1982, p. 2.

14. *Budget of the United States Government FY 1982, Appendix* (Washington, D.C.: U.S. GPO, 1981), pp. 1-12.

15. Conversation with Department of Education Budget Examiner Bayla White, August 4, 1982. Special note: According to OMB's FY 1983 *Budget Appendix*, the military-related portions of SAFAA will be transferred to the OMB defense function starting October 1, 1982.

16. U.S. Department of Commerce, "The United States Merchant Marine, A Brief History" (Washington, D.C.: Department of Commerce). Special note: The Maritime Administration was transferred from the Commerce Department to the Department of Transportation in August, 1981. Also, see U.S. Department of Commerce, *The Annual Report of the Maritime Administration for FY 1979* (Washington, D.C.: U.S. GPO, July 1980), p. 83.

Key to Table C.2

Abbreviation	Precise Name
FFO	Federal Funds Outlays
TID	Total Interest on the Debt
IAM	Interest Attributable to the Military
TMB	Total Military Budget
$\dfrac{\text{TMB}}{\text{FFO}}$	Total Military Budget divided by Federal Funds Outlays
TD/S	Total Deficit or Surplus
MD/S	Military Deficit or Surplus
TAD	Total Accumulated Deficit
AMD	Accumulated Military Deficit
IM	Interest Multiplier

Table C.1

Total Military Spending Budget
Fiscal Years
(Millions of Dollars)

Items	1940	1941	1942	1943
Defense Function	$ 1,490	$ 6,655	$28,266	$75,085
Veterans Benefits	557	563	556	605
Foreign Military Asst.				
a. FMS Financing Waived				
b. MAP Deliveries				
c. Excess MAP/MASF Deliv.				
d. IMET/MAP Deliveries				
e. Total	$ -	-	-	-
NASA				
a. Total				
b. 20% of Total	-	-	-	-
Coast Guard				
a. Retired Pay	$ 1			
b. Military Readiness	-			
c. Reserve Training	-			
d. Total	$ 1	-	-	-
MARAD				
a. NDRF	$ -	-	-	-
Impact Aid - SAFAA				
a. Military "a" child.				
b. Military "b" child.				
c. Payments to Fed. Ags.				
d. Total	$ -	-	-	-
Military-Related Interest on the Federal Debt	$ 0	215	457	1,112
Total Military Budget	$ 2,048	7,433	29,279	76,802
Federal Funds Outlays	$ 8,974	13,260	34,832	78,765
Total Military Budget as a Share of Federal Funds	22.8%	56.1%	84.1%	97.5%

1944	1945	1946	1947	1948	1949
$89,720	$90,501	$48,870	$11,601	$ 7,845	$11,761
743	2,093	4,411	7,325	6,457	6,599
-	-	-	164	259	239
-	-	-	-	-	-
			9	11	11
-	-	-	9	11	11
-	-	-	12	8	9
-	-	-	-	-	-
1,973	2,894	3,905	4,005	4,176	4,446
92,436	95,488	57,186	23,116	18,756	23,065
92,283	94,847	56,204	34,803	28,989	37,725
100.2%	100.7%	101.7%	66.4%	64.7%	61.1%

TABLE C.1   /Continued

Items	1950	1951	1952	1953
Defense Function	$12,407	$21,863	$43,351	$49,912
Veterans Benefits	$ 8,834	5,526	5,341	4,519
Foreign Military Asst.				
a. FMS Financing Waived	-	-	-	-
b. MAP Deliveries	$ 49	888	1,353	3,611
c. Excess MAP/MASF Deliv.	$ 28	279	177	134
d. IMET/MAP Deliveries	$ 1	25	71	87
e. Total	78	1,192	1,601	3,832
NASA				
a. Total				
b. 20% of Total	-	-	-	-
Coast Guard				
a. Retired Pay	$ 14	15	16	18
b. Military Readiness	-	-	-	-
c. Reserve Training		1	2	2
d. Total	$ 14	16	18	20
MARAD				
a. NDRF	$ 7	7	5	6
Impact Aid - SAFAA				
a. Military "a" child.				
b. Military "b" child.				
c. Payments to Fed. Ags.				
d. Total	$ -	4	23	48
Military-Related Interest on the Federal Debt	$ 4,735	4,567	4,640	5,079
Total Military Budget	$26,075	33,175	54,979	63,416
Federal Funds Outlays	$38,389	43,732	64,994	73,006
Total Military Budget as a Share of Federal Funds	67.9%	75.9%	84.6%	86.9%

1954	1955	1956	1957	1958	1959
$46,289	$39,834	$39,719	$42,915	$43,721	$45,961
4,614	4,676	4,892	5,006	5,350	5,443
-	-	-	-	-	-
3,012	2,235	2,896	2,591	2,261	2,059
88	88	93	72	207	176
52	55	64	51	55	49
3,152	2,378	3,053	2,714	2,523	2,284
-	-	-	-	-	29
18	20	23	25	26	28
18	14	15	18	19	20
3	3	4	7	12	15
39	37	42	50	57	63
007	7	7	007	7	6
46	54	45	43	47	54
4,720	4,757	4,964	5,256	5,512	5,647
58,867	51,743	52,722	55,491	57,217	59,487
65,922	62,338	63,921	67,190	69,746	77,078
89.3%	83.0%	82.5%	82.6%	82.0%	77.2%

TABLE C.1 /Continued

Item	1960	1961	1962	1963
Defense Function	$45,168	$46,633	$49,040	$50,142
Veterans Benefits	5,441	5,705	5,625	5,519
Foreign Military Asst.				
a. FMS Financing Waived	-	-	-	-
b. MAP Deliveries	1,703	1,250	1,074	1,528
c. Excess MAP/MASF Deliv.	216	228	240	210
d. IMET/MAP Deliveries	80	119	195	118
e. Total	1,999	1,597	1,509	1,856
NASA				
a. Total	401	744	1,257	2,552
b. 20% of Total	080	149	251	510
Coast Guard				
a. Retired Pay	29	30	31	32
b. Military Readiness	20	23	21	24
c. Reserve Training	16	16	16	16
d. Total	65	69	68	72
MARAD				
a. NDRF	5	5	5	6
Impact Aid - SAFAA				
a. Military "a" child.				
b. Military "b" child.				
c. Payments to Fed. Ags.				
d. Total	65	70	70	86
Military-Related Interest on the Federal Debt	6,715	6,282	6,636	7,399
Total Military Budget	59,538	60,510	63,204	65,590
Federal Funds Outlays	74,863	79,333	86,564	90,161
Total Military Budget as a Share of Federal Funds	79.5%	76.3%	73.0%	72.7%

1964	1965	1966	1967	1968	1969
$51,528	$47,456	$54,852	$68,243	$78,755	$79,417
5,680	5,721	5,921	6,899	6,882	7,640
–	–	–	–	–	–
1,180	1,361	1,017	934	721	605
141	175	190	380	442	530
80	81	77	58	60	38
1,401	1,617	1,284	1,372	1,223	1,173
4,171	5,092	5,932	5,425	4,724	4,251
834	1,018	1,186	1,085	945	850
34	37	41	45	48	53
30	12	13	21	31	33
19	21	23	24	25	26
83	70	77	100	104	112
6	5	5	5	5	5
84	78	102	112	127	100
7,788	7,661	8,835	9,622	10,290	11,488
67,404	63,626	72,262	87,438	98,331	100,785
95,776	94,830	106,569	126,815	143,138	148,810
70.4%	67.1%	67.8%	68.9%	68.7%	67.7%

TABLE C.1 /Continued

Item	1970	1971	1972	1973
Defense Function	$78,553	$75,808	$76,550	$74,541
Veterans Benefits	8,677	9,776	10,730	12,013
Foreign Military Asst.				
a. FMS Financing Waived	-	-	-	-
b. MAP Deliveries	499	499	524	515
c. Excess MAP/MASF Deliv.	511	474	370	377
d. IMET/MAP Deliveries	34	34	31	24
e. Total	1,044	1,007	925	916
NASA				
a. Total	3,753	3,382	3,423	3,315
b. 20% of Total	750	676	685	663
Coast Guard				
a. Retired Pay	59	65	71	76
b. Military Readiness	37	25	32	27
c. Reserve Training.	27	25	28	30
d. Total	123	115	121	133
MARAD				
a. NDRF	6	4	4	5
Impact Aid - SAFAA				
a. Military "a" child.				
b. Military "b" child.				
c. Payments to Fed. Ags.				
d. Total	164	132	162	145
Military-Related Interest on the Federal Debt	13,052	13,427	13,633	14,883
Total Military Budget	102,369	100,945	102,810	103,299
Federal Funds Outlays	156,300	163,651	178,I10	186,951
Total Military Budget as a Share of Federal Funds	65.5%	61.7%	57.7%	55.3%

1974	1975	1976	TQ	1977	1978
$77,781	$85,552	$89,430	$22,307	$97,501	$105,186
13,386	16,597	18,432	3,962	18,038	18,974
1,500	100	850	Contained	500	500
696	691	364	in 1976	109	220
305	103	45		63	6
27	25	27	Figures	25	29
2,528	919	1,286		697	755
3,256	3,267	3,669	951	3,945	3,983
651	653	734	190	789	797
86	105	122	33	139	157
24	25	20	6	38	44
27	28	31	10	36	38
137	158	173	49	213	239
5	5	5	1	6	7
140	155	150	018	191	192
18,082	19,502	21,342	5,216	22,228	25,478
112,710	123,541	131,552	31,743	139,663	151,628
199,918	240,081	269,921	65,088	295,756	331,991
56.4%	51.5%	48.7%	48.8%	47.2%	45.8%

TABLE C.1   /Continued

Item	1979	1980	1981	1982
Defense Functions	$117,681	$135,856	$159,765	$187,418
Veterans Benefits	19,928	21,183	22,988	23,955
Foreign Military Asst.				
a. FMS Financing Waived	500	500	500	
b. MAP Deliveries	157	319	245	
c. Excess MAP/MASF Deliv.	3	18	18	
d. IMET/MAP Deliveries	027	25	30	
e. Total	687	862	793	828
NASA				
a. Total	4,197	4,850	5,421	6,026
b. 20% of Total	839	97	1,084	1,205
Coast Guard				
a. Retired Pay	174	207	239	261
b. Military Readiness	42	48	55	77
c. Reserve Training	40	42	47	52
d. Total	256	297	341	390
MARAD				
a. NDRF	11	11	13	7
Impact Aid - SAFAA				
a. Military "a" child.				
b. Military "b" child.				
c. Payments to Fed. Ags.				
d. Total	228	173	172	180
Military-Related Interest on the Federal Debt	29,611	35,881	45,565	54,884
Total Military Budget	169,241	195,233	230,721	267,662
Federal Funds Outlays	362,396	419,220	475,171	526,113
Total Military Budget as a Share of Federal Funds	46.7%	46.6%	48.6%	50.9%

1983*	1984*	1985*	1986*	1987*	1988*
$214,769	$245,305	$285,268	$323,035	$354,277	$385,591
24,411	25,724	26,466	27,159	27,860	28,851
832	868	908	949	992	1,036
6,713	6,973	7,300	7,629	7,972	8,323
1,343	1,394	1,460	1,526	1,594	1,665
318	333				
81	85				
54	55				
453	473	495	517	540	564
8	8	8	8	9	9
189	197	206	215	225	234
55,941	62,011	67,727	72,388	76,945	79,350
297,946	335,980	382,538	425,797	462,442	497,300
603,047	610,467	666,167	719,266	771,262	822,515
49.4%	55.0%	57.4%	59.2%	60.0%	60.5%

* Projections.

Table C.2

Military-Related Deficit and Interest on the Debt
Fiscal Years
(Millions of Dollars)

YEAR	FFO	TID	IAM	TMB	$\frac{TMB}{FFO}$
1940	$ 8,974	$ 899	$ 0	$ 2,048	.228
1941	13,260	943	215	7,433	.561
1942	34,832	1,052	457	29,279	.841
1943	78,765	1,529	1,112	76,802	.975
1944	92,283	2,219	1,973	92,436	1.002
1945	94,847	3,112	2,894	95,488	1.007
1946	56,204	4,111	3,905	57,186	1.017
1947	34,803	4,189	4,005	23,116	.664
1948	28,989	4,341	4,176	18,756	.647
1949	37,725	4,523	4,446	23,065	.611
1950	38,389	4,812	4,735	26,075	.679
1951	43,732	4,665	4,567	33,175	.759
1952	64,994	4,701	4,640	54,979	.846
1953	73,006	5,156	5,079	63,416	.869
1954	65,922	4,811	4,720	58,867	.893
1955	62,338	4,849	4,757	51,743	.830
1956	63,921	5,076	4,964	52,722	.825
1957	67,190	5,352	5,256	55,491	.826
1958	69,746	5,596	5,512	57,217	.820
1959	77,078	5,750	5,647	59,487	.772
1960	$ 74,863	$ 6,937	$ 6,715	$ 59,538	.795
1961	79,333	6,704	6,282	60,510	.763
1962	86,564	6,877	6,636	63,204	.730
1963	90,161	7,731	7,399	65,590	.727
1964	95,776	8,189	7,788	67,404	.704
1965	94,830	8,579	7,661	63,626	.671
1966	106,569	9,369	8,835	72,262	.678

TD/S	MD/S	TAD	AMD	IM
$ - 3,095	$ - 706	$ - 3,095	$ - 706	.228
- 5,013	- 2,812	- 8,108	- 3,518	.434
- 20,764	- 17,463	- 28,872	- 20,981	.727
- 54,884	- 53,512	- 83,756	- 74,493	.889
- 47,004	- 47,098	-130,760	-121,591	.930
- 47,474	- 47,806	-178,234	-169,397	.950
- 15,856	- 16,126	-194,090	-185,523	.956
+ 3,862	+ 2,564	-190,228	-182,959	.962
+ 12,001	+ 7,765	-178,227	-175,194	.983
+ 603	368	-177,624	-174,826	.984
- 3,112	- 2,113	-180,736	-176,939	.979
+ 6,100	+ 4,630	-174,636	-172,309	.987
- 1,517	- 1,283	-176,153	-173,592	.985
- 6,533	- 5,677	-182,686	-179,269	.981
- 1,170	- 1,045	-183,856	-180,314	.981
- 3,041	- 2,524	-186,897	-182,838	.978
+ 4,087	+ 3,372	-182,810	-179,466	.982
+ 3,249	+ 2,684	-179,561	-176,782	.985
- 2,939	- 2,410	-182,500	-179,192	.982
- 12,855	- 9,924	-195,355	-189,116	.968
$ + 269	$ + 214	$ -195,086	$ -188,902	.968
- 3,406	- 2,599	-198,492	-191,501	.965
- 7,137	- 5,210	-205,629	-196,711	.957
- 4,751	- 3,454	-210,380	-200,165	.951
- 5,922	- 4,169	-216,302	-204,334	.945
- 1,596	- 1,071	-217,898	-205,405	.943
- 3,796	- 2,574	-221,694	-207,979	.938

TABLE C.2   /Continued

YEAR	FFO	TID	IAM	TMB	$\dfrac{\text{TMB}}{\text{FFO}}$
1967	126,815	10,258	9,622	87,438	.689
1968	143,138	11,077	10,290	98,331	.687
1969	148,810	12,694	11,488	100,785	.677
1970	156,300	14,374	13,052	102,369	.655
1971	163,651	14,837	13,427	100,945	.617
1972	178,110	15,474	13,633	102,810	.577
1973	186,951	17,346	14,883	103,299	.553
1974	199,918	21,449	18,082	112,710	.564
1975	240,081	23,244	19,502	123,541	.515
1976	269,921	26,711	21,342	131,552	.487
TQ	65,088	6,946	5,216	31,743	.488
1977	295,756	29,877	22,228	139,663	.472
1978	331,991	35,435	25,478	151,628	.458
1979	$ 362,396	$ 42,606	$ 29,611	$ 169,241	.467
1980	419,220	52,458	35,881	195,233	.466
1981	475,171	68,726	45,565	230,721	.486
1982	526,113	84,697	54,884	267,662	.509
1983*	603,047	88,936	55,941	297,946	.499
1984*	610,467	103,180	62,011	335,98	.550
1985*	666,167	114,210	67,727	382,538	.574
1986*	719,266	122,692	72,388	425,797	.592
1987*	771,262	130,415	76,945	462,442	.600
1988*	822,515	134,264	79,350	497,300	.605

TD/S	MD/S	TAD	AMD	IM
− 8,702	− 5,996	−230,396	−213,975	.929
− 25,161	− 17,286	−255,557	−231,261	.905
+ 3,236	+ 2,191	−252,321	−229,070	.908
− 2,845	− 1,863	−255,166	−230,933	.905
− 23,033	− 14,211	−278,199	−245,144	.881
− 23,373	− 13,486	−301,572	−258,630	.858
− 14,849	− 8,211	−316,421	−266,841	.843
− 4,688	− 2,644	−321,109	−269,485	.839
− 45,154	− 23,254	−366,263	−292,739	.799
− 66,413	− 32,343	−432,676	−325,082	.751
− 12,956	− 6,323	−445,632	−331,405	.744
− 44,948	− 21,215	−490,580	−352,620	.719
− 48,807	− 22,354	−539,387	−374,974	.695
− 27,694	$ − 12,933	$ −567,081	$ −387,907	.684
− 59,563	− 27,756	−626,644	−415,663	.663
− 57,932	− 28,155	−684,576	−443,818	.648
− 110,609	− 56,300	−795,185	−500,118	.629
− 207,708	− 102,608	−1,002,809	−602,726	.601
− 188,781	− 103,830	−1,191,590	−706,556	.593
− 194,197	− 111,469	−1,385,787	−818,025	.590
− 147,692	− 87,434	−1,533,479	−905,459	.590
− 142,113	− 85,268	−1,675,592	−990,727	.591
− 116,674	− 70,588	−1,792,266	−1,061,315	.592

Notes on Tables C.1 and C.2

To obtain accurate approximations of the military-related portion of programs in the defense function, we rely to a great extent on detailed budget breakouts, assembling the military-related components into annual totals for each program. For only one program, NASA, do we employ a flat percentage for estimating its military component. This is done because detailed budget data for NASA is classified.

Our calculations begin with FY 1940 because military expenditures prior to that year were relatively small, both in absolute terms and as a percentage of all federal expenditures. With minor exceptions, we report all budget figures in outlays because this is the amount of dollars that is actually spent in a given year, as opposed to budget authority, which represents funds committed over several years.

The Defense Function

For FYs 1940 and 1947 to 1988, U.S. Office of Management and Budget, "Federal Government Finances" (Washington, D.C.: OMB, February 1983), pp. 72-77. For FYs 1941 to 1946, *Budget of the United States Government for the FY Ending June 30, 1948* (Hereafter, *U.S. Budget.*) (Washington, D.C.: U.S. GPO, 1947), Table B, p. 1378.

Veterans' Benefits

For FYs 1940 to 1945, *U.S. Budget, FY 1947*, (Washington, D.C.: U.S. GPO, 1946) Appendix 6, p. 776. For FY 1946, *U.S. Budget, FY 1948*, Appendix 4, p. 1395. For FY 1947, *U.S. Budget, FY 1949*, Appendix 4, p. 1314. For FYs 1948 to 1988, U.S. Office of Management and Budget, "Federal Government Finances," *op. cit.*, pp. 19-23.

Foreign Military Assistance

No foreign military assistance figures were available for FY 1940. For FY 1947, *U.S. Budget, FY 1947*, Table 7, p. A24 under "Foreign Relief: National Military Establishment, Military Functions." For FY 1948 and 1949, *U.S. Budget, FY 1950* and *FY 1951* under "Funds for the President," Departments of Army and Navy allocations for Greece and Turkey, pp. 67 and 51 respectively. For the FYs 1950 to 1981, see U.S. Department of Defense, Data Management Division, Comptroller-Defense Security Assistance Agency, *Fiscal Year Series As of September ;1981* (backup document to a Congressional Presentation), pp. 2-3. FY 1982 to 1988 projections are the fiscal year 1981 figure adjusted for inflation. See U.S. Congressional Budget Office, *An Analysis of the President's Budgetary Proposals for FY 1984* (Washington, D.C.: C.B.O., February 1983), p. 14. (Hereafter, *An Analysis....*)

The National Aeronautics and Space Administration

For FY 1959 to 1980, U.S. National Aeronautics and Space Administration, "Budget History," Summer 1981, including figures for Research and Development, Program Management and Construction of Facilities. For FY 1981, *U.S. Budget, FY 1983*, p. 8-121. For estimates of defense activity funded in NASA's FY 1983 budget, see U.S. General Accounting Office, "Analysis of NASA's FY 1983 Budget Request for Reasearch and Development to Determine the Amount That Supports DoD's Programs," April 26 1982, p. 2. For FY 1982 and projected FY 1983 and FY 1984 outlays, U.S. Budget, FY 1984, p. 8-155. Subsequent projections are the FY 1984 figure adjusted for inflation. See U.S. CBO, *An Analysis...*, op. cit., p. 14.

Coast Guard

For FY 1940 *U.S. Budget, FY 1942*. Coast Guard figures are listed as part of the Treasury Department budget. All Coast Guard expenditures for the period FYs 1941 to 1946 are reported in the Defense Function because the Coast Guard was administered by the Navy during World War II. For FYs 1947 to 1983, *U.S. Budget*, annual Budgets and Appendices for FYs 1947 to 1984. Subsequent projections are the FY 1983 figure adjusted for inflation. See U.S. CBO, *An Analysis...*, *op. cit.*, p. 14.

Maritime Administration

No military component of MARAD was found for FY 1940. All MARAD budgets for FYs 1941 to 1946 are contained in the Defense Function. For the period 1947-1983, *U.S. Budget*, annual Budgets and Appendices for FYs 1947 to 1984. Subsequent projections are the FY 1983 figure adjusted for inflation. See U.S. CBO, *An Analysis...*, *op. cit.*, p. 14.

Impact Aid For Education (School Assistance for Federally Affected Areas)

For FYs 1951 to 1961, phone conversation with Susan Wiener, a Budget Analyst for the U.S. Department of Education. For FYs 1962 to 1979, U.S. Office of Management and Budget, *HISTFUN A*, *HISTFUN B*, and *HISTFUN C* budget tables published in 1980. For FYs 1980 and 1981, *U.S. Budget, FY 1982* and *U.S. Budget, FY 1983*.

Interest on the Federal Debt Attributable to Military Spending

U.S. Office of Management and Budget, "Federal Government Finances," *op. cit.* Interest on Federal Debt, Table 6, pp. 19-23. Deficit or Surplus and Federal Funds Outlays, see Table 1, pp. 5-7.

About the Author

Robert W. DeGrasse Jr. is a project director with the Council on Economic Priorities. Educated at Stanford University, he is the primary author of the Council's *Costs and Consequences of Reagan's Military Buildup* (1982), study coordinator of *Creating Solar Jobs: Options for Military Workers and Communities* (1978), and coauthor of *South Africa: Foreign Investment in Apartheid* (1978).